WHO'S AFRAID OF CHILDREN?

Ethics and Global Politics

Series Editors: Tom Lansford and Patrick Hayden

Since the end of the Cold War, exploration of ethical considerations within global politics and on the development of foreign policy have assumed a growing importance in the fields of politics and international studies. New theories, policies, institutions, and actors are called for to address difficult normative questions arising from the conduct of international affairs in a rapidly changing world. This series provides an exciting new forum for creative research that engages both the theory and practice of contemporary world politics, in light of the challenges and dilemmas of the evolving international order.

Also in the series

Old Europe, New Security
Evolution for a Complex World
Edited by Janet Adamski, Mary Troy Johnson and Christina M. Schweiss
ISBN 0 7546 4644 0

Peaceful Resistance
Advancing Human Rights and Democratic Freedoms
Robert M. Press
ISBN 0 7546 4713 7

The Ethics of Refugee Policy
Christina Boswell
ISBN 0 7546 4519 3

Justice and Violence
Political Violence, Pacifism and Cultural Transformation
Edited by Allan Eickelmann, Eric Nelson and Tom Lansford
ISBN 0 7546 4546 0

Global Ethics and Civil Society
Edited by John Eade and Darren O'Byrne
ISBN 0 7546 4214 3

In War We Trust
The Bush Doctrine and the Pursuit of Just War
Chris J. Dolan
ISBN 0 7546 4234 8

Who's Afraid of Children?
Children, Conflict and International Relations

HELEN BROCKLEHURST
University of Wales Swansea, UK

ASHGATE

Published by
Ashgate Publishing Limited
Gower House
Croft Road
Aldershot
Hampshire GU11 3HR
England

Ashgate Publishing Company
Suite 420
101 Cherry Street
Burlington, VT 05401-4405
USA

Ashgate website: http://www.ashgate.com

British Library Cataloguing in Publication Data
Brocklehurst, Helen, 1974-
  Who's afraid of children? : children, conflict and
  international relations. – (Ethics and global politics)
  1.Children and violence 2.Children and war 3.Children and
  politics 4.International relations – Moral and ethical
  aspects
  I.Title
  303.6 '083

Library of Congress Cataloging-in-Publication Data
Brocklehurst, Helen, 1974-
  Who's afraid of children? : children, conflict, and international relations / by
  Helen Brocklehurst.
      p. cm
    Includes index.
    1. Children and politics   Children and war. 3. Children--Government policy. 4.
World politics. 5. Internation relations. I. Title. II. Series

  HQ784.P5B76 2006
  327.1082--dc22   2006017127

ISBN-13: 978 0 7546 4171 1
ISBN-10: 0 7546 4171 6

Printed and bound in Great Britain by MPG Books Ltd. Bodmin, Cornwall.

Contents

Acknowledgements

This book began a long time ago, in a dark age when talking of children in an era of post cold war international relations was at best misunderstood and at worst ridiculed. I would like to thank the following people for their support beginning with my parents Jean and Malcolm to whom I owe everything. Thank you too to my sisters Anne and Lisa and to Gran and to Grandpa. This one is for you.

In Aberystwyth I would like thank the staff at the Department of International Politics and in particular Ken Booth and Marysia Zaleweski for their insight and patience in equal measure. I would like to thank Cynthia Enloe for her endorsement of this project which is but a footnote to her inspirational observations. To Stuart Shields and Sue Board, for office space and head space thank you. To a great group of friends – Helene Rhodes, Annaig le Mer, Diana Auwerter, Anthony Cannon Rosa, Mihir Patel, Nadeem Din, Anna Angelopoulou, and Michele Kingston – thank you for making post-grad insecurity totally bearable, and to the canteen ladies in Penbryn for always smiling in exchanges involving coffee.

In Northern Ireland thanks to Marie Smyth, Dominic Bryan and Martin Melaugh for your humour, encouragement and sound advice. I would also like to thank colleagues in the Department of Politics and International Relations at Swansea University for making the department an enjoyable place to work and for their unfailing support, particularly during the last two years following the death of my colleague on another project. To Michael Sheehan, Roland Axtmann, Mark Evans, Alan Finlayson, Robert Bideleux, Jonathan Bradbury, Sam Chambers, Mark Smith, John Baylis, Alan Collins, and Madeleine Rogerson, thank you. To Gunnar Bozenhard a big thank you for technical and esteem wizardry.

To Tom Lansford, Patrick Hayden, Kirstin Howgate and Margaret Younger at Ashgate, thank you for your professionalism and good will throughout. Finally, to Nicola Nieuwoudt, desk editor, my sincere appreciation for your dedication and expertise.

For children, whoever they may be

Chapter 1

Children

Beginnings

If children are people under 18 years old, it may be said that they form half of the world's population. Age however, in many respects, is not sufficient in itself as an indicator of childhood, nor does it illustrate why such persons are potentially receiving or deserving of different treatment throughout this time. In fact there is no single or agreed definition of childhood recognized or acted upon worldwide. As a unique and transient period of intense physical, mental, emotional and spiritual development; a time span delineated differently across and within communities and cultures; a managed societal or economic initiation; and a portal to romanticized and marketable evocations, images and memories, the consideration of childhood presents a unique empirical and theoretical challenge. Children are shaped not only by their underdevelopment as persons, but by conceptions earned and bestowed by the many individuals and groups who hold expectations of children, individually, collectively, simultaneously, arbitrarily and even contradictorily.

For the purposes of this book, however, all those considered to be children and childlike, are of interest. The construction or the image of a child, invoked in the minds of those fighting for their 'women and children' for example, is important to this discussion. It is also true that people can remain forever children in the eyes of their parents, regardless of age, as evidenced in the Latin American protest movement *Madres de Plaza de Mayo* whose grown-up children 'disappeared' during Argentine military rule. The choice of bestowed identity is of interest here despite the ambiguity.

The formal study of childhood, itself a young discipline, is another vital entry point. Childhood is often a clearly subdivided life phase though across different cultures and contexts these divisions may have no exact correspondence especially in later childhood. For the purposes of this book, all ages and stages of childhood are relevant. In the English language alone we may speak of early childhood, middle childhood and adolescence and 'baby', 'infant', 'child', 'teenager' and 'youth' to describe a spectrum of immature individuals with associated qualities and roles. As one identifies older persons, the terms 'child', 'juvenile', 'minor', 'youth' and even 'person' can be found interchangeably in international and customary law. The precise term used may also subtly bestow a social and political context. Youth describes a relatively older child though its use often suggests pejorative adult capabilities, notably in terms of the threat of physical strength and potential criminality.[1] The category of youth is thus included in this analysis of childhood by extension and because these social and political associations also inform the concept of child. 'Childhood' is clearly a concept which can be made and unmade. Through Military Orders imposed by Israel for example, Palestinians have been exclusively reclassified as adults from the age of sixteen. In Northern Ireland children throwing stones at the armed forces were described in the press as 'violent youths' or 'innocent boys' almost arbitrarily. Explicit or sensationalized portrayals of children in these political settings often unwittingly describe them as having *lost* their childhood. The idea that childhood and politics are mutually exclusive is one of the central building blocks of the book. No attempt to create a universal or comprehensive conception of the child will be made.

Concepts

In major works that attempt to conceptualize childhood, authors engaging in historical enquiries often admit to frustration with partial evidence and inconclusive arguments.[2] It appears uncommon for past societies to have recorded much of the nature and boundaries of this life phase, leaving us with a fragmented history, and particularly limited historical sources as lamented by Lloyd de Mause, in *The History of Childhood* (1974). This sustained the historical adage that 'the things that really matter are hardly ever committed to paper'.[3] Philip Aries' work, *Centuries of Childhood*, was the first historical study which advanced the notion of the modern 'conception' of childhood recognized in the last several centuries. He argued that the child is a contemporary concept of modern society. His crucial contention is that until the late seventeenth century there was no concept of childhood. The so called pre-modern ages distinguished only infants from adults, had no institutions to support the maturation process, and seemingly did not hold the child beyond infancy to be a separate or significant life stage.

David Archard, cautions against this view arguing that Aries cannot prove that pre-modern society lacked an awareness of children as different from adults, he merely shows that these societies held neither our present day conception of the child, nor the visible social support structures that we recognize in support of this conception.

[1]   See for example Monique Marks (2001), *Young Warriors: Youth Politics, Identity and Violence in South Africa* (Witswatersrand University Press).

[2]   For histories of childhood see: Urie Bronfenbrenner, *Two Worlds of Childhood – USA and USSR* (London: George Allen and Unwin, 1971); Philip Aries, *Centuries of Childhood* (Harmondsworth: Penguin, 1973); Lloyd de Mause, *The History of Childhood* (London: Souvenir, 1976); Lawrence Stone, *The Family, Sex and Marriage in England 1500–1800*; (New York: Harper and Row, 1977); Linda Pollock, *Forgotten Children: Parent–Child Relations from 1500–1900* (Cambridge, Cambridge University Press, 1983); Hugh Cunningham, *Children and Childhood in Western Society Since 1500* (London and New York, Longman, 1995).

[3]   De Mause, *op. cit.*, preface.

The presence of childhood – or the arrival of modern conceptions of childhood – is thus heavily contested as historical fact. In the present day, by comparison, our awareness or certainty over children as different to adults is seemingly indisputable. Many, at least from Western vantage points, would argue that we now have child-centered society and that since the end of the cold war in particular the child has become the quintessential icon or projection of apparent liberal values.

Archard, a theorizer of children's rights explains that '[t]he *concept* of children requires that children be distinguishable from adults in respect of some unspecified set of attributes. We may all then have a concept of them. A *conception* of childhood is a specification of those attributes'[4] and may be clearly deducible from their treatment and from legislation. Archard then identifies three aspects of conceptions of childhood, which are useful in separating out its form and content. These are 'boundaries' of childhood, its beginning and end; 'dimensions' of childhood, such as cultural, legal and social relativisms (which may end at different times), and the 'divisions' within childhood, that is, sub units of childhood.[5] Archard crucially argues that a very specific conception of the child that has dominated Western philosophical and political thought still operates today: that is the child is thought of, or described, as 'a comparative negative: an individual who is not yet an adult'.[6]

This view has a long 'enlightened' trajectory, and few dissenters. The dominant understanding of children, first employed by Western thinkers such as John Locke, clearly takes adulthood 'as a state of being', and from this 'childhood is correspondingly clearly defined against, and set apart from and below adulthood'.[7] This developmental[8] model of childhood conceives of adulthood as an achieved state. The child, for example, is thought not yet to achieve rational capabilities and has insufficient knowledge to make good decisions. Although attempts to quantify and apply time scales to the development of knowledge and rationality remain unresolved,[9] we continue to compare children in this way, with an adult being coterminous with a mature or developed norm.

Within the developmental model of childhood, there are two ways of seeing the maturation process, though these lead to the same outcome and neither are particularly generous. Either, it can be argued, that prior to becoming adults children have essential 'child qualities' and need specific nurturing and teaching in order

---

[4]   *Ibid.*, p. 22.

[5]   David Archard, *Children, Rights and Childhood*, 2nd edition (London: Routledge, 2004), p. 31.

[6]   Geraldine Van Beuren, *The International Law on the Rights of the Child* (Netherlands: Martinus Nijhoff, 1995), p. 33.

[7]   David Archard, (2004), *op. cit.*, p. 37.

[8]   On the developmental model see Archard *op. cit.*, pp. 34–6; William A. Corsaro, *The Sociology of Childhood* (Thousand Oaks, California: Pine Forge Press, 1997); and Jim, Goddard *et al.* (eds) (2005), *The Politics of Childhood: International Perspectives, Contemporary Developments* (Houndsmills, Basingstoke: Macmillan).

[9]   For a discussion see Michael Freeman, *Rights and Wrongs of Children* (London: Frances Pinter, 1983).

4 *Who's Afraid of Children?*

to change these into, or substitute them for, adult qualities; or, the child may be understood to be a partial or a lesser version of the adult, with adult qualities in place but yet to develop without assistance. Both views share however the anticipation of a time of end, when full adulthood is attained. In the former interpretation children's qualities are gradually transformed, in the latter, adulthood outgrows childhood. Critically neither view holds that childlike qualities may continue into adulthood, or that qualities are shared.

David Archard argues that the former developmental model of childhood, with its emphasis on the adult template and sudden transition is still privileged. He asserts that our conception of the child 'has been to a considerable degree infused with what are essentially myths or imaginative projections, deriving from a mixture of cultural and ideological sources'.[10] He goes on to say '[i]t is sometimes hard to separate the modern conception proper from what is in fact a symbolic ideal of childhood'. Of the modern conception recognized by Aries he writes (emphasis added):

> Children neither work nor play alongside adults; *they do not participate in the adult world of law and politics.* Their world is innocent where the adult world is knowing; and so on. We now insist upon a sharp distinction between the behavior demanded of children and that expected of adults; what is thought appropriate treatment of children is distinct from that of adults. There is a marked division of roles and responsibilities.[11]

Archard believes that the realization of a separate world for children to inhabit further fuels assumptions about their difference from adults. He questions this and asserts that there are scientific and cultural origins to the perception of separateness. In short, he alleges that children have been defined from the standpoint of adults and therefore perceived as the opposite of adults, a conception that privileges adult qualities:

> The ideal adult is equipped with certain cognitive capacities, rational, physically independent, autonomous, has a sense of identity and is conscious of its beliefs and desires, and thus able to make informed free choices for which it can be held personally responsible ... Childhood is defined as that which lacks the capacities, skills and powers of adulthood ... If childhood has virtues they are such only because of their very inappropriateness to adult life.[12]

The main alternative view of childhood suggested by Archard, is a process of maturation that has no point of complete separation from adulthood. 'Adulthood' can include and retain childlike qualities, and correspondingly virtues or disadvantages of adulthood may also be found throughout childhood. This model of gradual transition, which is more likely to be found outside of the West, makes clear that the child is as much a state of mind as a stage of physical maturity. There is no clear

[10]   Archard (2004), *op. cit.*, p. 37.
[11]   *Ibid.*
[12]   *Ibid.*, p. 39.

division between adults and children, and childlike and adult qualities and behavior can be held simultaneously. Archard writes:

> The individual can become more and more of an adult, but there is no guarantee that ageing brings with it maturity as understood normatively ... to that extent childhood is construed not so much as an actual period in one's life, but more as a metaphorical immaturity which can be present to some extent throughout a lifetime.[13]

Writers such as Farson have similarly argued that a modern-day conception of childhood is actually invented and forcibly so, through a desire to distinguish between adult and infantile qualities in ideological constructs, which in turn give adults greater powers.[14] As Archard echoes: 'it may well be our judgment as to what matters in being an adult which explains why we have the particular conception of childhood we do'.[15] Conceptions of childhood are lost and found at various junctures of history, in different locations and cultures, and within particular conditions of socio-economic climate. Perceptions of childhood and adulthood may vary with the (adult) priorities of society, particularly political priorities, as I later show. The following example is one illustration of how war acted as a catalyst for the separation and medicalization of the life phase of childhood. War was in this case 'good for children'.

Infantry Formula

Western liberal-democratic states, and indeed most cultures, recognize children as developing individuals in need of separate protection and health care until they are physiologically less vulnerable. However this simple division is relatively recent and the institutionalization of childcare in addition to 'healthcare', can be seen to have originated from specific links made between a population's health and the national interest in times of crisis. At the turn of the twentieth century, in what was a demanding era of imperialism, conquest and colonization, state strength and healthy, productive adults were vital. High infant mortality rates and slow population growth in Western Europe were thus a cause of concern and studied in a climate of military anxiety.[16] The Boer War and the First World War (WWI) further weakened populations and the cohort of young infantrymen were particularly frail. Scientific scrutiny of younger adults traced such soldier's vulnerability to inadequate care and nutrition in early life.[17] Consequently further separation of children's lives from adults, from infancy into childhood, so that they might benefit from additional health care, was advocated.

---

[13]   *Ibid.*, p. 45.

[14]   Richard Farson, *Birthrights* (London: Collier Macmillan, 1974), p. 31.

[15]   Archard (2004), *op. cit.*, p. 29.

[16]   See for example Maria Sophia Quine, *Population Politics in Twentieth Century Europe* (London: Routledge, 1996).

[17]   Valerie Fildes, Lara Marks and Hilary Marland (eds), *Women and Children First: International and Infant Welfare 1870–1945* (London: Routledge, 1992), pp. 1 and 97.

The need to regenerate society in this way led to specialized medicine for children, specific nurturing activities, and the popularization on the home front of an ideal, healthy childhood. Medical advances grew into child welfare structures, as is evident in the separation of children's health and welfare provisions. Though there is a medical and pediatric basis for this separation, it was not observed until war necessitated its consideration. It was thus a combination of development theory, culture and political prudence that led to increased separation and nurturing of the child in much of Western Europe.[18] The appeal of scientific conclusions concretized the public perception of childhood as a newly discovered but *natural* time of additional nurturing, and concomitantly, protection from adult experiences. To the present day this separation of children is sustained by behavioral analysis of what is natural and healthy for children of certain ages and stages.

Essential Childhood

Certainly, maturation is both a distinguishing feature of children and, importantly, one that affords them different or extra needs to adults. However physical development, though in many ways a defining characteristic of *childhood*, often continues into adulthood, finally stopping near the age of 25. Perhaps, then, there could be specified a certain degree of under-development which defines 'childhood'. And indeed though cell renewal and growth continues throughout both periods it is only during a certain span of early childhood that the physical *appearance and development* of particular vital organs, including the brain, takes place. This fact is significant in itself, pinpointing one of the very few characteristics that children do not share with other dependent persons. Concomitant with this threshold of 'vital' development are risks. Before the age of five, for example, a child's undeveloped body will absorb more toxins than for the rest of their entire adult lifetime. Their brains are also rapidly developing, leading to less tangible risks inherent in their immaturity, and common in war:

> While an adult may be severely affected by a traumatic experience and as a result suffer some personality alteration, a child's personality, in the absence of pre-existing development, may not be altered, but actually developed by a traumatic event. Any or all of a child's cognitive development may not only be altered but actually developed.[19]

Interestingly, in terms of both moral and cognitive development, children then reach levels comparable with adults between the ages of twelve and fourteen.

---

[18] See for example Denise Riley, *War in the Nursery: Theories of the Child and Mother* (London: Virago, 1983).
[19] G. Van Bueren, 'Opening Pandora's Box' in G. Van Bueren (ed.), *Childhood Abused: Protecting Children Against Torture, Cruel, Inhuman and Degrading Treatment and Punishment* (Dartmouth: Ashgate, 1998) p. 60.

Despite huge variations in the span of childhood experienced world-wide, such factors may help to explain why a majority of cultures hold a conception of a very young child or infant and deem a prepubescent person, that is up to the age of about twelve, to be unquestionably a child in at least some respects. Middle childhood, however, from approximately seven to eleven years may vary enormously and revolve around many roles and expectations also held of adults.

Major Variations in Minors

The most common marker of the boundary of childhood is the 'age of majority', which is not *directly* a physical quality so much as a social, religious, cultural or legal device by which societies identify the transition to adulthood. There is not necessarily correlation in its many levels of attainment.[20] Biological or mental issues of underdevelopment are not absent from this identification, of course. As the 'minority' of a community, children are most frequently deemed to lack the capacities necessary for running their lives as full members of it, comparable to the cohort of mentally impaired adults. In the West, majority typically functions as societies' means of acknowledging mature intellectual capabilities and legally endowing a child with membership of society in terms of citizenship and an entitlement to vote. In most of the world's sovereign states this is set at eighteen years.[21] The age of majority is also a symbolic stage of becoming an adult. The work of Boyden and Levison is worth citing here to capture its diversity and significance in relation to childhood:

> Many different kinds of criteria – although seldom age – are used to demarcate childhood. These criteria include the commencement of work, end of schooling, onset of menarche, betrothal, and marriage amongst others. ... Further, children in different social classes within the same society may reach adulthood at different ages, depending on their social and economic roles.[22]

Several processes of majority may unfold sequentially and simultaneously. Cadet soldiers in the UK for example may marry with parental consent at sixteen, make life, risk life and take life at 17, but not legally watch a violent or pornographic movie under any circumstance for another year. However as Boyden and Levison note, 'because they raise children's social and economic status and constitute public affirmation of community membership, such transitions far outweigh the universal age-based threshold in their significance for children'.[23]

---

[20] Guy Goodwin-Gill and Ilene Cohn, *Child Soldiers* (Oxford: Clarendon Press, 1994), p. 6.

[21] *Ibid.*, p. 7.

[22] Jo Boyden and Deborah Levison, *Children as Economic and Social Actors in the Development Process*, Working Paper 1, Stockholm: Expert Group on Development Issues, 2000, p. 28.

[23] *Ibid.*

Physical strength and labor capacity may mark a transition into adulthood, or at least partial adulthood. Occupation or apprenticeship may serve as a practical illustration of when adulthood is bestowed, or childhood qualities lost. In Afghanistan, an average life expectancy of 44 years[24] made it essential for community survival that most children learned and performed the same tasks as adults from an early age. In agrarian societies in particular, all physically capable people are an important economic asset, and are rapidly initiated into specific skills and social relationships. Across the world children, especially girls from the ages of six upwards, perform informal tasks at home. The age of a child worker does not necessarily render their employment exploitative. Many children imitate and learn the skills of work by choice and in ways that do not hinder their growth or development. Their working environment may be the home or the land outside the home, and their labor may form a positive part of their development, nurturing and education. In the West child work which occurs instead of formal education is generally recognized as an infringement of childhood rights and freedoms. For many in the West, childhood is seen as a natural period of protracted immaturity, play and learning.[25] Through this model, up to a billion people under the age of fifteen are considered to be experiencing a premature adulthood or a curtailed childhood. This conception of imperfect childhood would seem to weigh heavier in Western minds, than the conditions that prompt it. There has been similar indifference in most educational literature as to how work also functions as learning.[26] A child's physical and mental growth is however undoubtedly inhibited or permanently damaged by the labor often necessitated by absolute poverty.

The age of majority may also be coterminous with puberty. A sexual (hence 'adult') capability and/or readiness for marriage can allow the individual to fully contribute to the good of the wider community and its traditions. A religious ritual may be performed to mark this at a set age, 13 for example in Judaism, or later in the Islamic faith where the age of majority tends to be related to individual development. Puberty may begin from the ages of eight and sometimes earlier in non-Western cultures. Owing to the importance of puberty as a boundary in numerous cultures, sexual innocence and sexual incapacity are widely associated with or synonymous with childhood. These qualities clearly vary from child to child however, and puberty does not equate with loss of sexual innocence.

---

[24]   Molly Moore, John Ward-Anderson, and Chris McGreal, 'Fighting to Rescue a Lost Generation', *The Guardian*, 29 April 1995, p. 15.

[25]   Martin Woodhead, Paul Light and Ronnie Carr, *Open University: Child Development in a Social Context*. Vol. 3, *Growing up in a Changing Society* (London: Routledge, 1991) p. 3.

[26]   See for example George Kent, *Children in the International Economy* (London: Macmillan, 1995).

Law as Surrogacy

In Great Britain until comparatively recently, 'the child had no legal protection as an individual for fear that such protection would violate the sacredness of the family'.[27] The present-day conception of the child in the West is framed by a rights-based culture in which expectations about children and adults are tightly legislated in terms of adults', especially parents', responsibilities and duties. As children cannot themselves be bearers of rights according to traditional legal philosophy, the existence of laws themselves serve to act as a construction of childhood. As John Eekelaar notes:

> the central feature which traditionally marks minority status is that adults have a generalized legal power (exercisable either by parents or by legal authorities) to impose a course of action on minors on the basis of their assessment of the minor's best interests.[28]

The paradigm of 'best interests of the child' has led legal debate on children into the twenty-first century. Its wording alone implies guardianship and separation rather than partnership or agency. As Jo Boyden has argued, a gradual coalescence of factors, from capitalist development, changes in demography, Christianity, the role of the family and welfare laws have led to a climate in which the child is nurtured and protected from itself and from adult's society, as if from 'adult pollution'.[29] Indeed the entire legal apparatus surrounding children can be characterized as being about 'freedom from', rather than 'freedom to'. 'Freedom to' is associated with departure from childhood. That said, the former concept is not yet realized either; as Sara Ruddick notes: 'when you see children as demanding care, the reality of their vulnerability and the necessity of a caring response seem unshakeable.' Yet 'the presence of a child does not guarantee its care'.[30]

Childhood has also become associated with both legal protection and engagement with a sequential attainment of various rights. In terms of national and international law, age is the main criteria for distinguishing an adult from a child, or 'minor'. There are then also different ages at which someone is to be regarded as a child for the varying purposes of the law, such as criminal responsibility. There is also variance between national law, international humanitarian law and international and regional human rights instruments, in defining the parameters of childhood.[31] In Argentina, children are protected from the moment of conception and hold property rights from

---

[27] 'Child Welfare', *Chambers Encyclopaedia*, Vol. 3 (London), p. 400.

[28] John Eekelaar, 'The Interests of the Child and the Child's wishes: the role of dynamic self-determinism.' in Alston, *op. cit.*, p. 43.

[29] Jo Boyden, 'Childhood and the Policy Makers: A Comparative Perspective on the Globalisation of Childhood', in Jones, A. and Prout, A. (eds), *Constructing and Reconstructing Childhood* (1990), pp. 186 and 191.

[30] Sara Ruddick, *Maternal Thinking: Towards a Politics of Peace* (Boston, Mass: Beacon Press, 1990), p. 18.

[31] Guy Goodwin-Gill, *op. cit.*, p. 7.

this time.[32] Are newborns or even the unborn categorizable as children? Children in many American states for example cannot marry, vote, make a will or make a valid contract but can serve in the armed forces. Child marriage is discouraged but not outlawed in Muslim societies of Pakistan and Egypt.[33] In India it is legal for a child aged 10 to be fully employed in industry even if it is hazardous. In the United States, there is a minimum age at which children have criminal responsibility, varying from 15, to 7 in New York, to no minimum age in twenty-seven states.[34] Children may be deemed incapable of making decisions about their sexuality (as they may be taken advantage of) at an age when they may still choose to fight for their country (and not be taken advantage of). The issue of children's recruitment has fuelled perhaps most debate over whether young people between the ages of 15 and 18 are in fact adults or children.

It may be argued an internationalization of child care norms and rules, culminating in *The United Nations Convention on the Rights of the Child* (1989) created a coherent and universal approach to the problem of securing children's rights. The Convention states that 'children, because of their vulnerability, need special care and protection', and also that 'the child by reason of his physical and mental immaturity needs special safeguards and care, including appropriate legal protection'.[35] It is the most ratified human rights treaty in history: ratified by all countries except the USA and Somalia. Issues of cultural specificity however complicate the treaty's application in its current arguably rigid form. A Western and liberal model of childhood employed in the convention is identified for criticism. Debates over conceptions of children are however extremely complex beyond the evident differences in conceptions held across different cultures and jurisdictions. For example, Japan's ancient and family philosophies of harmony and unity uniquely connect mothers and children. Consequently, the Convention's requirement of parents' *partnership* with children are not accepted in Japanese society as they may be elsewhere.[36]

Perhaps more importantly the concept of the child is incommensurable with the concept of rights. In the Western legal framework children have been seen as people without responsibility, for whom obligations, that is the obverse of rights, are not applicable. Children, having no obligations to others, therefore hold a different claim to rights than do adults. In summary: '[o]bligations are the obverse of rights ... the only exception to this is the rights of children and especially small children. They

---

[32]   Cecilia P. Grosman, 'Argentina – Children's Rights in Family Relationships: The Gulf between Law and Social Reality', in Michael Freeman (ed.), *Children's Rights: A Comparative Perspective* (Aldershot: Dartmouth, 1996), p. 7.

[33]   John. L. Esposito, *Women in Muslim Family Law* (New York: Syracuse University Press, 1982).

[34]   Charlotte Faltermayer, 'What Is Justice for a Sixth Grade Killer?' *Time*, 6 April 1998, p. 48.

[35]   Defence For Children International, *The Convention on the Rights of the Child* (Geneva, 1990).

[36]   Yukiko Matsushima, 'Controversies and Dilemmas: Japan confronts the Convention', in Michael Freeman (ed.), *Children's Rights: A Comparative Perspective op. cit.*

have only rights. The obligations are ours and those of society'.[37] This assumption is contradicted by many children's experiences. In agrarian societies where children form the backbone of the workforce supporting their family, 'obligations' has a different significance. Children may be obligated to repay their families in return for their right to guardianship. In South Asia, Hindu law, describes children as holders of duties and obligations to the family and community and though these are not formalized legally they are central to tradition and community stability. Sons may be favored in a system of 'sonship', patriarchal or patrilineal inheritance, and hold the most important obligations from an early age.[38]

As David Archard argues: 'the young have been denied rights because, being young, they are presumed to lack some capacities necessary for the possession of rights'.[39] Until recently it has been assumed that children are less morally capable of making judgments than adults. This may be a key area where children's rights, and consequently the parameters and experience of childhood, have been significantly shaped by adult conceptions. The most radical development in the legal concept of the child therefore has been the realization that the child has a degree of self-determination and autonomy, and can be assisted into making choices rather than being the passive object of concern.[40] Being able to do something should not however be conflated with doing the right thing.

However, laws are culturally bound, may not be adhered to, and, in a sense, illustrate only idealistic projections of how child and adult roles should be maintained. Laws which prohibit particular activities may be subject to pragmatic alteration in times of crisis, thus allowing for greater use of children as a resource. Ages of military conscription and juvenile delinquency may be lowered in order to make recruits and victims of both kinds. One fundamental extension to the study of children's rights has been the recognition of different levels of care and guardianship that children receive based on their sex.

Gender Issues

One cannot account for dimensions and boundaries of childhood without looking at the role of gender. Gendered values may create separate experiences of childhood, determining its duration, opportunities and quality. Children's roles may be determined by their relative physical strength, sexual development, and gendered values held across society as a whole. The gender of a child may be the single

---

[37]   Simone Veil, quoted by Tarzie Vittachi, in *Making Reality of Children's Rights* (Stockholm: Radda Barnen, 1989), p. 53.

[38]   Savitri Goonesekere, 'The Best Interests of the Child: A South Asian Perspective', in Alston *op. cit.*, p. 129.

[39]   David Archard, *Children Rights and Childhood* (London and New York: Routledge, 1993), p. 58.

[40]   Michael Freeman (ed.), *Children's Rights: A Comparative Perspective* (Aldershot: Dartmouth, 1996).

most important explanation for differentiated experiences of childhood and explain variations of child status between cultures and within cultures.

Despite a legal basis from which to protect girls, discrimination against girl children is pervasive with millions of families resorting to infanticide of girls to make sure their one child is a boy. In China's 2000 census there were an estimated 19 million more boys than girls and a sex ratio of 100 girls to 120 boys, achieved through sex-selective abortion and a nutrition rights and care bias against girls. The perceived difference between a boy and a girl in cultural terms is often then a matter of life or death. In India, a boy will often be fed first and in the greatest amounts as he is valued and more useful to his family or community.[41] '[T]he apartheid of gender' starts early.[42] Children are both commoditized, and made vulnerable by gendered values within specific cultural and economic frameworks. In the Philippines, patriarchal society also creates this discrimination of male children over female children, reflected in their survival rates. A Filipino 'child prostitute', made pregnant by a US service member, may for example exchange a female infant in return for outstanding rent. If the baby is male, she is more likely to insist on keeping the child.[43]

(M)others

However, it is also obvious that experiences of childhood can be represented as if feminine for both girls and boys. Physical and emotional weakness can be described as a feminine and developmental phase that boys will 'grow out of'. The refrain 'Big boys don't cry' is still heard. Children's and women's bestowed qualities overlap in crucial areas perhaps leading to the feminization of childhood. Both women and children may be thought of as physically weaker, less rational and more emotional than (adult) males. In short, girl children are expected to maintain their girl-like qualities, most typically for the caring role of motherhood. In addition, children are closely associated with the mother and the maternal sphere or the realm of the family or home. In virtually all cultures mothers do overall spend more time with infants and newborn children than do fathers.[44] But though boys begin life in what may be thought of as a feminine sphere they are also more likely to be expected to lose any associated weakness and childishness, in readiness for masculine/adult roles.

Cynthia Enloe notes that the phrase 'womenandchildren' rolls easily off network tongues because in network minds women are family members rather than

[41] Radhika Balakrishnan, 'The Wider Context of Sex Selection and the Politics of Abortion in India', in Gita Sen and Rachel C. Snow (eds), *Power and Decision: The Social Control of Reproduction* (Boston: Harvard School of Health, 1994), pp. 268–70.

[42] Fildes, *op. cit.*, p. 10.

[43] Anuradha Vittachi, *Stolen Childhood, In Search of the Rights of the Child* (Polity Press, Cambridge, 1989), p. 28.

[44] Melvin Konner, *Childhood* (Boston: Little Brown and Company, 1991), p. 196.

independent actors, and presumed to be almost childlike in their innocence about international *realpolitik*.[45] The conflation of womanhood with motherhood ties children with women in a way that does not occur with men. Similarly, in many ways children are thought about in close connection with the female sphere, as natural consumers of a female sphere, and as therefore feminine regardless of their sex. The relationship between mother and child is an important component of the conception of childhood.

Aid agencies too have concretized this association of mothers with childhood. Mothers have been primarily represented as a physiological and emotional extension of the child; as indeed is correct in the sense that children's survival and sense of security is shared with their primary carers who are most likely to be mothers. In 1989 UNICEF (The United Nations' Children's Fund) realized that their commitment to helping children, was ineffective without also reaching mothers and potential mothers. At the Beijing Women's Conference, UNICEF advocated that:

> Everything UNICEF does relates to women. You cannot run programmes for women without tackling the injustice that begins for girls in their infancy or even before birth. Children are not treated as individuals, they are considered in the relationship with their parents or guardians. The quality of life for children depends on the status of women.[46]

The simultaneous direction of aid to children and mothers, in the absence of father figures, has also merely served to present mothers and children as a single, incapable unit, both subject to paternalist and protectionist politics. The absence of the mother in an image of a young child can sustain the concept of childhood as a time of vulnerability. Advertising consultants and fund-raisers for Oxfam maintain that in the context of famine images 'a child will bring in more than an adult, a girl child who cries will bring in more than a boy who does not'.[47]

'Children' Having Children

Reproductive capability also marks a change in children's status within the community. A psychologist writing in a popular psychology text of the 1960s casually claims that '[t]he ability to cope with family life is seldom attained before the twenties'.[48] What precisely is meant by coping is not made clear. Across the world however, and in the more recent past in the West, the (desired) age of motherhood and fatherhood was and remains far lower than twenty. In Niger for example half of all women give birth

[45]   Cynthia Enloe, *The Morning After: Sexual Politics at the End of the Cold War* (London: University of California Press, 1993), p. 166.

[46]   *Children First, op. cit.*, pp. 2 and 8.

[47]   Patricia Holland, *What is a Child? Popular Images of Childhood* (London: Virago Press, 1992), p. 156.

[48]   C. I. Sandstrom, *The Psychology of Childhood and Adolescence* (Great Britain: Pelican Books, 1968), p. 14.

before the age of 18.[49] Responsibility for a family may characterize the beginning of adulthood, if not the end of childhood. More developed or liberal societies such as the United States and Great Britain view 'children having children' as an anomaly, and for social commentators it is an opportune moment to question the stability and progress of the whole of society. In the West, the reasons for teenage motherhood are varied, and may be related to lack of education, and an impoverished life. In small, rural communities of Kentucky State, USA, poor health care has drastically shortened the average life expectancy, especially of women, placing expectations of marriage and motherhood on the girls remaining in the community. It is not unusual for girls here to become wives from age ten and mothers at age twelve. Society is however thought to be at fault for not protecting these children from these circumstances, and especially in not sustaining stable two-parent families, the perceived Western norm.

There are many examples in Britain and the United States of how the moral fabric of society becomes questionable if a child becomes pregnant, or children are found to be at home alone. The isolated child, without the buffer zone of the 'normal family', personifies helplessness and dependency, and calls society into question more than any other member of society. Although the notion of a family is itself a contested concept, the child is framed in terms of dependency on, and centrality to such guardians. The child as a mother is thus incongruous. These examples are in stark contrast however to the experience of young people in the other countries indeed the majority of young people who from an early age are effectively entrusted with the care of siblings. Of course this also takes place in the West, in the form of 'babysitting' or even play amongst siblings. This contradiction illustrates in part the fragility of seemingly uncontestable assumptions about children and their appropriate roles.

'Innocence'

The idea of innocence is impossible to ignore in any consideration of children or politics. Children are frequently cited as innocent or of losing innocence especially in a war zone. Rarely is the question asked 'Innocent of what?' Innocence and purity are two components of a conception of childhood which have gendered foundations.[50] It is contended by many that 'childhood innocence' is based on childhood being understood to be a time of *sexual* innocence.[51] Such assumptions of innocence may be not only inaccurate, but also further debilitating for children. Archard suggests that such a concept of childhood thus *becomes* sexualized and 'connotes a purity, virginity, freshness and immaculateness which excites by the possibilities of defilement. As has been noted of many men who frequent prostitutes

---

[49] 'Youngest and oldest brides', *The Guardian,* 28 January 1996, p. 22.

[50] Erica Burman, 'Innocents Abroad: Western Fantasies of Childhood and the Iconography of Emergencies', in *Disasters,* Vol. 18, No. 3, 1994, p. 240.

[51] Archard (1993), *op. cit.,* p. 40.

or abduct children for sexual gratification: '[t]hey're chasing after a particular look. And sexual value is attached to youth'.[52]

There is as yet no international agreement on what is unlawful sexual activity against children.[53] But publicity of child sexual abuse provokes a different and more powerful reaction by concerned groups than women's sexual abuse and slavery.[54] Children's enslavement is seen as more horrifying. 'This process distorts the reality of the situation, implying that it is tolerable to enslave women but not children.'[55] The discovery of Belgian girls who had been sexually abused, tortured and buried alive was hugely publicized and also served to draw attention to the world's first Congress Against the Commercial Sexual Exploitation of Children which later convened in Stockholm. *Time* Magazine, described at length the 'outrage' of the global phenomenon of sexual exploitation of children, that 'dramatized the plight of children in peril everywhere'.[56] But *Newsweek* seemed to catch the true nature of the shock felt in its comment: '[f]or if it can happen in a rural village in a country as benign as Belgium, surely it can happen anywhere'.[57] 'The world's dirtiest business',[58] the child-sex trade was not addressed until such crimes were committed on children – and on children who were particularly innocent on *home* soil in Belgium. This suggests that concepts of the child are also parasitic on notions of state respectability and development. The mentality of Western sex offenders abroad, would seem to bear this out as they too do not imagine they are abusing 'children'. They may resort to cultural relativisms and misogynistic excuses, conceptualizing the foreign children they use as 'others' or early developers.

Innocence and purity are characteristics also rendered in constructed images and conceptions of children.[59] An allegation of absence wielded almost exclusively at young people it is at best patronizing and at worst detrimental to development and rehabilitation, generating moral panic and rational paralysis in our attempts to form partnerships with children. These are perhaps the least considered and most opaque components of modern understandings of childhood. Jenny Kitzinger suggests that the child rendered as innocent and valued in this way further adds to their danger of becoming the idealized innocent of a certain male sexual desire – hairless,

---

[52]   Susan Greenberg, 'Children for sale', *Newsweek*, 2 September 1996, p. 11.

[53]   *Ibid.*, p. 12.

[54]   Kathleen Barry, 'Pornography and the global exploitation of women', in Diane Bell and Renate Klein, *Radically Speaking: Feminism Reclaimed* (London: Zed Books, 1996), pp. 448–55.

[55]   Robyn Rowland, 'Radical Feminism: History, Politics, Action' in Bell and Klein, *op. cit.*, p. 25.

[56]   *Time,* 2 September 1996, frontcover.

[57]   Susan H. Greenberg, *op. cit.,* p. 9.

[58]   *Newsweek,* 2 September 1996, frontcover.

[59]   Marina Warner, 'Outing of the family album', *Times Higher Education[al Supplement]*, 4 December 1998, p. 25.

vulnerable, weak, dependent and uncorrupted.[60] Such images of the child may be playing a central role in anchoring conceptions of the child and childhood.

Images and Iconography

The imagined child, most often realized in images and literary sources, is an important indicator of expectations of childhood.

> the familiar typology of childhood includes the energetic boy and the seductive girl, the dependent child in need of protection, the ignorant child in need of education, the playful child in the home and the violent child on the streets.[61]

It is an interesting fact that the images of beauty, or the aesthetic faces that we crave or are seduced by, are also typically identified as also young and feminine. The image of a child employed in visual culture is also often of a particular type. For example, the beautiful, feminine, infant child becomes the icon of vulnerability in war propaganda, polarizing and humanizing the threat, imploring protection. Propagandists retain infantile qualities even in depictions of older bodies, by making use of particular physical qualities. In Nazi and Soviet propaganda of World War Two (WWII), children were likely to be blonde, aesthetic, wide-eyed and pleading to receive attention and or be cared for; small, pre-adolescent, silent and still, and isolated from a familial context.[62] Such visual qualities also suggest purity, vulnerability, innocence and approachability.

As Archard explains, there has been a proliferation of the image of the child, not the everyday child but the aesthetic, pleasing, satisfying image of a young child. As a literary device and pictorial construct, it is used to provide contrast with the adult condition. As Archard notes:

> the English literary exploration of childhood is no more than two centuries old, and that this exploration, has, in many ways, been an exploitation of childhood as a symbol for what is deemed to be missing from and degenerate about adulthood.[63]

Images of childhood form a mainstay of nostalgic and sentimental recollection of better times; positive, innocent and free of pressure. Patricia Holland suggests that 'pictures of children are part of a set of interweaving narratives of childhood which are both public and private, and personal and social'. Holland asserts that within these images there are attempts to secure meanings within a structure of power.[64] In

---

[60]   Jenny Kitzinger, quoted in Archard, *op. cit.*, p. 40.

[61]   Holland, *op. cit.*, p. 12; Patricia Holland, *Picturing Childhood: The Myth of the Child in Popular Imagery,* (London: I B Tauris, 2004).

[62]   Toby Clarke, *Art and Propaganda in theTtwentieth Century: The Political Image in the Age of Mass Culture* (London: Weidenfeld and Nicolson, 1997).

[63]   Archard (1993), *op. cit.*, p. 39.

[64]   Holland, *op. cit.*

the West, innocence of adult experience and threat are thought to be self-evident in the concept of the child, particularly the young child. This is evidenced in the near exclusive pictorial use of the child in the Western media to illustrate or epitomize crises and disasters, thus simultaneously compounding societal and childhood innocence or degradation.

Victims

Focusing on the plight of the child is a technique frequently employed in the reporting of international news and foreign conflicts. Crises in far away places intrude on our consciousness through the work of the media. The children whose faces and terror are zoomed in on, are part of what Erica Burman describes as the iconography of emergencies, or disaster pornography.[65] Children's faces demand responses. Positioned alone and out of place in a situation that is not of their making, they are a compelling illustration of wrongdoing. Children are sole agents of disaster aesthetics, allowed to illustrate a story because they actually explain very little. Particular images of children seem to symbolize or concretize at least the horror of a situation in the mind of the observer. Pictures of starving children dominated the film footage of the Ethiopian famine in 1985. When Russian troops invaded Chechnya in 1995, pictures of blood-smeared Chechen children were on the front pages of most British newspapers.[66] Similarly, British reporting of the Rwandan massacres has used the case studies of children to portray the crisis in graphical clarity.[67] The questions remain: is the child that is represented in the news, the same as the child in the societies in question, and how is that choice of representation intended to inform the observer?

Other individuals if not whole sectors of population can be attributed with childlike qualities or personified as infantile. Reducing different and 'other' people to children was a visual tool in the propaganda of the British Empire. Today, the images of these same developing countries are also presented, as both full of children, and childlike. Holland asserts that the growing awareness of humanitarian issues in the West, is fuelled by the desire to protect such children. She writes that consequently, this desire may have far-reaching implications for these children and their society:

> women, Black people and the whole of the Third World are among those who stand in a childish relation to the exercise of power. The non-white nations are regularly represented as if they themselves lack potency, and it is among the children of the developing countries – in stark contrast to the well-fed, well-equipped mini-consumers of the domestic image – that we find the most frequent pictures of childhood suffering.[68]

---

[65] Burman (1994), *op. cit.*

[66] Andrew Higgins, 'Yeltsin takes over army', *The Independent*, 12 January 1995, p. 1.

[67] See for example, Jenny Matthews, 'A holocaust we chose not to see', *The Observer*, 2 April 1995, p. 14; and Lindsey Hilsum, 'Rwanda's time of rape returns to haunt thousands', *The Observer*, 26 February 1995, p. 17.

[68] Holland, *op. cit.*, p. 148.

The condition of children and the length of childhood are strongly correlated with the condition of a society or state. It may, for example, be asserted that children who are exposed to society's ills have *lost* their childhood.[69] Likewise, security, development and progress can be clearly epitomized by the condition and health of children. Holland asserts that 'the western public has become familiar with an imagery of extremity at the expense of context, and the wrenching of emotion at the expense of understanding'.[70] Children have remained at the center of images of hardship as photographers work to create the most striking images. The charity: *Save the Children* requires shocking images to gain fast results. Through their visual representation and manipulation, the apparent 'truth' they possess also simplifies to the point of obscurity, their context.

'Children may express emotions that are universal, while remaining separate from those other qualities that make humanity so diverse.'[71] Through such use of the victim-child to headline disasters, an entire support network, perhaps the family, and community and state to which a suffering child belongs is mentally by-passed in the viewer. In the visual absence of other authority figures, a temporary surrogacy by the viewer is also encouraged. 'Iraqi children are dying – you can save them.'[72] In media stories, the public are then congratulated on rescuing the children, shown corresponding 'before' and 'after' faces, and thus the beginning and end of a foreign disaster.[73] Children are inherently victim-like and help reduce a story into sound bites and essentials.[74] Aid and development are conflated and femininity and childish dependency are collapsed to evoke sympathy.[75] Erica Burman and Holland share the view that children act as visual 'indices of vulnerability that transcend culture and politics'.[76] Moeller too has uncovered systematic and often distorted use of children in international news reports regardless of their actual relevance to the story.[77]

Containment

Above all, the imagery drawn on above, 'displays the social and psychic effort that goes into negotiating the difficult distinction between adult and child. There

---

[69]   See for example, 'Growing up Scared: How America's Kids are Robbed of Their Childhood', *Newsweek*, 10 January 1994, frontispiece and p. 37.

[70]   Holland *op cit.*, p. 151.

[71]   *Ibid.*, p. 157.

[72]   *The Independent*, 6 March 1998, Headline, p. 1.

[73]   For example, the widely publicized rescue of Irma from Bosnia in 1995, and Mariam Hamza from Iraq 'by' Labour MP George Galloway in 1998.

[74]   Holland, *op. cit.*, p. 152.

[75]   Burman (1994), *op. cit.*, p. 242; Burman, Erica (1996), 'Constructing and Deconstructing Childhood: Images of Children and Charity Appeals', in J. Haworth (ed.), *Psychological Research: Innovative Methods and Strategies* (London: Routledge).

[76]   Burman (1994), *op. cit.*, p. 243.

[77]   Susan D. Moeller, 'The Media's Use of Children in the Telling of International News', *Press/Politics*, Vol. 7, no. 1, 2002, pp. 36–56.

is an active struggle to maintain childhood – if not actual children – as pure and uncontaminated'.[78] As I shall show throughout the book, this negotiation of meaning is inherent in the projection of a *contained* concept of the child, in a world society where multiplicities of concepts are possible. Holland summarizes the idea of containment as follows:

> ... yet the public discourse of which imagery plays so important a part strives to produce a childhood which, as well as being different from adulthood, is its obverse, a depository for many precious qualities adulthood needs but cannot tolerate as part of itself. The dichotomy child/adult is linked to other dichotomies that dominate our thought: nature/culture, primitiveness/civilization, emotion/reason. In each pair the dominant term seeks to understand and control the subordinate, keeping it separate but using it for its own enrichment.[79]

As Erica Burman notes, 'discourses of childhood are central to definitions of adulthood: each relies upon and secures the boundaries of the other'. She notes that key areas that threaten to blur this boundary include children's 'knowledge' (especially sexual knowledge) and activity (especially political, economic and violent activity).[80] I argue that the concept of the 'political' in particular is formulated and projected as if separate from children. This *containment* is to an extent, recognizable in the study of childhood and of children's development. This shift in understanding may be the narrow end of a wedge that firmly opens up concepts of childhood and adulthood and with this destabilizes many other social identities.

The current paradigm shift underway in childhood studies shows that we are late in recognizing the multiple ways in which children have agency and power. By agency I mean the ways in which they are able to participate and inform social practices. By power I mean their agency and their contribution. This new phase in the study of childhood is itself in its infancy. It is also represented in popular culture and the media as a 'crisis' in childhood.[81] Though crises in childhood are not new, it is clear that how the political is constituted in childhood is being questioned:

> Children are seen as 'presocial', unable to articulate a set of coherent political views (Sears and Valentino, 1997). The social science community has thus treated children's political participation as a contradiction in terms. A political community has an exclusive adult membership with children unable to provide qualifications for entry. ... these research assumptions connect with broader social forces of convention. For many the very essence of childhood, at least in contemporary western terms, prohibits political participation such that the 'political child' is seen as the 'unchild', a counter-stereotypical image of

---

[78] Holland, *op. cit.*, pp. 13–14.
[79] *Ibid.*, p. 14.
[80] Burman, (1994) *op. cit.*, p. 241.
[81] Anne Higonnet, *Pictures of Innocence: The History and Crisis of Ideal Childhood* (London: Thames and Hudson, 1998).

children that does not fit with the way we commonly view childhood (Stainton-Rogers and Stainton-Rogers, 1992: 32–3).[82]

The contribution children may make to a community is often not recognized as political until it is invited to be so by adults. Competence to vote is one such marker. In Brazil, Croatia and Cuba children may vote from 16. In the UK and across Europe this potential is eclipsed by evidence of children's apparent political apathy. This apathy is perhaps borne of a particular framing of politics and society more generally. As Archard notes, those in power might also be failing to communicate with children.[83]

Political contribution is thus also an essential aspect of how adulthood is conceived. The last section of this chapter returns to the academic debates on understandings of childhood at the end of the twentieth century, which challenge the contained dimensions of childhood illustrated above.

Agency

Scientific approaches to childhood span barely a hundred years and are supplemented by studies of childhood across nearly all the social sciences. The realization that children are worthy of study as a separate group, has meant therefore a gradual proliferation of approaches across academia with the prefix 'child'. The *Encyclopaedia Britannica*, for example refers to child-development, child-labor, child abuse, child-psychiatry, child-psychology, and child-welfare without defining parameters of the subject or child.[84] Each field of enquiry is thought to merit a child sub-category by virtue of the child's developing qualities, physically, emotionally, intellectually and morally, which create different demands in providing for children. More recently, the psycho-social field of development studies has become the arena of contestation for mapping and charting the phenomena of childhood.

It is only in the last two decades however that systematic attempts to study children's socialization, and their own agency have emerged, concomitant with 'the need to reappraise our understanding of childhood as a rehearsal for adult life', and grant children recognition and respect in their right and on their own terms.[85] Recent constructivist and interpretive approaches taken from the social sciences have led to a reexamination of apparently natural boundaries and dimensions of childhood, the role of social forces in shaping children and the role of children in forming social forces:[86]

---

[82]   Wyness, M., Harrison, L., and Buchanan, I. (2004), 'Childhood, Politics and Ambiguity: Towards an Agenda for Children's Political Inclusion', *Sociology*, Volume 38(1).

[83]   Archard (2004), *op. cit.*, p. 101.

[84]   *Encyclopedia Britannica Micropedia* ,Vol. 3, 15th edition (1989).

[85]   Jo Boyden and Deborah Levison, *op. cit.*, p. 42.

[86]   See for example Alison James and Alan Prout, A. (eds), *op. cit.*; Corsaro, W., *op. cit.*

[t]he new emphasis on context in child development represents a long overdue rapprochement between the individualism of psychology, the social structural concerns of sociology and the cultural descriptions of anthropology.[87]

The construct of the child is now firmly on the agenda of social science research and has recently been the subject of a £3 million project by the Economic and Social Research Council.[88] It is also newly recognized that concepts of childhood may be culturally created. Across all social science disciplines there is an awareness that children's environment can shape their development, thus posing a unique challenge for researchers to observe children's experience without privileging adult assumptions in that observation process. Most notably the last decade or so of sociology and childhood studies has brought new-found recognition of children's abilities to comprehend political issues and make political decisions perhaps from the ages of nine.[89]

Sociologists increasingly question the validity of literature, which has hitherto treated children as objects rather than subjects. Childhood is inseparable from the adult world that constructs it, which includes the political world. Children too are still being understood as agents in their own identity, rather than mere recipients of adult interpretation. The concept of children observed by adults may not be that which is experienced by the subjects themselves, a phenomenon of duality and misinterpretation which is unique to this cohort, since they cannot represent themselves. As childhood becomes less certain, the popularization of perceived threats to childhood, and reported anomalies of the child's role, particularly in areas of world politics, evidences norms or expectations of childhood. Contemporary media reportage often draws attention to the contamination of childhood by apparently non-childlike experiences such as violence, politics, and sexual activity. These common social norms of acceptable child experiences allow for a great deal of socio-political comment and interference, particularly when such boundaries are overstepped. Holland, argues therefore that the child is a symbol of common humanity.[90] It is however a Western construct of childhood, as a time of protection whilst adulthood is being attained, against which many 'damaging'/non-Western practices and ideas are measured and criticized. It is an easy step to export blame to developing countries because of their inability to conform to our projected model of childhood.[91] Norman Stone has noted how

---

[87] Martin Woodhead, Paul Light and Ronnie Carr, *Open University: Child Development in a Social Context*, Vol. 3, *Growing up in a Changing Society* (London: Routledge, 1991), p. xi.

[88] ESRC *Children 5-16* Research Programme for the 21st Century 1996–1999.

[89] See Archard (2004), *op. cit.*; Sharon Stephens, *Children and the Politics of Culture* (Princeton: Princeton University Press, 1995) and Jim Goddard, Sally McNamee, Adrian James and Allison James (eds) (2005), *The Politics of Childhood: International Perspectives, Contemporary Developments* (Houndsmills, Basingstoke: Macmillan).

[90] Holland, *op. cit.*, p. 157.

[91] Vanessa Pupavac, 'The Deviant South: The Globalisation of Childhood and the Creation of a New Moral Order', paper presented to British International Studies Association, 1997, p. 28.

the globalization of American Liberal values, particularly a universal protectionist concept of childhood,[92] carries with it moral or ethical weight which has allowed the United States to wield heavy blows in its discourse with other states.

From this brief tour of childhood it would be difficult to isolate or evaluate the relative importance of the many social, cultural, national, and economic factors which contribute to the construction of the child at any one time. The prominent and recent journal of child studies, *Childhood*,[93] defines itself as interdisciplinary in approach and spanning divisions between geographical regions, disciplines, social and cultural contexts. Again, it is arguable if one could produce an equivalent journal of *Adulthood*, which could collate adult experiences and also be defined against childhood. Childhood fluidity and temporality however does mark it out for special attention. A perceived endpoint of childhood may be experienced as no more than a dimension of childhood or adulthood elsewhere. As such it is a powerful construction that can be harnessed readily and subtly. Shifts of meaning in childhood have often occurred within national rather than cultural or social borders as a consequence of national and military mobilization.

Boundaries and dimensions of childhood, are thus concretized at various points in history. In civil wars, where a nation or ethnic group is under threat, particularly in the developing world, childhood has been shown to be contracted, informally and formally, in order that children are freed to perform adult roles earlier. Parents of children in cultures in sub-Saharan Africa have privileged and brought forward puberty rites through fear that their daughters may be violated whilst away from the home. Girls may thus undergo premature puberty rites which take them into the realm of womanhood, respectful marriage or pregnancy, and consequently abandon schooling earlier. In addition their informal education is perceived as beginning at home and formal education is deemed as irrelevant for local needs.[94] In this area, childhood for girls is thus increasingly delimited by the means taken to avoid the shame of sexual encounters before adult initiation rights. Education is not seen as a right but an indicator of child status. The relative instability of the societal experience of war, particularly in Africa where poverty has deepened and wars with small arms have proliferated, can require an early appropriation of adult roles and behavior by children. The lack of maternal education on childcare, and the inadequate financial provision for health, may also be responsible for a shorter time of acknowledged childhood, compared to the West. A Liberian ten-year-old may be thought of in his community as a child, before and after conflict takes place. Though, for the purposes of participating in a conflict, he may be made forcibly into

---

[92]   Norman Stone, 'The New Age of Interventionism: the Globalisation of American Liberal Discourse', paper presented to the British International Studies Association, 1997.

[93]   *Childhood: A Global Journal of Child Research* (London: SAGE, 1995 ff).

[94]   B. Rwezaura, 'The Concept of the Child's Best Interests in the Changing Context of Sub-Saharan Africa,' in Philip Alston (ed.), *The Best Interest of the Child. Reconciling Culture and Human Rights* (Oxford: Clarendon Press, UNICEF, 1994), pp. 102–103.

an adult through a militarized initiation rite and thus think of himself as one.[95] Child soldiers in Africa may hold the responsibilities of an adult, and think of themselves as taking on adult roles if military obligations come into force at an earlier age than is usual. In 1992 UNICEF reported that in Sudan, 12,500 boys aged between nine and sixteen were kidnapped by rebel fighters to be trained as soldiers. In this case the conscription criterion was two molar teeth.[96] Acquisition of responsibility may thus indicate a transformation of status. It has long been documented in Northern Ireland and Palestine that war is an initiation right for boys.[97] Militarization and masculinity are seen as directly related to maturity.

Chapter 2 continues the uncovering of conceptions about childhood by looking at children's engagement in areas of global politics. Constructs of the child are embodied in their roles, exploitation, and in expectations held of them. Thus dominant constructions of emasculated or unpolitical childhood and the assumed separation of children from the adult political world are brought into question. The multiplicity of understandings of the child and the specificities of socio-economic, cultural, national, gendered and legal dimensions to childhood, outlined in this chapter, also inform these practices.

---

[95] Human Rights Watch/Africa, *Easy Prey: Child Soldiers in Liberia* (New York: Human Rights Watch, 1995).

[96] Molly Moore, John Ward-Anderson, and Chris McGreal, 'Fighting to rescue a lost generation', *The Guardian*, 29 April 1995, p. 15.

[97] For an overview see Morris Fraser, *Children in Conflict* (Harmondsworth: Penguin, 1972).

Chapter 2

Children in Global Politics

Chapter 2 continues to uncover constructs of the child through various ways that children's bodies and minds are harnessed in the global political economic system. Having outlined the fluidity of the construction of the 'child' in Chapter 1, this chapter now challenges the perceived partiality of children as political people and demonstrates children's agency and vital political capital. Organized into cultural, historic and socio-economic and political contexts it includes state-building measures, employment and slavery, education and indoctrination and children's changing experiences in warfare and security practices.

State-building and Family Planning

Harry Hendrick, in a history of child welfare in England, divides children into dualisms of bodies and minds. His study illustrates how the concept of the child changed as their physical and mental health was increasingly recognized as being of political significance.[1] Hendrick notes that changes in family structure, the welfare state, the Boer War, WWI and the British Empire played their part in changing perceptions of the child. The child's body rather than mind was of national interest to the British between 1870–1914, as the role of nutrition, welfare of the mother and medical care, were recognized as being of strategic importance in the propagation of much needed healthy soldiers. Society was informed by their government that 'an Empire such as ours requires a race vigorous and industrious and intrepid'.[2] As shown in Chapter 1, military requirements led to the demarcation of a period of childhood in medical science and practice. After the Boer war for example, the role of responsibility for child-care taking was stated in rather more direct terms. The British public were told that 'an unhealthy schoolchild is a danger to all society'.[3] In Canada, children were described as a national asset, a constituent part of the state's defenses, embodying the future of Canada. 'The Great War has impressed upon us as never before the grave necessity not only of conserving the children, but also of affording them every opportunity to develop normally. It has become a patriotic

---

[1]   Harry Hendrick, *Child Welfare in England, 1872–1989* (London: Routledge, 1994).
[2]   Valerie Fildes, Lara Marks and Hilary Marland (eds), *Women and Children First: International and Infant Welfare 1870–1945* (London: Routledge, 1992), pp. 1 and 97.
[3]   Hendrick, *op. cit.*, p. 13.

duty as well as a professional one'.[4] Pronatalist policies and attention to the relative birth rates of European states illustrate an increasing perception of children as future investments in terms of state manpower and security.[5]

Keep Britain Tidy

The corollary of generating and caring for larger numbers of younger people to shore up the future state was that their unhealthy counterparts necessarily drained resources which could further strengthen 'healthy' children. It was at this time that British nationals were needed to populate the Empire and these two factors alone prompted the British government's twin-track strategy of removing and exporting less desirable children from the British slums to the Dominions. Child emigration had already begun in the 1860s.[6] The forced or arranged mass migration of smaller bodies abroad dealt with unwanted children and acted as a safety valve on civil discontent, reducing numbers of the degenerate poor who posed dangers to respectable society. These children were seen as 'bricks with which the empire would be built – the young colonists of the future ... who would help to consolidate the Empire and form the living link between the Dominions and the mother country'.[7]

Children were thus a constituent part of nation-building, and the means employed to counter fear about declining birthrate. As Beveridge stated, reduced numbers of children could contribute to a decline of 'the security and influence of Great Britain'.[8] Opinion in the Dominions echoed this racial insecurity. In 1938 the Archbishop of Perth had stated that 'if we do not supply from our own stock, we are leaving ourselves all the more exposed to the menace of the teeming millions of our neighboring Asian races'.[9] Many agencies in Britain, including Barnardo's, the Catholic Child Welfare Council, National Children's Homes and the Salvation Army, 'exported' children to Australia and New Zealand from 1850 until as recently as 1967. From the late 1860s, 10,000 children alone were sent to Canada.[10] In 1994 an article by Margaret Humphreys, entitled: 'Empty Cradles: one Woman's fight to Uncover Britain's Most Shameful secret', drove an ironically 'new found' moral panic over these grown up children, and through the media and churches, further

---

[4]   In Cynthia R. Comaccio, 'The infant soldier: early child welfare efforts in Ontario', in Valerie Fildes, Lara Marks and Hilary Marland, (eds), *op. cit.*, p. 107.

[5]   Hendrick, *op. cit.*, p. 14.

[6]   *Ibid.*, p. 82.

[7]   *Ibid.*, p. 14.

[8]   *Ibid.*, p. 285.

[9]   Alexandra Frean, 'Empire's forgotten children strike back', *The Times*, 18 May 1998, p. 7.

[10]   Patrick, A. Dunae, 'Gender, generations and Social Class: the Fairbridge Society and British Child Migration to Canada, 1930–1960', in Jon Lawrence, Pat Starkey (eds), *Child Welfare and Social Action in the Nineteenth and Twentieth Centuries: International Perspectives* (Liverpool: Liverpool University Press, 2001), p. 82.

publicity and compensation were sought.[11] Sherington notes how contrary to this drive, many of 'the lost children of empire' were not shamed but celebrated at the time by exporters and importers, the media and the family. A spectrum of complicity and victimhood is evident however. Children of Aboriginal and Torres Strait islander peoples were forcibly removed from their parents and fostered and assimilated into white society. This practice also remained legal until 1967.[12]

Such practices suggest that children were conceptualized as embodiments or potential vessels of national security or strength and also a conveniently mobile collective body that could be moved at will. A contemporary example might be shown in the mass baby-lift organized by the Americans when they left Vietnam in 1975. Vietnamese 'orphans' were taken from villages to prevent them from being further exposed to the Communist threat and given new adoptive parents in the United States.[13] In all these cases children's lesser size, strength and cognition may have allowed them to be subject to this attention and manipulated by the 'surrogate' state. Children may be particularly vulnerable to state manipulation if they are also homeless or without family. In practices not dissimilar to those outlined above, children in present day Central America are removed from the streets and killed. Their physical condition and presence can be regarded as sufficiently threatening to warrant their removal. Guatemalan street children, for example, have been targeted by government-sponsored hit squads in order to cleanse cities of sources of crime and evidence of poverty. The killing of small street children and child traders fulfils state requirements of public 'cleanliness'. In Colombia these children are described as *limpieza social*, or disposables. This 'social cleansing' – ridding the streets of vermin[14] – was first initiated in the 1950s by police squads to combat rising crime. There are up to 7.5 million children in Brazil's streets vulnerable to this practice which has attracted a great deal of attention in the West as a human rights abuse. Sixty-eight death squads are reportedly active in one neighborhood of Rio de Janeiro alone. The phenomenon has also been reported in India, Turkey, Bulgaria and Kenya,[15] and it is interesting that there is no such parallel practice in which homeless adults are targeted in the streets of their cities. In these examples children are physically moved and renationalized, or in the case of Latin America, 'taken out'.

---

[11]   G. Sherington, 'Suffer Little Children': Between child migration as a study of journeyings between centre and periphery', *History of Education,* September 2003, vol. 32, no. 5, pp. 461–76.

[12]   See the 'Open letter from the International Supporters of Australian Native Title to H.M. Queen Elizabeth II', in *The Independent*, 19 June 1997.

[13]   Bridget Daly and Jenny Vaughan, *Children at War* (London: Macdonald, 1988), p. 25.

[14]   Susan Kobrin, 'Killed like cockroaches', *Amnesty*, January/February 1996, pp. 16–17.

[15]   Caroline Moorhead, 'All the world's children', in *Index on Censorship,* 2, 1997, p. 159.

Population Wars

Children's presence may also be alluded to by states in the context of population policy and antinatalist and pronatalist practices. Children may feature prominently in discourses of population policy, though it is the mother, as container of the future child who is used and targeted in practice. In times of perceived national threat children may be essentialized as a number, reduced to a statistical concept. In Britain, children were invoked and motherhood deployed as a means of managing British identity, or of controlling what wasn't British identity:

> The concern for proper mothering was often couched in terms of national and imperial interests, and a concern for racial degeneration. Children were posited as 'citizens of tomorrow' and a 'national asset' upon which the future of the country and empire depended. Consequently, concern over the (white) British population's birthrate intensified. Fears over depopulation mushroomed and the focus turned to women and mothers as a site of the reproduction of the nation and the maintenance of racial health and purity. Women became 'mothers of the race'.[16]

French pronatalist policies during the Third Republic and Fascist Italy's 'battle for births', are evidence of the perception of children's increased numbers as an emblem and guarantor of state health. In 1919, the Italian government created 'Children's Colonies' – free summer holidays for thousands of children in order to preserve their health and Mussolini's closest advisors suggested annulling childless marriages and criminalizing celibacy.[17]

In war, however, the nationality as well as the number of children may become of paramount importance. Where territory is disputed and national identity under threat, pronatalist practices may be pursued with more urgency as an additional means of securing the political body. In Croatia for example, a legislative program to encourage the propagation of the Croatian family and the biological control of the nation was introduced.[18] Forced impregnation of women and the legal channeling of motherhood essentialised women's identity in relation to her capacity to bear children and childless women were specifically referred to as 'non-women'. Pronatalist practices may also serve as a dual strategy of violence and renationalization against the enemy, for example, in the mass rape of women. In the Serbian occupied territories of Bosnia Hercegovina and Croatia for example, Serbians have combined ethnic cleansing and population policy by committing mass rape and serial rape to populate and maintain the greater Serbian state. Women already pregnant prior to

---

[16]   Omnia Shakry, 'Schooled Mothers and Structured Play: Child Rearing in Turn-of-the Century Egypt', in Lila Abu-Lughod (ed.), *Remaking Women. Feminism and Modernity in the Middle East* (Princeton University Press, 1998), p. 133.

[17]   Maria Sophia Quine, *Population Politics in Twentieth Century Europe* (London: Routledge, 1996), p. 42.

[18]   Cynthia Enloe, *The Morning After: Sexual Politics at the End of the Cold War* (London: University of California Press, 1993), pp. 241–3.

assaults had their fetuses removed[19] and women and girls interned in various types of Serbian concentration and rape/death camps were kept for at least 21 to 28 days to ensure pregnancy.

Evidence such as this is standard in accounts of the break-up of the former Yugoslavia. Though these children would be born of 'enemy' mothers they were forcibly conceived as part of the (re)nationalization of territory of which women's bodies formed a part. The rapists verbally emphasize that the women will give birth to their children.[20] The enemy was thus able to create a future national asset and a prize of war. Croatian and Bosnian men have also been attacked, specifically to make them sterile, to prevent them from fathering Croatian children. Survivor accounts detail systematic sterilization in various concentration camps by Serb forces using medical radiation, complete and partial castrations and beatings of the genitals.[21]

As has been shown, in times of state expansion and insecurity the propagation of more children may be high on the agenda. Conversely, in peace time the abundance of children may be rendered as a threat to the state, a source of instability, rather than an example of 'national' health. Antinatalist practices may be enforced by states in order to slow down population growth. National policies and programs to influence population size and growth rates are particularly common in developing countries where a link has been established between population growth, economic security and the health of society. Egypt, India, the Philippines and Zambia each began population reform after the population size was shown to be hindering economic development. China has perhaps demonstrated the most aggressive and restricted population policy. Between 1977 and 1990 family planning was specifically linked to economic production[22] and from 1980 tight legislation forced families to have only one child per couple. As Yuval Davis points out however, it was concern for 'political security in the 3rd world which in turn would create security problems to the US' that in part provoked and funded these measures and invoked the necessary gendered and cultural frames of reference which helped to make it happen.[23] It is interesting to note that in the states which have implemented population reform and its associated antinatalist practices, surprisingly little 'political' debate has incurred.[24] From the 1990s the world's population has been deliberately and systematically imbalanced where there is pressure to reduce the number of children, though states may not even declare this gendered information in their census return.

---

[19] Natalie Nenadic, 'Femicide: A framework for understanding Genocide', Diane Bell and Renate Kline, *Radically Speaking: Feminism Reclaimed* (London: Zed Books, 1996), pp. 458 and 459.

[20] *Ibid.*, p. 460.

[21] *Ibid.*, p. 459.

[22] John W. Thomas and Merilee S. Grindle, 'Political Leadership and Policy Characteristics in Population Policy Reform', in Jason L. Finkle and C. Alison McIntosh (eds), *The New Politics of Population: Conflict and Consensus in Family Planning* (New York: Oxford University Press, 1994).

[23] Nira Yuval Davis, *Gender and Nation*, (Sage: London, 1997), p. 34.

[24] *Ibid.*, p. 57.

This suggests that the sphere of the family and maternalism are not recognized as political by the majority of the polity, or that its political importance is deliberately played down. The latter is perhaps borne out by an example taken from Palestine where the sphere of child care is specifically identified as an 'antidote' to political participation. Palestinian women have noted that their family responsibilities and care of children are allowed to become extremely woman-oriented activities for the purpose of distracting, deterring and disassociating women from the sites of 'political' activities. Day-care centers, for example, are disallowed by the Israeli government and so children are seen and used as natural shackles on women in the community.[25] Children are encouraged to be 'seen to' by mothers, so that politics is not.

Workers, Laborers and Slaves

Children can play an active part in communities by securing themselves economically from an early age. Until the last decade, the children who sustained economies were barely even documented. Dominant paradigms of childhood illustrated earlier, have yielded little information on children as economic agents. Importantly this means that children's decisions or autonomy are ignored. Boyden and Levison have exposed the comprehensive nature of children's exclusion, the challenges for their appropriate inclusion and the numerous changes, recalculations and policy reforms necessitated through recognition of children as agents and participants in economic and social capital.[26] World wide, a majority of children's bodies – up to a billion, perhaps two billion – are contributing to the international economy. However in literature on the economy, children have been, and still are, subsumed within the category of adult workers or not documented at all if their labor is taking place informally, at home, within the family or unpaid. Disproportionately participating in labor, children are also, like women, disproportionately affected when structural reforms move them into the realm of goods and exchange. As suggested in the last section, children can perform roles, not by what they knowingly accomplish, but by their presence or constructed presence. A brief look at children in the global economy will first illustrate how children's bodies or presence can be commoditized, and then move on to illustrate some of the roles they perform and how they have been constructed.

Child Slaves

By definition, slaves have no power over how they are used. What distinguishes many child slaves from child laborers is the trade of their bodies and the use *of* their

---

[25]   Cynthia Enloe, *Bananas, Beaches and Bases: Making Feminist Sense of International Politics* (London: University of California Press, 1989), p. 58.

[26]   Jo Boyden and Deborah Levison, *Children as Economic and Social Actors in the Development Process*, Working Paper 1, Stockholm: Expert Group on Development Issues, 2000, p. 28.

bodies as opposed to the harnessing of their skills and their production of goods. The slave trade is centered on children and is perhaps the least visible example of human trafficking taking place on a large scale in the international economic system.[27] Female children's bodies are particularly valued in the sex trade, which itself forms a large, illicit and largely undocumented part of the international economy. Sexual slavery and associated employment of women and children has only recently been recognized as significant.[28] Sexual exploitation is defined as a practice by which person(s) receive sexual gratification or financial gain or advancement, through the abuse of a person's sexuality by abrogating that person's human right to dignity, equality, autonomy, and physical and mental well being.[29] Conceptions of children, outlined earlier, explain their value in the trafficking and sex industries. Consumers 'buy women who act like children, or girls who act like adult women'.[30] Children's enforced isolation further legitimizes their use and commoditization. Their removal and isolation from the familial sphere and their state encourages the adults who employ or use them to believe that they are also their guardians.

In conflict, children may be particularly susceptible to abduction and use in the slave trade. For example, since 1989 the Sudan People's Liberation Army and the National Islamic Front (the militant Islamic regime in power in the South until 2005), have both abducted young boys aged from nine years from their families and schools. Child slaves, described as being coercible and at the complete disposal of a master, are kept by army soldiers and militia.[31] Christians from the South have been given Arab names, 'converted' to Islam, branded with hot irons, and kept in houses in the North. They perform unpaid labor or are later exported to the Gulf, Libya, Chad and Mauritania. Few escape to tell their story and many may be being trained to become child combatants.[32] They have also been used to donate blood for Northern soldiers fighting the Sudanese civil war.

Child Laborers

This section now moves to illustrate examples of children as laborers, a role undertaken by most children worldwide. Child 'labor' indicates the degree of labor that is performed, and its relative impact on a child. It does not include all children's

---

[27]   *Children of Sudan: Slaves, Street Children and Child Soldiers* (USA: Human Rights Watch Africa, 1995).

[28]   Robyn Rowland and Renate Klein, 'Radical Feminism: History, Politics, Action', in Bell and Kline *op. cit.*, p. 9. See also Jan Jindy Pettman, *Worlding Women* (London: Routledge, 1996).

[29]   From a Convention on Sexual Exploitation quoted in Kathleen Barry, 'Pornography and the Global Sexual Exploitation of Women', in Bell and Klein *op. cit.*, p. 453.

[30]   *Ibid.*, p. 448.

[31]   Human Rights Watch Africa, *op. cit.*, p. 32.

[32]   Shyam Bhatia, 'Sudan revives the slave trade', *The Observer*, 9 April 1995, p. 14. Professor Ushari Mahmoud was jailed for two years for exposing the revival of slavery in Sudan.

work in the informal economy and reasonable labor undertaken within the home. Nossent defines child labor as:

> any activity done by a child which either contributes to production, gives adults free time, facilitates the existence of the child, facilitates the work of others, or substitutes for the employment of others and which endangers the safety, health and welfare and/or development of that child – whether that development be physical, mental, emotional, moral or intellectual.[33]

Like many authors and campaigners on the subject, she distinguishes between work that a child is reasonably capable of, and work, in such a quantity or quality that hinders the child's development. Although child labor is monitored by non-governmental organizations and IGOs such as the International Labor Office, a large proportion of children's labor in the strictly pejorative sense remains undocumented. Debts through bonded labor are never usually paid off and are taken up by subsequent generations. There are over 11 million bonded child laborers in India, working to pay off the debt incurred in a verbal contract of employment. Even unborn children may be pledged to factory owners against maternity loans to the parents.[34]

Invisible Girls

Natasha Nossent has shown that children, especially girl children are often missing from official statistics even as recently as a decade ago. The informal nature of their work and the gender of child laborers may have contributed to their invisibility and a downplaying of the scale of their presence and contribution. Girls in fact may be used as workers without acknowledgement of their labor by their families, employers or the state. She cites evidence of girls as young as three undertaking tasks in factories as servants and socialized into sewing forces from the age of four.[35] Nossent points out that reports such as those made by the ILO usually only refer to paid labor in a strictly defined 'formal' sector and as such many workers are not counted. 'Talk' of children working most often means boys. Given that 80 per cent of all child labor is estimated to be unpaid, many children are yet to be taken into account.

Most analysis of labor hides the vast numbers of children who work outside cities and in illegal occupations. Girls may not be considered to be 'workers' though they often work for longer hours than boys. Girls are also most often unpaid or paid less than boys for the same jobs. This gendered division of labor extends into other spheres of social life. According to Nossent: 'Girls spend their childhood close to the household domain while boys are encouraged to spend more time outside the home and thus participate in community affairs.'[36] Girls remain inside

---

[33]   Natasha Nossent, 'When the division of child labour in gendered, but civil society's approach to this phenomenon is not', unpublished paper (University of Amsterdam, 1996).
[34]   Urvashi Butalia, 'So many Shivas', in *Index on Censorship*, 2, 1997, p. 162.
[35]   Nossent, *op. cit.*, p. 5.
[36]   Nossent, *op. cit.*, p. 10.

the community, doing the majority of the work. Boys, however, may have greater opportunities through their status as workers outside the home and also by their increased pay, enabling them to act within and represent the community. It could be argued, therefore, that the gendered division of labor within economies, allows boys to gain adult responsibilities and opportunities sooner than their female counterpart laborers.

George Kent's seminal study, *Children in the International Political Economy,*[37] illustrated how children are intrinsically part of the international economy. Kent argues that children take on specific roles within the economy because of their physical and mental attributes and focuses on the most highly dependent young children in society. In Brazil, seven and a half million young workers, of which three million are aged between ten and fourteen, provide very cheap labor because companies do not need to pay the same benefits as to adults. Seventy per cent earn half of the minimum wage – typically £2.50 a week – in the sisal industry.[38] As a result, children are sought after as workers whilst their parents often go unemployed. The reduced pay that a child commands also brings down labor rates and working conditions. This in turn ensures that more children in a family have to be employed. They are often described as hard workers who are easy to manage. These children's lives and futures are shaped primarily by their physical capacity for labor and their low wages. Child laborers often work in appalling conditions and have virtually no protection afforded by labor law. Children's working conditions often coupled with extreme poverty can drastically harm their physical and emotional well being. Quite often they are under the legal permitted working age, and this illegality contributes to their non-recognition. Children in India or Thailand for example, may work as competently and for the same duration as their adult counterparts in carpet factories and prostitution rings, where smaller bodies are appreciated. Their adult labors, however return a child or female's wages. Such children may have been brought into the world solely for future economic security, to fulfill a function, and nurtured only for their relative capability as a worker. Under difficult circumstances or harsh working conditions the child may be correspondingly less important to a community if he or she is unable to contribute to labor needs.

The next section will move on to look at how children are instrumental and take on roles in what for adults can be a legitimate occupation – warfare.

Warfare

The earliest documented use of children being *active* in warfare begins with the mythologized Children's Crusade in 1212 where children set out to join the

---

[37]   George Kent, *Children in the International Political Economy* (London: Macmillan, 1995), p. 5. See also Alison M. S. Watson, 'Seen but Not Heard: The Role of the Child in International Political Economy', *New Political Economy*, Vol. 9, No. 1, 2004.

[38]   Valerie Franca and Joachim de Carvalno, 'Children in Bondage' in *Veja*, Sao Paulo, 30 August, reprinted in *World Press Review*, January 1996, Vol. 43, No.1, pp. 10 and 11.

Christians fighting to capture the Holy Land, though most perished from exposure before reaching their battleground. Throughout history, children of soldiers have joined their parents and become involved in war as soon as they are physically capable. During the Napoleonic wars young boys joined the navy in such numbers that their ships were called 'nursery ships'. They could join up at the age of ten or eleven as officers' assistants suited to many small tasks. Frederick the Great of Prussia is recorded as allowing child soldiers to enlist from the age of eight. Armies raised through conscription however have since considerably reduced the need and opportunity for young boys to join the armed forces in many states.

The use of children in conflict has however increased as a consequence of the changing character of warfare, particularly in the late twentieth century. Total war and people's war, for example, have mobilized citizens outside the traditional boundaries of battlegrounds. During the final days of WWII, Hitler used thousands of children aged between eight and seventeen on the front line. Most died, perhaps in greater numbers because they had less experience than their adult counterparts.[39] New, lighter weaponry coupled with extreme poverty, Western training techniques and educational indoctrination have however considerably advanced the capacity of the child soldiers and young resistance fighters and with this also created new opportunities for children's abuse. Guerrilla war and very light weaponry alone make it possible for children to fight and kill from as young as six years. 'New rifles weigh less than 3 kilograms and fire 600 rounds a minute ... making them genuine equalizers'.[40] African and Palestinian children have been at the forefront for change and participation in military activity. During the Palestinian *intifada* in the Israeli occupied territories, children and youths were the catalysts and initiators of violent strife against Israeli troops.[41] Stone throwing in Palestine has been elevated to a military art with specific roles assigned to children of all ages.[42]

Roles that children are given and/or take up war include:

- soldiers/combatants
- sex slaves and prostitutes
- human shields
- targets, killed or maimed or captured
- minesweepers
- 'consequences' of war rape

[39]   Jean Bethke Elshtain, 'Sovereignty, Identity, Sacrifice', in V. Spike Peterson (ed.), *Gendered States: Feminist (Re)Visions of International Relations Theory* (Boulder: Lynne Riener, 1992), p. 150.

[40]   Mark Frankel, *et al.*, 'Boy Soldiers: Special Report', *Newsweek* , 7 August 1995, p. 15.

[41]   Guy Goodwin-Gill and Ilene Cohn, *Child Soldiers* (Oxford: Clarendon, 1994), p. 22.

[42]   Ed Cairns, *Children and Political Violence* (London: Blackwell, 1996), pp. 112–13.

- stakeholders
- moral and political agents or agitators
- peacemakers.

The international age limit for soldiers' voluntary recruitment and use is currently set at sixteen and many are much younger than this. Over forty-five states now use approximately 300,000 child soldiers.[43] (Their lives are highly expendable and, as such, the total figure must run far higher.) It is estimated that the majority are active in government armed forces and the youngest are to be found in armed groups.[44] They may constitute 10 per cent of current combatants.[45] In addition girl soldiers are now occupying more silent, hidden or risky roles often forced to participate in sexual servicing of other combatants as well as a range of roles upon which camps depend. The late recognition of girl soldiers and the consequent inadequacy of current disarmament, demobilisation and reintegration (DDR) attempts tells it own story.[46] Soldiering or armed combat roles do not assume that the child's status is shared or agreed by all parties concerned. These children may be solely in adult company, with other children, under the direction of adults, or even under the command of older children. They may be active agents with varying degrees of self-awareness. They may or may not be willing combatants. In today's conflicts the distinction between voluntary and enforced recruitment is often blurred, given the fact that militias may offer far more to children than just a life of combat. The more unstable a country is, the more the military may even resemble a safe harbor in some senses. Children may be motivated to enlist to ward off poverty and insecurity, attracted by the familial-style environment, food and clothing. Orphaned and traumatized children may 'simply' receive food or treats in return for using guns. Their role may primarily be a means of survival in the face of other threats: starvation, isolation, or abduction to name but a few. Children may therefore join to *live* – not to kill or be killed. Conversely, child soldiering may be experienced as a well-founded and complex site of development and apprenticeship, particularly in longstanding guerrilla campaigns. Groups such as the Tamil Tigers of Sri Lanka have been known to provide education integrated with military experience, tutoring boys from the age of nine in the importance of discipline, honesty and respect for the rights of ordinary citizens.[47] Here, child soldiers may be allowed to imitate adults in combat but only in

---

[43] Alstri Halsan Høiskar, 'Under Age and Under Fire: An Enquiry into the Use of Child Soldiers 1994–8', *Childhood*, 8 (3), 2001 p. 342.

[44] Rachel Harvey, *Children and Armed Conflict: A Guide to International and Humanitarian Human Rights Law* (Essex University and the International Bureau of Children's Rights: The Children and Armed Conflict Unit, 2003).

[45] Peter W. Singer, 'Caution: Children at War', *Parameters,* Winter 2001–2002, pp. 40–56, at http://carlisle-www.army.mil/usawc/Parameters/01winter/singer.htm accessed (20/10/04).

[46] See works by Andy White, especially 'Children and Armed Conflict: Impact, Protection and Rehabilitation', Research Project. [Website] http://www.arts.ualberta.ca/childrenandwar/research_methodology.php.

[47] Goodwin-Gill and Cohn, *op. cit.*, pp. 29, 97.

specific positions that do not exceed their strengths or place them at risk of physical harm – 'apprentices' behind the frontline. They are also free to leave.

In the midst of a war, military obligations may come into force at an earlier age than is usual and child soldiers such as those in Africa may assume many of the responsibilities of an adult. Indeed conscription may be an initiation process into adulthood. Forced participation in war means that children now occupy a position in armies where they are capable of subjecting others and being subjected to the experiences of adults in war though, unlike some soldiers they may have no choice but to be soldiers.[48] Children's roles as soldiers may overlap with those of adults and some children may clearly relish taking control.

Other roles may be specially designed for them based on pejorative assumptions about their physical and mental underdevelopment and opportunities these afford. In Colombia child soldiers are 'nicknamed "little bells" by the military, which uses them as expendable sentries, and "little bees" by the guerrillas, because they "sting" their enemies before they know they are under attack'.[49] In war 'the choice' for many children has been to shoot or be shot. Children below fifteen have been forcibly recruited in Ethiopia, Angola, Mozambique, Liberia, Sri Lanka and the Sudan.[50]

Children may also join armies as their last means of protection from poverty and insecurity. In Uganda in 1986 the army recruited 3,000 children including 500 girls who had lost their parents and needed food and shelter.[51] In Myanmar, parents volunteer their children for the rebel Karen army because they know that the guerrillas will provide clothes and meals.[52] The war in Liberia has itself created the many orphaned and traumatized children who are forced to enlist or starve. The Liberian Red Cross has witnessed children as young as seven using guns in return for food.[53] Some joined because the Liberian rebels made promises of football games and other treats.[54] Alternatively, they may be attracted by the familial style environment and protection that the army appears to offer. The Iranian government made a special point of recruiting children who had lost their fathers in the war. Children were taught the basic precept that the state president was now their father and that it was their duty as 'men' to go to war and to sacrifice themselves for their country.[55] Thus their mental status as dependent was identified and used to ensnare them. Conversely for *adults* in Cambodia, a new-found dependency was wielded on them via the Khmer Rouges' relationship with children.[56] Children:

---

[48]   Bellamy, *op. cit.*, p. 17.

[49]   *Ibid.*

[50]   UNICEF, *op. cit.*, p. 19.

[51]   Bellamy, *op. cit.*, pp. 17–19.

[52]   *Ibid.*, p. 17.

[53]   Goodwin-Gill and Cohn, *op. cit.*, p. 33.

[54]   *Child Soldiers in Liberia*, Human Rights Watch Africa (1995), p. 28.

[55]   Cairns, *op. cit.*, p. 131.

[56]   Boyden, J. (2003), 'The moral development of child soldiers: what do adults have to fear?' *Peace and Conflict: Journal of Peace Psychology*, 9 (4), pp. 343–62.

became its foot soldiers, its workers, its spies, policing family and community life and leading the relentless marches through the countryside that resulted in so many deaths. It was decreed that children must be served before adults in the communal halls and addressed by adults with terms of deference.[57]

In Sierra Leone too, The Revolutionary United Front (RUF) deliberately broke down the social fabric of a community by letting children target adults.[58] Child soldiers may be specifically useful to armies by virtue of their childlike qualities, physically and mentally. Children, 'being small and inconspicuous' have been used as mini-messengers or spies.[59] Their ability to mingle and hide with crowds has meant that the Ugandan National Resistance Army has found an ideal use for them as hand-grenade throwers.

A significant change in child soldiering, thought to have been actually promoted by agencies from the West during the bitter proxy wars of the Cold War, is the deliberate use of children as combatants because of their perceived limitations or weaknesses. Children are increasingly used to play at 'dirty war' – doing the things that adults have thought of but do not want to do themselves or think that children can do better. A Renamo Party Delegate described his soldiers as working out 'quite nicely in the field. You know they always did what they were told to do, they were fiercely loyal and brave in battle.'[60] Children have also been encouraged to see war as a game, to not understand what they do so that they will have no inhibitions. In this way children have been manipulated differently compared to adults. They have been drugged into committing atrocities which adult soldiers refuse to do. The United Nations Operations Officer in Liberia commented that '[i]t's a children's war. Kids get promoted in rank for committing an atrocity. They can cut off someone's head without thinking'.[61] These children probably are thinking however. As a Save the Children field worker noted: '[c]hildren make awesome soldiers. Children are effective because they are easy to organize, and they don't ask questions. In wartime a commander wants total submission. You can get that only from a child.'[62] Again, it is unlikely that children do not have some 'questions' about what they are doing. It is also unlikely that they have the opportunity to ask them. Child soldiering is often cruelly dependent on naivety and vulnerability, qualities that cannot be lost at will (though it is arguable whether adults lose them in war either). Mimicking adults whilst high on drugs or 'playing the game' of war in Sierra Leone, such children are treated as neither child nor

---

[57]   *Ibid.*, p. 6.

[58]   Jo Boyden (2003), *op. cit.*

[59]   Bellamy, *op. cit.*, p. 18.

[60]   Peter Nkhonjera, quoted in 'Children in Bondage', *World Press Review*, January 1996, Vol.43, No.1, p. 10.

[61]   Human Rights Watch , Africa, *Easy Prey: Child Soldiers in Liberia* (New York, 1995), p. 31.

[62]   Nkhonjera, *op. cit.*, p. 8.

adult, victims nor aggressors but both.[63] Reports suggest that after political and
military socialization some cannot distinguish their actions from fantasy. If these
children survive they often attend rehabilitation centers to try and make sense of
the atrocities that they were encouraged to participate in.[64] In Northern Uganda,
the Lord's Resistance Army led by Joseph Kony has been abducting children since
the 1990s. The army has now been cited by the UN as creating one of the most
systematic and brutal humanitarian disasters in the world.

Young children are more vulnerable to harm than other soldiers by virtue of their
susceptibility to terror and less developed faculties, though older children may be
no less vulnerable than some adults and perhaps some are more resilient. The roles,
circumstances and responses outlined above illustrate the ambiguities of children's
status as combatants. The dominant representation of child soldiers however is
unambiguously of persons who have attained premature adulthood though inhabiting
a child's body. However as P.W. Singer notes, the prospect of ambush by such
children is increasing, as evidenced in British Operation 'Barras', carried out by the
Special Air Service (SAS) against the West Side Boys militia in Sierra Leone.[65]

Children may also perform a role in conflict by virtue of their presence. Three
widely different examples can illustrate this. When the Serbs laid seige to Srebrenica
in April 1993, children and their mothers were not evacuated out of the city. Moslem
leaders believed instead that their particular presence strengthened Moslem claims
to territory. In effect, children remained hostages in their own homes to their own
fathers. Their bodies were kept in place as a physical claim to territory and a
symbol of nationalism.[66] Children's presence may also be used to temporarily halt
conflict and begin negotiations. The idea of children as 'zones of peace' emerged in
Norway in the 1980s and the most successful example of this practice, pioneered
by UNICEF, occurred in Sudan.[67] The Executive general of UNICEF met with the
leaders of the Sudan People's Liberation Army and the Government to negotiate
a temporary ceasefire in order for humanitarian aid workers to reach children. In
'Operation Lifeline Sudan', eight corridors of relief were created allowing food to
reach up to 90,000 children.[68] Aid agencies were able to negotiate peace zones for
children, by reference to children's innocence in war and their need to be protected.
In El Salvador from 1985 to the end of the war in 1991, three-day tranquility spaces
allowed 20,000 health workers to immunize 250,000 children against polio. Similar
zones were organized in Uganda in 1986 and in Lebanon in 1989.

---

[63]   Chris McGreal, 'Africa's child troops fuelled by drugs and revenge', *The Guardian,*
21 February 1995, p. 7.
[64]   *Ibid.*
[65]   Singer, P. W (2005), *Children at War* (Pantheon) and see also 'Western militaries
confront child soldiers threat', *Jane's Intelligence Review*, January 2005.
[66]   Kent, *op. cit.*, p. 84.
[67]   Carol Bellamy, *The State of the World's Children 1996* (Oxford and New York: Oxford
University Press, 1999), p. 34.
[68]   Bellamy, *op. cit.*, p. 36.

In other conflicts, however, such recognition of children's vulnerability has given rise to the reverse, their targeting by the enemy group. Children's status as precious or valued within a family gives purpose to their systematic killing; an act which might normally be explained as simply aggressive. In the Rwandan civil war male Tutsi children were deliberately targeted as a means of eradicating the Tutsi Army of the Future.[69] Children were thus killed strategically. As one political commentator broadcast to Rwanda before the violence erupted: '[t]o kill the big rats you have to kill the little rats'.[70] Thus, children have different political instrumentalities. Bosnian Moslem children were kept in place as indicators of nationalist resolve, Sudanese children were presented as embodiments of innocence and thus constituted within peace tactics and Tutsi children became a targeted presence. Their demobilization and rehabilitation is now of primary importance to the stability of their war-torn region.

The intergenerational status of children as embodiments of future internal stability is beginning to be recognized. Many studies of children in crisis situations have found that they respond differently to adults, and are in need of longer term care. Their mental and emotional experiences may lead to a different set of problems when they become adults. 'Approximately 50 per cent of children in Rwanda had seen other children killing, 66 per cent had witnessed massacres, and 56 per cent had seen their family killed.'[71] The cyclical impact of children's experience of war on their future has yet to be analyzed. It is possible, that the identification of the war child as weak being may be a short-sighted interpretation. Weakness and vulnerability are likely to manifest themselves in other ways when the child reaches adulthood, to the extent that the consequences may be quite profound. Weakness may be translated into agency later on, perhaps resilience or in defiance such as through future civil revenge killings. Though their situation is extraordinarily complex, Tutsi children who suffered in the Rwandan civil war of the 1970s have identified themselves as the aggressors of the recent Rwandan conflict.[72]

During the Iran–Iraq war, children's immaturity was deliberately employed to the Iranian army's advantage. Thousands of children were sent out into the battlefields as 'kamikaze' mine-sweepers.[73] The Minister of Education in Iran said that in 1987, 150,000 children (making up 60 per cent of its ranks) 'volunteered' to fight.[74] This was only possible because the children involved were first manipulated into believing that it was a worthwhile exercise. As a human rights lawyer has observed: '[t]hey received intense religious indoctrination, emphasizing the value of martyrdom to

---

[69]   Carolyn Hamilton, 'Children in armed conflict – New moves for an old problem', *The Journal of Child Law*, Vol.7, No.1, 1995, p. 46.

[70]   Bellamy, *op. cit.*, p. 14.

[71]   See for example, Human Rights Watch, Africa, *Easy Prey: Child Soldiers in Liberia* (New York, Sept. 1995).

[72]   Anuradha Vittachi, *Stolen Childhood: In search of the rights of the child* (Cambridge: Polity Press), p. 46.

[73]   Bellamy, *op. cit.*, p. 18.

[74]   Kent, *op. cit.*, p. 85.

the Islamic faith. These children were sent into the minefields to clear mines for the advancing Iranian army, armed only with keys around their necks for opening the gates of heaven.'[75] When these atrocities came to light, Iran was widely criticized and the United Nations called for an end to this practice. The justification given by Iran reveals a different, if not gratuitous, assumption of the responsibilities of the child. An Iranian minister said: '[i]t was an honor for my country that those young people had become sufficiently mature to understand the seriousness of their country's situation. Their heroism and enthusiasm were based on the notion of martyrdom, which materialists are unable to understand'.[76] It is interesting that he did not call them 'children'. This example of martyrdom was made possible by political socialization and the manipulation of the belief system held by Iranian children. The following section will look at examples of how children's minds have been the object of a different form of political interest and appropriation.

Conflict in the Curriculum

Propaganda is described as '[t]he deliberate and systematic attempt to shape perceptions, manipulate cognitions and direct behavior to achieve a response that furthers the desired intent of the propagandist'.[77] Due to children's noted capacity to learn new information it is not surprising that an interest may be taken in what political information they learn. The Sri Lankan LTTE (Liberation Tigers of Tamil Eelam) typically uses schools as a means of propaganda and indoctrination. Young soldiers are paraded before schoolchildren, military training given inside school grounds and military lessons take place in classrooms. One observer noted of a school that it had 'a combination memorial hall and playground, full of photos of young martyrs and a play area with toy guns mounted on see saws'.[78] Children were also encouraged to watch 'Rambo style' movies. By contrast in other schools in Sri Lanka, the government had launched a program of peace education in order to counter the impact of the civil war.[79] Philosophy, based on Buddhist and Hindu traditions encouraged children to think about compromise and inner-peace. These lessons were integrated into the whole curriculum. The campaign was then extended to reach parents and the wider community. This example is unusual however. In most civil wars children are encouraged to learn about or be aware of threats and military preparation rather than peace. Sixty per cent of Peru's 7.7 million school children, for example, live in areas where the guerrilla forces (*Sendero Luminoso*) may exert complete control over schools.[80]

---

[75]   Carolyn Hamilton, *op. cit.*, p. 38.

[76]   *Ibid.*

[77]   Garth S. Jowett and Victoria O'Donnell, *Propaganda and Persuasion* (London: Sage, 1992), p. 4, and Lyndley Fraser, *Propaganda* (London: Open University Press, 1957), p. 1.

[78]   Goodwin-Gill and Cohn, *op. cit.*, p. 29.

[79]   Bellamy, *op. cit.*, p. 32.

[80]   Goodwin-Gill and Cohn, *op. cit.*, p. 32.

In Afghanistan, thousands of children were removed by the Soviets for long term indoctrination and training as spies on, and assassins of, the Mujahedin resistance fighters.[81] If captured by the Mujahedin, however, they were sent back to Russia, though this time as 'double-agents'. Two and a half million child refugees are known to have been subject to Pakistani education and preparation for their future ideological or military 'role' against the Russians. In the refugee camps in Pakistan, girls were kept out of United Nations schools by their fathers. Their nationalist identity clearly threatened by education, it is preferred that they learn within their families.[82] Formal and familial channels may be equally effective conduits of political information during and outside of conflict. Chilean mothers for example have attempted to *de*militarize their children by discouraging imitation of practices of the Pinochet regime in their play activities.[83]

Civil defense was incorporated into American public education at the height of the Cold War. American children were subject to preparation for nuclear attack and education about their role as citizens. As Dean Acheson commented in 1947, civil defense was 'a perception, a state of mind ... The nation must be on permanent alert'.[84] And as President Truman declared after creating the Federal Civil Defense Administration in 1951: '[e]ducation is our first line of defense'.[85] Joanne Brown, an historian of this phenomena, comments: '[e]mergent civil defense professionals and embattled school professionals developed a kind of symbiotic relationship in the 1950s that determined what kind of information about war reached a whole generation of schoolchildren'. Civil defense programs in schools included classroom drills, the study of pamphlets and films, and the distribution of material which would be taken home to parents.[86] Cover drills were routinely practiced and dog tags issued from 1950. Three million comic books were issued featuring 'Bert the turtle' who advised children to take cover in nuclear attack because '[t]hings will be knocked down all over town'.[87] This benign assimilation of the unthinkable into children's everyday life also 'taught a generation to equate emotional maturity with an attitude of calm acceptance toward nuclear war'.[88]

Children may be considered as susceptible to political and military values in the informal education sector. For example, in West Germany and France, it was reported that 10 per cent of toy manufacturers made only war toys. Worried by this, the European Parliament passed a resolution in 1982 recommending the banning

---

[81]   *Ibid.*, p. 37.

[82]   Cynthia Enloe, *The Morning After: Sexual Politics at the End of the Cold War* (London: University of California Press, 1993), p. 57.

[83]   *Ibid.*, p. 100.

[84]   Elaine Tyler May, *Homeward Bound: American families in the Cold War Era* (New York: Basic Books, 1988), p. 90.

[85]   JoAnne Brown, '*A* is for atom, *B* is for Bomb: Civil Defense in American Public Education, 1948–1963', *The Journal of American History*, Vol. 75, no. 1, 1988 , p. 74.

[86]   Brown, *op. cit.*, p. 71.

[87]   *Ibid.*, p. 84.

[88]   *Ibid.*, p. 90.

of realistic war toys.[89] Children's assimilation of military skills in their play and recreation may however be desired by states. The Soviet Ministry of Retail Trade declared in 1980 that:

> Military toys and war games are important from an educational point of view, as they arouse children's interest in, and knowledge of, military techniques, and war games also inspire patriotism.[90]

President Reagan, in an address to high school children in 1983 about 'Star Wars' styled video games, commented:

> Many young people have developed incredible hand-eye-brain coordination playing these games. The air force believes these kids will be outstanding pilots should they fly our jets. Watch a twelve-year-old take evasive action and score multiple hits while playing Space Invaders and you will appreciate the skills of tomorrow's pilots.[91]

Such superpower opinions clearly show that children in the Cold War were exposed to implicit training for war. Schooling may be used more explicitly to denigrate another state or ethnic group and to reproduce the values of the dominant groups within states.[92] Xenophobic teaching and curricula were employed in the former Yugoslavia in 1994 and in Serbian schools in Kosova. It may be an important factor in mobilizing xenophobic hostility.[93] Schools may use language as a means of cultural and social reproduction, and consequently schools and the curricula are one of the battlegrounds of a nations' secession, and one of the first areas to be reformed. The newly created Central Asian republic of Tajikistan reformed education by implementing the Tajik language and textbook reform within a flexible cultural curriculum to mirror ethnic diversity.[94] The Council of Europe has regularly initiated and assisted with cross-cultural History teaching programs in newly reformed states. For a recent report, Bush and Salterelli, listed 'peace-destroying and conflict-maintaining' impacts of education that agencies hope to counter:

- the uneven distribution of education as a means of creating or preserving positions of economic, social and political privilege
- education as a weapon in cultural repression
- denial of education as a weapon of war
- education as a means of manipulating history for political purposes
- education serving to diminish self-worth and encourage hate

---

[89]   Daly and Vaughan, *op. cit.*, pp. 20–21.
[90]   *Ibid.*
[91]   Helen Caldicott, *Missile Envy: The Arms Race and Nuclear War* (New York: Bantam, 1984), p. 145.
[92]   David Coulby, 'European Curricula, Xenophobia and Warfare', *Comparative Education* Vol. 33, no.1, p. 39.
[93]   *Ibid.*
[94]   See Nick Holdsworth, 'Tajiks opt for revival of the fittest', *Times Higher Education[al Supplement]*, 6 November 1998, p. 16.

- segregated education as a means of ensuring inequality, inferiority, and stereotypes
- the role of textbooks in impoverishing the imagination of children and thereby inhibiting them from dealing with conflict constructively.[95]

They note that 'restricted access to education should be viewed as an indicator of deteriorating relations between groups' and therefore 'a warning signal':[96]

> the systematic ethnic cleansing undertaken by the Serbian military forces in late 1999 was in no way a spontaneous event. The precursor to abuse on such a massive scale is the systematic dismantling of the social, political and economic institutions that provide order and stability for a community. This was certainly the case in Nazi Germany, and in Cambodia under Pol Pot.[97]

Children's comprehension about conflict and history may also be thought of as an important part of their identity and be managed by states through citizenship education and the formal transmission of inherited culture. Education and historiography, particularly history curricula and history teaching remain the subject of contemporary debate in Great Britain.[98] The concept of *Education for Citizenship* was revived in 1990 to develop skills of 'tolerance and constructive questioning of the world around them', taught not as a substitute for but complementary to history.[99] An ethnically diverse British population also places a high degree of responsibility on the way British history is presented. Additionally international events illustrate lessons about human behavior which cannot be gleaned in any other subject. In a Working Committee Report on History in the National Curriculum,[100] Anthony Polonsky expressed the view that history was the intellectual discipline which appeared the most obvious means to transmit knowledge and understanding of the Holocaust. Despite its publicity, the Holocaust is still not a substantial element in WWII history teaching. Yet, the history of Nazi Germany is.

History that children learn is however underpinned by what history has been written. Up to 50 million civilians may have died under Stalin, in the Gulag, through collectivization, the Political Terror and genocidal famine, yet it has received very little attention from Western historians.[101] No photographs and few survivor's testimonies exist, but this alone does not account for the lack of general information

---

[95]   Kenneth D. Bush, and Diana Salterelli (2000), *Two Faces of Education in Ethnic Conflict*, United Nations Children's Fund, Innocenti Research Centre, Italy, p. 34.

[96]   *Ibid.*, p. 9.

[97]   *Ibid.*, pp. 6–8.

[98]   Neil Burtonwood, 'Culture, Identity and the Curriculum,' *Education Review*, Vol. 48, no. 3, 1996, p. 227.

[99]   Blunkett David, 'The minister's view', *The Guardian Education Supplement*, 22 September 1998, p. 3.

[100]   John Plowright, 'Teaching the holocaust: A response to the report of a survey in the UK', *Teaching History*, No. 45, 1991, p. 28.

[101]   Norman Davies, *Europe: A History* (London: Pimlico, 1997), p. 965.

in academia. The lack of photographs and pictures of such events may however account for the limited coverage in books for younger children which are heavily reliant on imagery in their communication. The silence, however, suggests that we in the West may be more interested in what we think of as nations 'like ours'.[102] Information in children's textbooks may contribute to dominant and incorrect interpretations of history. Researchers point out, for example, that from the vast photographic libraries of photos for use in children's textbooks on WWI or WWII, the thousands of black soldiers are not included, or if they do exist they are not selected for publication. Such under-representation towards an audience who are not in a position to draw contrary conclusions contributes to this generation's mental picture of *who* was doing what to whom.[103] Similarly, whether the Holocaust is singularly or plurally defined, its teaching may be a central and critical component of future issues of ethnicity, pluralism, and human rights. Little research, however, has taken place on children's reaction to learning about these kind of events and their understanding of the sphere of human rights and wrongs.[104] There is a similar lack of research on political socialization of children through the media.[105]

Throughout this section assumptions about children's roles as recipients of political knowledge have been shown. The final section returns to ways children are represented, by focusing on how they are collectively and frequently identified and counted as *victims* in political and international contexts.

Victims and 'Victims'

Children are vulnerable in different ways to adults: Children may experience physical, mental and emotional harm differently to adults and they may be specifically maltreated with this intention. In the multitude of ways that war is harmful, it is typically more so for children; civilian children along with women form 90 per

---

[102] See for example Ian Grosvenor and Maria Green, 'Making subjects: history writing, education and race categories', *Paedegogica Historica,* Vol. 33, no. 3, 1998 and Robert Guyver, 'National Curriculum History: Key Concepts and Controversy', in *Teaching History*, No. 88, 1997.

[103] Gillian Wilson, 'History – Ours or Yours? Pt 1', *Teaching History*, No. 19, 1986, p. 7.

[104] Carrington Bruce and Short Geoffrey, 'Holocaust Education Anti-racism and Citizenship', *Educational Review*, Vol. 49, no. 3, 1997, p. 271. See also Bruce Carrington and Geoffrey Short, 'Reconstructing Multiracial Education: A Response to Mike Cole', *Cambridge Journal of Education*, Vol. 28, No. 2, 1998 and Mike Cole 'Re-establishing Multiracial Education; A Reply to Short and Carrington', *Cambridge Journal of Education*, Vol. 28, no. 3, 1998.

[105] See for example Margot Brown and Ian Davies, 'The Holocaust and Education for Citizenship: The Teaching of History, Religion and History in England', *Education Review*, Vol. 50, No.1, 1998.

cent of casualties in ongoing conflicts.[106] The unique vulnerabilities of very young children may make them first in the queue for protection.

A key way in which children are represented in an international context is as victims, of senseless wars, grinding poverty or natural disasters and famine. This is evident in aid appeals and literature made by international organizations and widely publicized in the media. Perhaps more than any other term, 'victim' is used to describe and isolate children in such times. By definition, it takes away agency from children and obscures the instrumentality bestowed on and found in children, explored throughout this chapter. This representation allows children to be used as an emotive construct or resource for political purposes, particularly in propaganda, and is a prominent example of a construct of the child in use across national borders. Statistics on children as victims proliferate in information sources from international governmental organizations such as UNICEF, and the International Labor Organization and international non-governmental organizations, such as Anti Slavery International, Defense for Children International, the International Catholic Child Bureau, International Save the Children Alliance, and many other NGOs such as WarChild and Oxfam. The following statistics have been used during the last decade, particularly in the turn towards the third millennium, to draw attention to the plight of children:

- The United Nations Children's Fund estimate that over 90 per cent of casualties in war are civilian women and children, compared to 5 per cent at the time of WWI.[107]
- There are 23.6 million internally displaced people, the majority are women and children.[108]
- Twelve million children aged between one and five die each year from poverty-related diseases.[109]
- Up to two billion children are laborers.[110]
- One million children work in the Asian sex trade.[111]
- Two million children under twelve are genitally mutilated each year.[112]

---

[106] See Olarra Ottunu (1999), 'Protection of Children Affected by Armed Conflict: Note by the Secretary General', United Nations General Assembly, 1 October, 99-28333, p. 6; and Carlton-Ford *et al.*, 'War and children's mortality', *Childhood*, Vol. 7, No. 4, 2000, p. 401.

[107] Otunnu, O. (2000), 'The Impact of Armed Conflict on Children: Filling Knowledge Gaps, Draft Research Agenda.' http://www.mofa.go.jp/policy/human/child/survey/annex2.html.

[108] Human Security Report 2005, Canada.

[109] Jesse Banfield and Nevine Mabro, 'Children in Statistics', *Index on Censorship*, 2, 1997, pp. 132–3.

[110] *Ibid.*

[111] *Ibid.*

[112] *Ibid.*

- In 1987, UNICEF reported that 3.5 million children a year were dying of diseases which can be prevented by immunization at an additional yearly cost which is less than the price of five advanced fighter planes.[113]
- Measles kills more children every year than all the world's wars and famines put together.[114]
- About 40,000 children will die each day mainly from curable diseases.[115]
- The majority of one billion people who endure chronic under nourishment and poverty are women and children.[116]
- In Somalia, half or more of all children alive on 1 January 1992 were dead by the end of the year.[117]
- One million children lose their mothers in childbirth or through complications from pregnancy each year.[118]
- Pregnancy in the developing world makes the chances of dying or being disabled one in four.[119]

However, as Nordstrom reminds us, 'it is both dangerous and unrealistic to look at the abuse of children, in war, in another country, in another context as if that were somehow different and more barbaric than the patterns of abuse that characterize our own everyday cultures, in peace and war'. Citing examples of child abuse in the USA she says: 'we should be asking instead what it is that makes such behaviors possible where they are found'.[120]

Children attract attention in aid appeals and in propaganda, graphically sign-posting abuse within or to a state, but not the analysis Nordstrom seeks. The emaciated condition of children in orphanages in the former Communist countries of Romania, Moldova and Bulgaria caused the launch of an immediate aid appeal in Britain in 1989.[121] UNICEF figures suggest that at this time there were one million children in state orphanages, placed there because their families were no longer able to support them. There are now over half a million more, and media and charitable interest in these children has subsided. Victim status was accurate in every sense.

The street children of Latin America are often portrayed as victims in literature by charitable organizations. Their apparent distance from the familial sphere and

---

[113] George Kent, *op. cit.*, p. 5.

[114] James P. Grant, *The State of the World's Children 1994* (New York: Oxford University Press), p. 1.

[115] James Roberts, '1996: 37,000 Children Die Each Day', *The Independent,* 12 June 1996.

[116] Robyn Rowland and Renato Klein, in Bell and Klein, *op.cit.*, pp. 18 and 19.

[117] Bellamy, *op. cit.*

[118] *Ibid.*

[119] Roberts, *op. cit.*, p. 8.

[120] Carolyn Nordstrom (1999), 'Visible Wars and Invisible Girls, Shadow Industries and the Politic of Not-Knowing', *International Feminist Journal of Politics*, vol. 1, no. 1, 1999, p. 26.

[121] Don McReady, 'Children of chaos', *The Guardian,* 17 November 1998, p. 20.

the school makes them seem out of place and isolated, and attracts attention from philanthropic Western agencies. Hence UNICEF came to estimate the presence of millions of street children when in actual fact the number for whom the street was their actual home and bed has been re-estimated at hundreds. Most children work and play in the street but survive elsewhere. Duncan Green notes that the singular image of the street child as a charitable cause, created by aid agencies, conflated 'the cheeky urchins of the morning who can easily become the glue-sniffing muggers of the afternoon and the terrified children of the night'.[122] It is interesting to note how Western-led assistance attempts primarily to find and remove children from the street, and does not address how they came to be there.

For many children, especially for girls, the streets are safer than home. Children are on the streets through the need to work, because of domestic violence and out of sheer boredom. As a consequence of being misunderstood in this way, Brazilian children have formed their own organization: the National Movement of Street Boys and Girls (MNMMR). It has so far proved successful, resulting in a new children's statute, giving them a voice and allowing them to be seen as more than just victims.[123] Listening to these 'working children' has consequently revealed that they often do not want to stop working and that their alternatives are more dangerous. Such children may be semi-skilled but are able to survive, make good and complex decisions and support each other. The most effective teaching and education programs have been those in which the children have taught and protected each other. These particular Brazilian children were victims only in name – not in practice.

Significant a 'new paradigm of adversity' is emerging where challenges and trauma are understood as contextual and constructed, and potentially generating dynamic and often positive responses from children. Responding to children as inert victims may further disable them. The major implication is that children should be active agents in negotiating their protection.[124] Returning to an early issue of contained childhood, it is apparent that other aspects of survival, including children's resilience are only now being explored.

Conclusion

This chapter has illustrated the variety of constructions of children manifested in the practices in world politics. It has shown that while children have been invisible in the standard literature of academic international relations, they have in fact been present in the workings of global politics. Two particular themes seem to emerge from the discussion so far. Children perform military roles, knowingly and unwittingly in all forms of conflict. They are the foci of security-driven, antinatalist and pronatalist practices and can be moved, propagated or renationalized as a collective body when

---

[122] Duncan Green, *Hidden Lives: Voices of Children in Latin America and the Caribbean* (Cassell, 1998), p. 64.

[123] *Ibid.*

[124] Boyden and Levison, *op. cit.*, p. 40.

security is perceived to be under threat. The child's mind has been shown as subject to political and military socialization in education, from the schools of Sri Lankan Tamil Tigers to the leisure activities of Soviet and American children. Secondly the chapter illustrates how children seem uniquely suited for use in propaganda as icons of 'the threatened' and the insecure. The construction of the child as a victim considerably undermines their status as political beings.

Conflict is the context of both these major themes, and therefore would seem to merit further analysis. The construction of children as politicized bodies will now be further examined through an exploration of the nationalization and militarization of children in Nazi Germany, Northern Ireland, Mozambique and South Africa. These cases allow a critical and parallel examination of nationalization and militarization. Each case illustrates the centrality of the child in aims and objectives of war, the *interdependence* of the child and the political world, and the management of a particular concept of the young child for political ends, here explored as '*infant power*'.

Chapter 3

Reproducing the State:
Children in Nazi Germany

Making the Link: Children and Security

Although Nazism is often thought of as a temporary aberration in the history of a nation, it was, in fact, based upon various strands of intellectual thought that go back at least a century. This was the *völkisch* doctrine, which was essentially a product of late eighteenth-century romanticism. The four major themes that recur in nazi propaganda during this period reflect the roots and antecedents of *völkisch* thought: 1) appeal to national unity based upon the principle: 'The community before the individual' (*Volksgemeinschaft*); 2) the need for racial purity; 3) a hatred of enemies which increasingly centred on Jews and Bolsheviks, and 4) charismatic leadership (*Führerprinzip*). Both the original doctrine and the manner in which it was disseminated by nazi propaganda led inexorably to the mobilization of the German people for a future war.[1]

This chapter begins with the links made between children and state security over a century ago by prominent politicians and scientists; connections which became embedded as pronatalist and antinatalist foundations to Nazi racial security. It illustrates how children came to feature on political agendas from several directions, and also how the realm of childhood accumulated political capital: as the stakes of war increased so children's roles were harnessed in ever more blatant ways. Linkage began with the threat of population decline and its reverse image: new birth and state renewal. Germany's slowing population growth in 1900, became a significant political issue, receiving attention at the highest levels. An increased child mortality rate escalated fears of depopulation and the advice of scientists was sought. At this time the work of scientists and biologists in Western Europe and the United States was coalescing towards an ideology of racial hierarchy based on eugenic principles.[2] The term 'eugenics' for example had been first used in 1883 by the British naturalist and

---

[1]   David Welch, 'Nazi Propaganda and the *Volksgemeinschaft*: Constructing a People's Community', *Journal of Contemporary History*, Vol. 39, No. 2, 2004, p. 217 (213–38).
[2]   See for example Paul Weindling, *Health, Race and German Politics between National Unification and Nazis, 1870–1945* (Cambridge: Cambridge University Press, 1989), and Michael S. Teitelbaumn and Jay M. Winter, *The Fear of Population Decline* (Orlando: Academic Press, 1985).

mathematician Francis Galton (1822–1911), who was also Charles Darwin's cousin.[3] Genetic improvement of the human race became subsumed into 'racial hygiene'[4] practices. Scientists found grist for their mill and state support, and the equation of security and population lent a crucial social dimension to Germany's concept of military strength. As articulated by politicians of the time, low population growth indicated a potentially weak state, less capable of either defense or expansion. And framed in this way, *internal* and *international* securities were perceived as mutually reinforcing[5] a point which was to come to characterize Nazi objectives. Across Western Europe population growth was studied within the context of these military anxieties.[6] Such organicism was 'subsumed in the integrationist social philosophies of Friedrich Naumann' who confidently declared the birth rate to be synonymous with national vitality; the '*Lebensbejahung des volkes*'.[7] This message had particular resonance in Germany where the *volk* were understood to *embody* state and national security. In the decade prior to the outbreak of the WWI, descriptions of the state as a living entity or body filtered into national consciousness and popular literature. The resulting discourse of new terms and ideas were also disseminated in the school classroom, particularly in the textbook teaching of biology where 'the state was popularized as an organism, the family as an elemental cell, and the decreasing family size as a cancer'.[8]

With this conceptual fusion of body and state, a broad consensus emerged for the extension of German patriotic duty through pronatalism and associated medical interventions. In a short space of time institutions formed which allowed the state to take on the role of 'child' guardian. Child care for new-borns was institutionalized and security codified within it. The opening of the *Kaiserin Auguste Viktoria Haus* (KAVH), an institution for maternal and infant health with the mission of combating child mortality was of patriotic importance. The first volume of Germany's *Magazine for Youth Welfare*, published in 1909, claimed that the foundations for military capability were laid in earliest childhood and mothers could improve their children's fitness levels by up to 50 per cent by breastfeeding them.[9] This twin-track 'infantry formula' typifies the merging of private and public spheres. The 'racial hygiene'

[3]   M. Burleigh and W. Wipperman, *The Racial State: Germany 1933–1945* (Cambridge: Cambridge University Press, 1991), p. 29.

[4]   The term was coined by Alfred Ploetz, see Burleigh and Wipperman, *op. cit.*, p. 32; see also Henry Friedlander, *The Origins of Nazi Genocide, From Euthanasia to the Final Solution* (Chapel Hill and London: University of North Carolina Press, 1995), p. 4.

[5]   Michael S. Teitelbaumn *et al.*, *op. cit.*, see the Introduction.

[6]   *Ibid.*, pp.18–19. See for example Maria Sophia Quine, *Population Politics in Twentieth Century Europe* (London: Routledge, 1996).

[7]   Paul Weindling, *op. cit.*, pp. 83, 291.

[8]   *Ibid.*

[9]   Jurgen Reulecke, 'Mobilising Youth in Wilhelmine Germany', in Mark Roseman (ed.), *Generations in Conflict: Youth Revolt and Generation Formation in Germany 1770 –1968* (Cambridge: Cambridge University Press, 1995), p. 95.

movement led to action groups such as the Society for Inner Colonization;[10] and the name itself perfectly illustrates Germany's attempt at strengthening from the inside outwards. It is worth noting that these issues, their patriotic implications and scientific responses, made a notable contribution to the perceived sense of social cohesion and stability within the German state. As Paul Weindling has observed, eugenics, here framed as a product of *volkish* nationalism, generated an heroic rather than purely scientific image. It was a logical move then, for the state to further promote health and welfare policies so that they work as a national unifying device and 'a means of mobilizing nationalist sentiments'.[11] As Weindling explains:

> [S]cience and medicine provided an alternative to party politics, by forming a basis for collectivist social policies to remedy social ills ... The concept of a fit and healthy social organism provided a means for realising renewed stability, social integration and national power.[12]

The potency of this relationship is also indicated in the careful management of child care establishments during the regime change; namely the retention of the KAVH institution after 1914 as a symbol of cohesion, mitigating popular fears of total societal upheaval or state decline. '[M]aternal and infant health became symbols of national unity in their own right'.[13] Young children were clearly publicly associated with German politics and foreign affairs through their 'embodyment' of future military and racial strength. The administrator of The Society for Child Health stated that 'infant health was vital to Germany's position as a world power' and that children were barometers of a nation's fitness and future military potential.[14] As Weindling notes, the spread of socialism provided further impetus towards promoting fitness in older children and the centralizing of their fitness facilities.[15] World events were to add their own momentum to this partnership. By 1914, for example, two million youths were already taking part in camps, drills and sports.[16] By the end of that decade, the WWI's heavy cost to life and the influenza epidemic had impacted significantly on the populations across Europe. The toll on young men, like the child mortality of the previous generation again lent weight to influential protagonists of population science who played on fears that 'the German *volk* had lost its vitality and would die unless the will to have large numbers of children could be engendered into people'.[17] The German Right's fear of attack from the Eastern Slavs secured another urgent expression of support for population management. But now German concern was exacerbated by French popular propaganda which demonstrated how her population

---

[10]   Paul Weindling., *op. cit.*, p. 298.
[11]   *Ibid.*, p. 209.
[12]   *Ibid.*, p. 1.
[13]   *Ibid.*, p. 209.
[14]   *Ibid.*, p. 208.
[15]   *Ibid.*, p. 209.
[16]   *Ibid.*, p. 213.
[17]   *Ibid.*, p. 342.

insecurity was also to be met with pronatalism and in 1919 Prime Minister George Clemenceau placed population concerns in the shadow of her vulnerability after the Treaty of Versailles.

In return, German politicians drew attention to the prescribed 'two-child system of France', and described it as an 'enemy' phenomenon. This rhetoric thus facilitated fear of the enemy or 'other' to permeate into previously private decisions on family size.[18] And to not have children at all was to risk considerable social criticism for being egotistical, materialist or against German state interests. In 1920 this downturn was thoroughly attested to as Germany experienced a further decline in birth rate. All political parties were in favor of national reconstruction through population policy and, in this desperate climate, eugenicists were to find an audience for their theory that society would not strengthen if attention was directed to the sick alone. The strong would also benefit from health care. It is perhaps here that the scene was set for a shift towards 'selection' as a population policy. As one legal scholar lamented at the time, there was a 'glaring disjunction between the sacrifice of thousands of dead youth and the care of the worthless'.[19] Interest in eugenics was again heightened by the depression of 1929, where in a worsening economic climate, costly healthcare, and the inheritance of this cost were publicly debated by eugenicists and politicians. With a healthy population now perceived primarily as a means to a political end, it was not surprising that attention would eventually fall on those perceived to be 'unhealthy', especially those who might weaken others. As the state became interested in reducing the number of sickly children, and mitigating the cost of their care, so their future *prevention* rather than cure was considered.

Alfred Ploetz, an influential racial hygienist (1869–1940) argued that conception should be regulated according to prescriptions of science. Deformity for example was an issue of citizenship, to be solved by physicians who would prepare 'a gentle death'.[20] Absence of such people would allow additional resources to be directed at strengthening the strong. The case for compulsory sterilization in Germany was actually introduced in 1923, not on anti-Semitic grounds but in order to eradicate those deemed to be 'racially unfit'.[21] Population 'scientists' acquired prominence from their claims that neglected or inferior children's bodies and minds could leave the state with an uncertain future. They were an internal weakness. 'Put simply, welfare was obstructing the natural elimination of the unfit.'[22] A degree of public acceptance of sickly children as 'racially' undesirable was an essential foundation for the practices that characterized the postwar period.

---

[18] *Ibid.*, p. 292.
[19] Karl Binding cited in Friedlander, *op. cit.*, p. 15.
[20] Burleigh and Wipperman, *op. cit.*, p. 32.
[21] Weindling *op. cit.*, pp. 406–7.
[22] Burleigh and Wipperman, *op. cit.*, p. 33.

Sterilization

From the mid 1920s, Hitler had consistently articulated his views that the 'master race' was not already there, but had to be produced. The work of the nineteenth-century zoologist Ernst Haekel, had impressed Hitler, particularly his reasoning that through selective breeding and culling, elite races might be preserved, leading to a strengthening of the human race.[23] He exemplified the ancient Spartans who reputedly owed their racial strength and heroism to this breeding and selection: they killed their weak children and only allowed strong children reproductive rights.[24] Hitler thus created the racial ideology in *Mein Kampf* on the need to prevent miscegenation, whilst also promoting racially selective breeding. In *Mein Kampf* he had written that individuals were not equal to each other and must be evaluated separately on their right to have children,[25] and in a 1929 party rally Hitler advocated eugenics for up to 700,000 individuals.[26] As Weindling summarizes, mutual financial and political benefit derived by interested parties involved in eugenics and Nazism was to give rise to powerful and well propagandized population control measures. As Weindling stresses in his interpretation:

> … eugenics was authoritarian, in that it offered the state and professions unlimited powers to eradicate disease and improve the health of future generations. But it was neither a product of the theory of a superior Aryan race, and nor was it inherently Nazi. The synthesis between Nazism and eugenics was a process of adaption and appropriation on both sides.[27]

The doctrine of selection (*Auslese*) was established in 1930 and the Reich sterilization law drafted in 1932. A year later, Wilhelm Frick, Minister of the Interior, publicized his ideas on eugenics and sterilization, arguing that the cultural and ethical decline of Germany could be curtailed by preventing the procreation of the hereditarily unfit. In his estimation 20 per cent of the population was undesirable as producers of the next generation. Other policy experts including Swiss eugenicists calculated that six million Germans were 'less than full value'.[28] After 1934, men and women could be legally sterilized to prevent the replication of the following diseases: feeblemindedness, schizophrenia, manic-depressive syndrome, St. Vitus's dance (Huntington's Chorea), epilepsy, blindness, deafness, dumbness, severe alchoholism, and marked physical handicaps.[29] Sterilization experiments took place in secret and

---

[23] Weindling, *op. cit.*, see Chapter 1.

[24] Burleigh and Wipperman, *op. cit.*, pp. 29–30.

[25] *Ibid.*, p. 115, see Adolf Hitler, *Mein Kampf*, with an introduction by D. C. Watt, translated by Ralph Manheim (London: Hutchinson, 1969).

[26] Claudia Koonz, 'Eugenics, Gender and Ethics in Nazi Germany: The Debate about Involuntary Sterilization', in Childers and Caplan (eds), *Reevaluating the Third Reich* (New York: Holmes and Meier, 1993), p. 68.

[27] Weindling, *op. cit.*, p. 7.

[28] Koonz, *op. cit.*, p. 68.

[29] *Ibid.*, p. 70.

included the use of x-rays concealed in desks which burnt the genitals.[30] Official commentary stated that sterilization would bring about a gradual 'cleansing' of the people's body or *volkskorper*. Those sterilized on grounds of 'moral weakness' included single mothers,[31] regarded as 'weak' in the absence of a father figure.[32] In 1935 castration was decreed necessary for homosexuals. Himmler argued that their presence worsened the demographic problem of excessive numbers of women, and that they were a waste of fatherhood.[33] Covert sterilization operations on less racially desirable women and mothers were the crucial beginning in this rapidly escalating control over family life. Between 1933 and 1945, 0.5 per cent of those of childbearing age were sterilized on eugenic grounds amounting to over 320,000 operations evenly divided between men and women. This is compared to 11,000 sterilizations in the same period in the USA.[34] Gisela Bock estimates that up to half a million may have been sterilized in total, inside and outside the law. (It has also been calculated that the state prevented 1.6 million births by sterilization.[35]) In 1933 a 'racial problem' identified by the Third Reich was that of 'Rhineland bastards', part Negro children born after the Rhineland occupation by French colonial troops. Intra-ministerial discussions and a Special Commission of the Gestapo, eventually led in 1937 to the secret, and illegal sterilization of 600 child *mulattos*.[36] This attempt to prevent continuation of mixed races illustrates that these 'black' children were as unwanted as Jewish children.[37] Interestingly plans to then 'deport them were vetoed on the grounds of the possible impact of world opinion'.[38]

Abortion

The life of the fetus in Nazi Germany was also subject to laws of 'prevention'. Nazi decision makers counted the fetus as a child, and the mother as a container of a future problem or a future Aryan. The rights of the mother were thus subordinated to the right of the state to protect itself from the 'diseased' child. In 1933 Wilhelm Frick declared a 'War of births' against the enemy,[39] a misleading concept, as in that same year the law was passed which could also curtail the life of the fetus for the greater interests of the state. Eradication (*Ausmerze*) has led the historian Gisela Bock to argue that from its beginning the Nazi regime was essentially anti-

---

[30]   Robert N. Proctor, *Racial Hygiene: Medicine under the Nazis* (Cambridge, Mass: Harvard University Press, 1988), p. 110.

[31]   Weindling, *op. cit.*, p. 533.

[32]   Bock, *op. cit.*, pp. 113–14.

[33]   Weindling, *op. cit.*, p. 535.

[34]   Burleigh and Wipperman, *op. cit.*, p. 253.

[35]   Proctor, *op. cit.*, p. 126.

[36]   Burleigh and Wipperman, *op. cit.*, p. 130.

[37]   Proctor *op. cit.*, pp. 108 and 110.

[38]   Burleigh and Wipperman, *op. cit.*, p. 130.

[39]   Proctor, *op. cit.*, p. 125.

natalist.[40] The 'law for the alteration of the law for the prevention of hereditarily diseased progeny', sanctioned compulsory abortion up to six months. In 1935 legal, eugenic and medical indications for abortion were introduced,[41] and a year later the pregnancies of 'genetically unfit' women could be terminated without their permission.[42] The importance of the unborn Aryan child to the Nazis is evident from the consequent proliferation of abortion control measures. In 1934 penalties for the sale of abortion and birth control devices had been introduced and voluntary abortions were forbidden. By 1943 women attempting to abort racially valuable pregnancies risked the death penalty. The charge made was that of 'racial sabotage' or contributing to the 'dying out' of the German nation during the crisis of war.'[43] A strategy employed by some Polish and Russian women was to use pregnancy as a means of avoiding war work but as of 1941 these women were 'encouraged' or forced to have an abortion, often given heavy men's work to induce miscarriage, followed by sterilization.[44] Where pregnancy was advanced, birth was allowed and the babies placed in child collection centers, although they were only 'collected' after they had died of starvation or lethal medication.[45] In one such 'home for Foreign Children', run by the Volkswagen factory or *Kinderheim* in Rühen, children frequently died of neglect including all those taken there after 1944.[46] A child judged to be of racially 'good stock' was taken to a foster home.[47]

Euthanasia

The Nazis capitalized on the vulnerability and weakness of children, paradoxically with recourse to children's future capacity to debilitate the race. Henry Friedlander writing of the child euthanasia programme comments that the killing of children 'commenced the euthanasia killing program. The children were considered especially crucial because they represented posterity ....'[48] The prevention and elimination of particular births also featured heavily in the SS plans for the conquered Eastern territories: *Deutchesplan Ost*. Prior to the invasion of Poland and the Soviet Union, the SS considered the isolation of ethnic Germans in Eastern territories and, using

---

[40]   Gisela Bock, 'Antinatalism, maternity and paternity in National Socialist racism', in David F. Crew (ed.), *Nazism and German Society* (London: Routledge, 1994).

[41]   Bock, *op. cit.*, p. 122.

[42]   Koonz, *op. cit.*, p. 70.

[43]   Jill Stephenson, 'Women, Motherhood and the family in the Third Reich', in Michael Burleigh (ed.), *Confronting the Nazi Past: New Debates on Modern German History* (London: Collin & Brown, 1996), p. 181.

[44]   Bock, *op. cit.*, pp. 129–30.

[45]   Burleigh and Wipperman, *op. cit.*, p. 263.

[46]   Klaus-Jorg Siegfried, 'Racial Discrimination at work: forced labour in the Volkswagen factory', in Michael Burleigh (ed.), *Confronting the Nazi Past: New Debates on Modern German History* (New York: St. Martin's Press, 1996), p. 42.

[47]   Burleigh and Wipperman, *op. cit.*, p. 263.

[48]   Friedlander, *op. cit.*, p. 61.

racial biology as the basis of their social policy and military strategy, decided on a program of abortions, sterilization and mass infant neglect.[49] Removing racially inferior babies from their mothers, placing them in undisclosed hospitals and letting them die, was a small but efficient step towards restructuring the population.

At the Nuremburg rally of 5 August 1929, Hitler declared that 'If Germany was to get a million children a year, and was to remove 700,000 to 800,000 of the weakest people, then the final result might even be an increase in strength'.[50] Non-Aryans, Jews, Gypsies, foreigners, disabled and retarded were categorized as weak and diseased – they represented a threat to the strong. In 1935 Hitler admitted that war would be useful in solving the problem of these children. Not only could security needs be invoked in justification of euthanasia, but the escalating climate of violence and military activity would subdue its impact.[51] Initially euthanasia was administered to children under three years old who were mentally ill, retarded, or malformed at birth. In 1938 this definition covered most newborn babies with diseases. The condition and fate of these children was determined by midwives who were paid to observe 'idiots' and 'monguls', spastics and malformed.[52] The Child Euthanasia Program began in 1939, and led to the deaths of tens of thousands of children from infants to adolescents aged seventeen. This included an initial group of 5,000 handicapped children under three years whose mothers (and fathers) could not be identified.[53] By 1941 the program was expanded to include more children between eight and seventeen to compensate for the ending of adult euthanasia. Healthy children of unwanted races and unhealthy Aryan children were deliberately neglected until they died.[54] Euthanasia was perhaps easy to administer by virtue of its benign methods. Putting a small child to sleep or allowing hypothermia or starvation to occur was, as one medical doctor boasted: 'a method least likely to incur criticism from the foreign press'.[55] Comments made by Directors during tours of institutions and other contemporary justifications show how a 'clean' or 'natural' process of death, albeit by neglect was strong enough to satisfy the consciences involved.[56] The foreign press accordingly observed only a high number of cot deaths. In total, there were twenty-two hospital wards, each for up to 200 children.[57]

---

[49]   Paul Weindling. *op. cit.*, p. 541.
[50]   Burleigh and Wipperman, *op. cit.*, p. 142.
[51]   *Ibid.*
[52]   Paul Weindling, *op. cit.*, p. 543.
[53]   Bock, *op. cit.*, p. 131.
[54]   Proctor, *op. cit.*, p. 188.
[55]   *Ibid.*, p. 187.
[56]   Friedlander, *op. cit.*, p. 50.
[57]   *Ibid.*, p. 48.

Amnesia

What is of interest here is how easily child deaths were accomplished, tolerated and justified in the scientific realm of euthanasia and in the normally protective hospital environment. 'Euthanasia' provides an interesting example of how children, especially neonatals could be killed with apparent ease, often blaming the mother for having produced inferior offspring and by allowing (forcing) mothers to neglect their children. The proximity of mothers to their children, and their semi-complicity, served to distance the actual perpetrators physically and notionally from the killing of children. And interestingly, it seems that this line was only reluctantly crossed even at the height of the regime's barbarity. Outside of a hospital environment children were not killed outright, even in concentration camps, where one at least was solely for children. A child isolated from a familial or science environment, for example in an execution queue, had a sobering impact on Nazi officials. This will be explored further through an analysis of the child, particularly the constructed child as an embodiment of the state's security needs, and in the case of Aryan children, with the state as a surrogate parent. Children thus far had been a germ-cell of the nation, either protected and under close guardianship of mothers and the state, or dying within and by via their mother and the state. The isolated child *might* have unsettled the Nazi conscience and called into question the nationalist construction of child-centered welfare and a cult of motherhood – in short Nazism as being in the best interests of the child.

> We came to the question: what about the women and children? I decided to find a clear solution here too. In fact I did not regard myself as justified in exterminating the men – let us say killing them or having them killed – while letting avengers in the shape of children grow up.[58]

Himmler made this statement awkwardly to a troop of doubting executioners in nearby woods, ill-prepared for the task of shooting women and children in the back. Himmler suggested that the mental strength necessary was in preparation for the difficult times ahead, although by 1943 he and fellow members of the SS, including Adolf Eichmann were less confident about killing children in execution camps. They had 'psychological difficulties', and became sick when watching the shootings.[59] New massacre methods such as gas chambers disguised as shower rooms, were originally introduced to avoid actually 'killing' and Gisela Bock writes that the first mobile gas vans were provided solely for the killing of women and children. Bock notes how 'men women and children' was the frequent description of the victims[60] despite the fact that mostly Jewish women, and those with children were selected for death right upon arrival; '[e]very Jewish child meant automatically death to its mother'.[61]

---

[58] Gisela Bock, in Crew *op. cit.*, p. 132.
[59] *Ibid.*, p. 131.
[60] *Ibid.*
[61] *Ibid.*, p. 132.

Perhaps the term 'men' was added because it suggested that complete families were killed and women and children were not singled out; a completeness creating an effect of normalization to counteract possible criticism or doubts over killing women and children. Evidently women's and children's deaths were understood to be more abhorrent or unsettling than the deaths of men. The uncomfortable contradiction that they should be protected but were to be shot was ameliorated by 'adding men' to the description of events. Adding virtual male victims to events specific to children and women, hides, and also prevents the questioning of the isolation of women and children and the interests that necessitated their deaths. Similarly the differential 'victim' status of women and children was recognized and concealed by the camp commandants and by the Nazi doctors who preferred the foreign press to know that children died in their sleep alone rather than were killed. Women and children warrant 'protective' behavior towards them. This is illustrated by the initial difficulty experienced by the camp guards in visibly harming them, and thus damaging this ideology, and the unwillingness to recognize their isolation.

The everyday experiences of children in Nazi Germany were often linked to the powerful ideology of gender difference that typified certain males as protectors, and allowed certain notions of the (Aryan) family to serve the function of a normal and valued sphere of activity against which policies of extermination were rationalized. This is exemplified in the following quotation by Rudolf Hoess, who said: 'I am completely normal. Even while I was carrying out the task of extermination I led a normal family life and so on.'[62] Hoess, commandant of the concentration and extermination camp at Auschwitz, made this final point whilst being tried as a war criminal by the Polish Peoples' Supreme Court. This recourse to family values was applied with the intention of distancing and counteracting a brutal past by signifying the 'normality' of a family home, to which he returned each day. Over fifty years later, the observation that 'Hitler loved children and animals; he was human too', can be heard in Bavaria where promoters of the newly constructed Hitler Museum are intent on the inclusion of his informal family photographs.[63]

This refuge within the reality and construct of the loving family may have been an important reason why the cult of motherhood and the family was retained, despite practices to the contrary. In a recent German documentary, former women in the SS agreed that they had provided an atmosphere of normality and an emotional background to extermination policy by also attending to children, their nursery care and associated socializing. As Jill Stephenson notes: 'in the Nazi view the family was the "germ cell" of the nation – a fundamentally important basic unit and a microcosm of the "national community"'.[64] Racial superiority became a powerful metaphorical image and reality and so too the ideal of motherhood, propagandized in pronatalist policies, became an indelible image of care and nurture of the future

---

[62]   Rudolf Hoess, cited in Joachim C. Fest, *The Faces of the Third Reich*, translated from the German by Michael Bullock (London: Weidenfeld and Nicolson, 1970), p. 276.

[63]   *Newsnight* Report, BBC2, aired on 20 November 1997.

[64]   Stephenson, cited in Burleigh, *op. cit.*, p. 168.

German state. It was an image strong enough to permeate into all aspects of life and withstand the blatant antinatalist policies that coexisted with racial hygiene. This championing of the mother's role was a necessary prerequisite for the state's shared interest in the child. Von Saldern contends that getting on with 'normal family life' served a political purpose and some German women experienced 'social motherhood' in that their ideals of motherhood merged with a social responsibility for attending to the state. This dissolution might also prevent us from assigning guilt. Their private sphere became a much propagandized and managed 'special female public sphere'.[65]

Possibly the intense or totalitarian regulation of the private sphere served to draw mothers' attention away from extermination or genocide. Each woman (or future mother) had a defined role and place in the fight for the survival of the nation, and perhaps it was hoped, not enough time to think about the death of other people's children. Tim Mason believes that the Nazis stumbled upon the 'reconciliatory function' of the family which was extolled and became attractive as Nazi policies became more extreme and economic and political pressures increased.[66] He writes: '[t]he nightmare world of dictatorial government, huge industrial combines, all encompassing administration and organized inhumanity was parasitic upon its ideological antithesis, the minute community of adults and children'.[67] However the continued existence in a real or perceived sense of a relatively intact private sphere, a household and family containing a mother with children, strengthened the dichotomies of mothers and soldiers, home front and battlefront. Political leaders openly stated that they were dependent on the effective functioning of the private sphere where mothers were controlled and subject to instruction and instrumental rationalization.

Motherlands

In practice Nazis depended on a carefully controlled engagement with, and representation of mothers, and women as future mothers. A delicate balance was to be achieved between encouraging a 'natural process', controlling it, and making it a national duty. Mother and child, or family, constituted a political and military resource, legitimized by and subject to Nazi principles: a means to a greater end. Women then were reduced to vessels, and in the case of the unhealthy or childless, not even acknowledged. Although the family was protected and publicly reified as the bastion of civil defense, it was also broken down or infiltrated, regulated and subjugated to the public Nazi arena, to such an extent that it is suggested that 'a non-

---

[65]   von Saldern, *op. cit.*, p. 146.

[66]   Tim Mason, 'Women in Germany, 1925–1940: Family, Welfare and Work. Part II', *History Workshop* (1976), p. 24.

[67]   *Ibid.*

political private sphere simply did not exist'.[68] In the framework of Ernst Fraenkel, von Saldern argues that 'the apparent division between the private and the public spheres actually dissolved under the Third Reich' and the private sphere became politicized.[69] Women's organizations were told that:

> the rights of parents over the bringing up of their children ... have become a duty undertaken at the behest of the nation and under the supervision of the state and involving unlimited responsibility.[70]

And Nazi literature on motherhood explained how a home for children:

> ... represents a place where nationalist and racialist culture is nurtured. It means realising in the community of the family a part of the ideal national community and giving to the nation, in the form of grown up children, people who are physically and emotionally developed to the fullest extent, who are able to cope with life and face it boldly, who, are aware of their responsibilities to the nation and race, and who will lead their nation onwards and upwards.[71]

In Prussia for example, social hygiene had been made part of the curriculum and eugenics was taught in biology lessons. Girls learnt their duties of healthcare and motherhood[72] and textbooks were rewritten in order to instill in pupils a sense of responsibility to the nation and race.[73] The child or infant featured frequently and prominently in political addresses, and in statements made to women's organizations. In return women's organizations were polarized around the function of the mother and other nurturing roles. The NSF had, by 1932 enshrined the following basic first principle: that 'the whole education, training, careers, and position of women within the nation and state must be organized in terms of their physical and mental tasks as mothers.'[74] Hitler's speech to the Nationalist Socialist Women's Organization in 1934, typifies this early centrality of the child in propaganda and rhetoric:

> [T]he programme of our National Socialist movement has in reality but one single point, and that point is the child, that tiny creature which must be born and grow strong and which alone gives meaning to the whole life struggle.[75]

---

[68]   A. von Saldern, citing the work of Ernst Fraenkel, who differentiated between the 'prerogative state', or *Massnahmenstaat* – the sphere dominated by Nazi illegality and injustice, and the *Normenstaat*, where the norms of pre-Nazi bourgeoise society survived, in 'Victims or Perpetrators? Controversies about the Role of Women in the Nazi State', in Crew, *op. cit.*, p. 148.

[69]   *Ibid.*, p.146.

[70]   J. Noakes and G. Pridham (eds), *Nazism: 1919–1945,* Vol. 2. *State, Economy and Society 1933–1939* (Exeter: University of Exeter, 1984), p. 455.

[71]   *Ibid.*

[72]   Weindling, *op. cit.*, p. 410.

[73]   *Ibid.*, p. 411.

[74]   J. Noakes and G. Pridham , *op. cit.*, p. 461.

[75]   *Ibid.*, p. 450

The Nazis made clear the dual role of mothers and children in the racial and military strengthening of the state and in this sense the private was also conceptualized as both political and international; or to use the terminology of the time – the 'big world' would not survive if 'the small world' was not secure.[76] 'Providence has entrusted to the woman the care of the world which is her very own, and only on the basis of this smaller world can the man's world be formed and built up'.[77] Invoking the rhetoric of war again when he addressed the Nazi Women's League in 1935, he said:

> What the man gives in courage on the battlefield, the woman gives in eternal self-sacrifice, in eternal pain and suffering. Every child that a woman brings into the world is a battle, a battle waged for the existence of her people.[78]

Women were not expected to hinder their reproductive capacities or natural talents. In May 1934 the Reich Mother's Service (*RMD*) was introduced. Its purpose: 'the training of physically and mentally able mothers to make them convinced of the important duties of motherhood, experienced in the care and education of their children and competent to carry out their domestic tasks'.[79] As Goebbels stated, 'a woman's primary, rightful and appropriate place is in the family, and the most wonderful task that she can perform is to present her country and people with children'.[80] From 1938, the 'Honour Cross of the German mother', was awarded to all women with four or more children. Medals or crosses were inscribed with words 'the Child ennobles the Mother'.[81] Mothers with medals were entitled to be saluted by Hitler Youth members in public and large families designated *kinder-reich* (rich in children) received preferential treatment and specific entitlements. Children's welfare was also represented by two organizations for women, the *NS Frauenschaft* – (National Socialist Womanhood) and sub-ordinate to this, the *DFW* – *Deutsches Frauenwerk* (German Women's Enterprise). As Dr Krummacher, Reich leader of the NSF and leader of the DFW wrote in 1933 'the German woman belongs in the first instance to her family'. The DFW played an active role supervising traditional child-minding and housekeeping skills, as well as monitoring of pregnant women to deter abortion.[82] In addition, from 1934 to 1936 the Racial Political Office and the Expert Committee for Population and Racial Policy were both engaged in management of the family. Maternity advice was also given by the 'mother and child' section of the Nazi Welfare Organization, the NSV, and in addition the regime launched a comprehensive propaganda campaign to raise the status of mothers and housewives

---

[76]   Tim Mason, 'Women in Germany, 1925–1940: Family, Welfare and Work. Part I', *History Workshop* (1976), p. 74.

[77]   Hitler speech to the Nationalist Socialist Frauenschaft in 1934, cited in Noakes and Pridham, *op. cit.*, p. 449.

[78]   Noakes and Pridham, *op. cit.*, p. 449.

[79]   Noakes and Pridham, *op. cit.*, p. 459.

[80]   Cited in Burleigh and Wipperman, *op. cit.*, p. 242.

[81]   Noakes and Pridham, *op. cit.*, p. 452.

[82]   Stephenson, *op. cit.*, pp. 170–71.

and to formalize their role as part of the war effort. The state assumed and shared a high level of guardianship of the child, in addition to the surveillance of mothers, and the economic conditions made available to them. Firstly, as responsibility for family welfare shifted from the private family sphere to the state, scientific and medical channels opened up and directed policy.[83] Nazi concern with the next generation was comprehensive, public and invasive, including the monitoring and assisting of births and an attempt to reduce miscarriages (spontaneous or contrived), still births, infant and maternal mortality and childhood diseases.

The Nazis believed that policies of the Weimar Republic had allowed the family to become a corrupted unit, as did the availability of birth control and acceptance of women's aspirations outside the home.[84] The child thus seemed to offer a single point of coalescence for Nazi objectives of control, both of women and of a future generation. By 1935 the Nuremberg laws to 'Protect German Blood and Honour' were also in place. These aimed to prevent marriage and children which was not deemed to be in the interests of the state. New marriage laws prevented intermarrying between healthy and diseased Jews, and by 1935 philanthropic social policies and concessions were aimed only at those of higher racial value.[85]

Despite motherhood being propagandized as the most *natural* condition for women to be in, the intensity of state monitoring and regulation would seem to suggest that a specific idealized motherhood was pursued by the state, which mothers alone were not capable of. The esteem which mothers received publicly was not also held within elite circles. They were thought to be naturally stupid and engaged in a simpleton's task (a perception evidenced by the ability of mothers to remain undetected as underground agents by virtue of their status.)[86] At a more abstract level childbearing was said by some eugenics experts to be far from ideal as it distracted women from such state allegiance. In 1934 Nazi brochures distributed in millions explained that 'women's 'task was not prolific propagation but "regeneration"'.[87] As Bock notes, the female characteristic of maternalism (*Mutterlichkeit*) became the object of racist polemic and was treated as contemptible 'sentimental humanitarianism'. Maternalism was a phenomenon to be controlled and curtailed lest it threatened the values of the state. One early race hygienist Agnes Blum in a 1934 edition of the magazine *Die Frau*, emphasized the danger of maternalism which 'like any egoism acts against the race'.[88] Ultimately motherhood was expected to be a transient phase and the child would be 'given' up to the Führer's care; a currency of allegiance. For although Hitler explained: '[i]n my State the mother is the most important citizen',[89]

[83]   Weindling, *op. cit.*, p. 208.
[84]   Stephenson, *op. cit.*, p. 168.
[85]   Burleigh and Wipperman, *op. cit.*, p. 48.
[86]   Claudia Koonz, *Mothers in the Fatherland: Women, the Family and Nazi Politics* (London: Methuen, 1987), p. 336.
[87]   Bock, *op. cit.*, p. 119.
[88]   *Ibid.*
[89]   Adolf Hitler in 1933, cited in Burleigh and Wipperman, *op. cit.*, p. 242.

this attention came with a vital caveat: as he also stated, 'children belong to their mothers as at the same moment they belong to me'.[90]

Bock notes from Nationalist Socialist policies that fathers were privileged over mothers in status and financial reward. The 'duty' of begetting children was considered more valuable than that of bearing and rearing children, and women's contribution to procreation inferior to men's.[91] The Nazi Minister Hans Frank claimed that the concept of fatherhood, handed down through age old processes of natural law, 'is unambiguous and must be placed at the centre of the financial measures'.[92] Motherhood then was a political territory between the child and the fatherland. In practice it was often reduced to an act of biological reproduction, whilst conceptually it was harnessed as an emotive, easily transferable image of the new Aryan nation. As Bock argues at length, Nationalist Socialist family policy consisted 'of antinatalism and a cult of fatherhood and masculinity' not motherhood as we might think about it.[93] It was a process to be controlled, a means to an Aryan end, leading historians to argue that the slogan '*Kinder, Küche, Kirche*' is misappropriated to the regime.[94] The regime was friendly to *some* children and mothers, not 'mother and child-friendly'. In Bock's view the established belief then and now, that Nationalist Socialist policies were pronatalist and created a cult of motherhood, is in need of revision. Sterilization, abortion, *Lebensborn* homes, child-abduction, and euthanasia, marked the progress of the gradual intensification and institutionalization of racial hygiene in Germany. A sequence of population control measures of increasing capacity, 'produced the technology and mentalities' for the holocaust and genocide.[95] Sterilization as Bock argues, was the first step towards the final solution, and crucially desensitized those same doctors who later executed women and children.[96] In the practices of raising the population's 'quality' or *Aufartung*, it can be shown that the regime directed more attention to preventing unwanted life than encouraging births. Bock writes that *antinatalism* was the key functioning device used by the Nazis. Motherhood was only encouraged only in healthy women, whereas antinatalist policies were aimed at a broad cross-section of women, and some men, most evidently through forced sterilization.[97] Although the birthrate did increase marginally, historians of social history, such as Timothy Mason question how much this can be attributed to National Socialism.[98] It was imperative that women capable of child-bearing understood their duty, and participated in what was in effect a selective breeding program. Hitler made clear that protection of such children also fulfilled their parents' duty to the state and race. Pronatalism was too specific and limited in application to significantly

[90] Joachim Fest, *op. cit.*, p. 269.
[91] Bock *op. cit.*, p. 124.
[92] *Ibid.*
[93] Bock *op. cit.*, p. 129.
[94] *Ibid.*, p. 120.
[95] *Ibid.*, p. 111.
[96] *Ibid.*, p. 130.
[97] *Ibid.*, p. 132.
[98] Mason, *op. cit.*, pp. 102–3.

increase the birthrate amongst healthy women.[99] Their forced employment made this less practicable.[100] The limited achievements of pronatalism on the birthrate should not however belittle its other consequences. This discourse of procreation and protection for example, perhaps helped to mask the practices of invasion and violation it heralded. The control of the child led to control of the mother, either her compliance through fear or compliance as a consequence of the absorbing nature of her heavily propagandized task. Children were removed from parents who did not comply with the state policies for parenting. As Stephenson comments on the scale of the Nazi preoccupation with children's welfare, '[n]one of this was merely for the benefit of individual Aryan families: all these efforts were geared single-mindedly to promoting the regime's racial and power-political objectives'.[101] Motherhood was a state-managed fiction for the production of an Aryan race and the control and protection of the Aryan child. As Goebbels' Ministry for Propaganda later made clear: '[t]he goal is not: "children at any cost", but: "racially worthy, physically and mentally unaffected children of German families"'.[102] As late as 1944 the German Girls' League was still telling its 'daughters' that if they could not find a husband they should at least donate a child to the Fuhrer.[103] Teenage pregnancy was thus considered to be a political act, as state became father, and the image of a 'family' was maintained.

Aryanization

One particular practice of Aryanization, was intended for new-born children, yet took place in the absence of their mothers. SS baptism ceremonies were secretive, stage-managed displays of paternal protection. The sole preserve of the SS, they complemented the Nazi aim of making the boys into men and soldiers, but perhaps also acted as a symbolic point of focus for the Aryan elite soldier. Racially pure children represented the embryonic German state in its most desired form, and were to be nurtured and protected as such. Babies represented an extension of the soldier's honor. The birth of an SS child was ritualized and celebrated in a naming ceremony, in which a large ceremonial sword was rested on the child's stomach to the strains of the German anthem. A senior SS officer addressed the service, saying the following words over the baby: '[w]e take you into our community as a limb of our body, you shall grow up in our protection and bring honour to your name, pride to your brotherhood and inextinguishable glory to your race'.[104] The ceremony was also of

---

[99]   Bock, *op. cit.*, pp. 126–7.

[100]   Stephenson, *op. cit.*, pp. 175–7.

[101]   *Ibid.*, pp. 170–71.

[102]   Bock in Crew *op. cit.*, p. 120.

[103]   Richard Grunberger, *A Social History of the Third Reich* (Harmondsworth: Penguin, 1974), p. 317.

[104]   Catrine Clay and Michael Leapman, *Master Race: The Lebensborn experiment in Nazi Germany* (BCA and Hodder and Stoughton, 1995), p. 34.

symbolic significance since though his physical worth and machismo was already bestowed, the child would not be old enough to bring honor to his race for some time. The importance invested in the child as a mirror of the father is suggested by the example of SS men who could not stand the 'shame' of caring for retarded *minderwertige* offspring. Some children, such as the disabled 'Knauer kid', were murdered before the war began.[105]

Himmler ensured that his elite SS men who had already proven their purity, should have the opportunity to leave their blood line behind with guaranteed safekeeping even if death of the father ensued.[106] He issued a procreation order to the entire SS, privately stating that: '[i]n defiance of existing laws I have systematically influenced the SS to consider children, irrespective of illegality or otherwise, the most beautiful and best thing there is'.[107]

Himmler thought of his men as acting as 'conception assistants', ideally after surviving the front. Promiscuity was alleged to be a symptom of having survived war, and as survival of the fittest was the aim, such fathering was deemed logical. Divorce laws were also relaxed so that either partner could more rapidly enter into other productive relationships.[108] The offspring of SS men were to receive optimum benefits. The SS's 'Well of Life Agency' was directly subordinate to Himmler and in 1936 he created *Lebensborn* homes for married and unmarried women to receive prenatal and postnatal care.[109] These were state-run maternity homes of a high standard to assist children born of racially elite fathers. All valuable mothers and children who might be in want of care, not just those connected with the SS, would be able to seek refuge in these homes.[110] There was no such refuge for non-Aryan children, and from 1937 the Reich adoption service only dealt with those deemed 'racially healthy'.[111]

The *Lebensborn* agency took on responsibility for illegitimate children of German soldiers born in Norway and Polish or Russian women made pregnant by German men were also taken to special delivery camps and subjected to racial selection before they were admitted to homes.[112] Their children were then selected or rejected under the euthanasia regime. Himmler termed this sorting and selection of Eastern babies 'fishing for blood' in Occupied Europe. In 1939 *RuSHA*, a subdivision of the SS Race

---

[105] Proctor *op. cit.*, p.184.

[106] Jill Stephenson, 'Women, Motherhood and the family in the Third Reich', in Burleigh (ed.), *Confronting the Nazi Past: New Debates on Modern German History* (London: Collin & Brown, 1996), p. 174.

[107] Richard Grunberger, *A Social History of the Third Reich* (Harmondsworth: Penguin, 1974), p. 316.

[108] Burleigh and Wipperman, *op. cit.*, p. 252.

[109] *Ibid.*, p. 73.

[110] Burleigh and Wipperman, *op. cit.*, p. 252, Jill Stephenson, in Burleigh, *op. cit.*, p. 174.

[111] Burleigh and Wipperman, *op. cit.*, p. 71.

[112] *Ibid.*, p. 298.

and Settlement Office established in 1932,[113] issued a paper titled 'The treatment of the population in former Polish areas according to racial political criteria.' It stated that Polish children should only be educated in German, and this should not exceed more than rudimentary skills such as counting and advocated that:

> [There] must be an attempt to exclude racially valuable children from the resettlement [of Poles] and to educate them in suitable institutions, such as the former military institutions in Potsdam, or in a German family.[114]

It is interesting that the age is given before which re-nationalizing or conditioning is most effective:

> To be suitable children must not be more than eight or ten years old, because as a rule a genuine ethnic transformation – that is, a final Germanization – is possible only up to this age. The first condition of this is a complete ban on all links with their Polish relatives. The children will be given German names of Teutonic origin. Their birth and heredity certificates will be kept by a special department.[115]

In a secret order of 1942, Himmler requested the Germanization of Norwegian children, that is, their secret removal from their mothers and homes in order to increase the Nordic blood in German stock.[116] Burleigh and Wipperman cite estimates that the SS kidnapped or abducted up to 200,000 blond and blue-eyed children from the occupied territories within Eastern Europe. From 1942, children under six, kidnapped from Ukraine, Yugoslavia and Romania were placed in 'Child collection points' and categorized.[117] It is worth providing Burleigh and Wipperman's summary in full:

> Racially, 'especially valuable' children were taken by the SS 'well of Life' agency; the 'racially valuable' by the NSV, which then farmed them out for adoption. The racially worthless were starved to death in the 'Care Centers for Foreign Children. Their corpses were packed into cardboard boxes and incinerated'.[118]

Valuable children that were placed in homes were bullied and brutalized to build Aryan 'character' and then further tested for racial qualities before being given to German foster parents. Those that 'failed the tests' but did not die, were sent back to Poland.[119]

This chapter has thus far illustrated the importance attached to the presence and absence of particular children in Nazi policies of nationalization. The link

---

[113] Clay and Leapman, *op. cit.*, p. 36.
[114] *Ibid.*, p. 92.
[115] Clay and Leapman, *op. cit.*, p. 93.
[116] Burleigh and Wipperman, *op. cit.*, p. 66.
[117] Clay and Leapman, *op. cit.*, p. 163.
[118] Burleigh and Wipperman, *op. cit.*, p. 73.
[119] *Ibid.*, p. 66.

made between their bodies and the survival of the nation, was further concretized in practices of racialization and militarization in schooling and other spheres of education.

> The family was, then, to cease to be a private institution, becoming instead an instrument of Nazi policy, one partner in a triangular relationship, along with school and the Hitler Youth Organization of the National Socialists (NSDAP). These three agencies were to cooperate in the continual and unceasing indoctrination of the young.[120]

Aryan-nation: Education and Leisure

> I am beginning with the young. We older ones are used up. Yes, we are old already. We are rotten to the marrow. We have no unrestrained instincts left ... but my magnificent youngsters – are there finer ones anywhere in the world? ... Look at these young men and boys what material! With them I can make a new world.[121]

Hitler made these statements in 1939, by which time extensive revision of the school curriculum, removal of many sectors of society from the teaching profession, and an overarching application of the *Führerprinzip* to the whole structure of education was underway to help shape new National Socialist minds.

Children were clearly regarded across the Reich Ministries as a resource to be propagandized, nationalized and socialized. In 1934 Wilhelm Frick, the Minister of the Interior, announced to the public that 'the political task of the school is the education of youth in the service of nation and state in the National Socialist spirit'.[122]

Education had already been a conduit of political reform during the 1920s when the issue of depleted troop numbers and the need for national unity in the wake of WWI were addressed through health education and compulsory physical activity. The racial hygiene movement, capitalizing on a swing towards unity and population preservation, used textbooks to promote popular explanations of racial hygiene in schools. Authors then believed that eugenics, blended with the laws of heredity could 'instill in pupils a sense of responsibility to the nation and race'.[123]

These ideas, of racial health and physical fitness again provided an easy foundation for Nazi education policy. Though by 1934 the Reich government established central control over the whole education system[124] the education system did not reform effectively, owing to Hitler's lack of interest and aptitude in providing accurate policy. He had only crudely suggested the following attributes on which

---

[120] Stephenson, *op. cit.*, p. 168.

[121] Martyn Housden, *Resistance and Conformity in the Third Reich* (Routledge: London, 1997), p. 68.

[122] Lisa Pine, 'Nazism in the classroom', in *History Today*, April 1997, pp. 22–7, and p. 23.

[123] *Ibid.,* p. 411.

[124] Noakes and Pridham, *op. cit.*, pp. 433–5.

teaching should be based: 'contempt for intellect, a strong emphasis on sport, and the need for indoctrination in Nazi values'.[125] In effect most children were able to spend time doing what they enjoyed, playing rather than thinking. This was noted by the compilers of the *Deutschland-Berichte Sopade* reports. The Social Democratic Party's observations on the population and the regime reported that: '[t]he new generation never had much use for education and reading. Now nothing is demanded of them; on the contrary knowledge is condemned'.[126] Hitler's tenet of education found in *Mein Kampf* was that 'our goal is not the contemplative man but the man of action'.[127] After 1935, reason, knowledge and intellect were increasingly criticized as cowardly.[128] In *Mein Kampf* Hitler elaborated on the need for young people to receive intellectual instruction and physical training. He recommended boxing in particular because it encouraged the 'spirit of aggression' and required 'lightning decisions'.[129] The call for more sport was also intended to turn boys' attention away from prostitution which was propagandized as a Jewish disease. Sport was a convenient introduction to the strong mind and healthy body desired by racial theorists.[130] Hitler saw strength as a prime virtue of the secure German state. In a speech to the German people he said:

> I intend to have an athletic youth – that is the first and the chief thing. In this way I shall eradicate the thousands of years of human domestication. Then I shall have in front of me the pure and natural noble material.[131]

The curriculum demanded a great deal of participation in sport rather than intellect. From the age of four Aryan children were to experience a significant increase in sports activity, in some cases up to five hours in one day.[132] Physical tests were the means of graduating to the next class. Noakes writes that Hitler Youth activities complemented the reformed schools by imprinting upon children emerging stereotypes such as contempt for the intellectual and respect for brutality, often to the regret of parents and teachers.[133] The physical education teacher was considered second only to the head master.[134] Teaching camps that were provided for teachers also used sporting activities as a means of breaking down barriers of status and encouraging collective enthusiasm. It was believed that the teachers themselves had to experience such team spirit through sport in order to pass it on enthusiastically to children. Wearing a uniform, singing, listening, marching, playing sport, communal

---

[125] *Ibid.*, p. 434.
[126] Welch, *op. cit.*, p. 63.
[127] Noakes and Pridham, *op. cit.*, p. 437.
[128] Fest, *op. cit.*, p. 232.
[129] Burleigh and Wipperman, *op. cit.*, p. 201.
[130] *Ibid.*, p. 202.
[131] Housden *op. cit.*, p. 68.
[132] M. Freeman, *The Atlas of Nazi Germany* (London: Croom Helm, 1987), p. 86.
[133] Noakes and Pridham, *op. cit.*, p. 429.
[134] Grunberger, *op. cit.*, pp. 365–6.

eating and sleeping in camps was made a compulsory experience.[135] In 1943 it was decreed that all sporting organizations had also to become affiliated with Hitler Youth.[136] An agreement between Baldur von Schirach and the Reich Sports Minister granted the Hitler Youth a monopoly on sports activities up to the age of 14 and later up to the age of 18.[137]

During the regime, alternative schools were specifically set up as elite education centers for future top-ranking government and army personnel. Parents volunteered children for *Napolas* or National Political Educational Institutes, established by Bernhard Rust, Minister of Education, for pupils aged between ten and eighteen.[138] These institutions, modeled on old Prussian cadet schools, aimed to train bodies and minds through paramilitary style sport. By 1940 there were 5,000 pupils, almost all of them male, training as the functionaries of the Third Reich. Rival Adolf Hitler Schools were set up by von Schirach and Robert Ley in 1937 for children aged between twelve and eighteen, and were operated and financed exclusively by the Nazi Party. Pupils in Adolf Hitler Schools were selected by virtue of physical appearance and capability from Hitler Youth and were intended to be future Nazi leaders.[139] Such competition illustrates the interest in elite education, particularly when resources were already stretched as to make duplicity imprudent. There was no clear or consistent curriculum in place in either school.

Within Nazi education, experience was considered to be more important than learning in terms of personal development. Students were encouraged to feel united by a common racial heritage, demonstrated by success in sport for example. The Nazi Prussian Minister of Education explained this to a group of students involved in vocational education. '[T]he true great practical school, is not over there (the University), and not in grammar schools, it is in the labor camp, for here instruction and words cease and action begins.'[140] The emphasis on education thinly disguised what was also war labor and indoctrination. Children were so familiar with receiving instructions from every sphere, an experience typical of Western childhood, that they may have had little opportunity to reflect on their actions. A set of ten laws of behavior for German students, published in 1934, included the following instruction 'As a leader be ... helpful and kind, never petty in the judgment of human weaknesses, generous in the recognition of the needs of others and modest in your own.'[141] These honorable guidelines may have enabled young people to believe they were capable of doing well whilst they were engaged in less desirable racist activities. Nazi ideology was so diffuse that its approach to learning could not be applied holistically, nor discussed in great detail.[142] It was, as Ian Kershaw has observed, initiated by

---

[135] Noakes and Pridham, *op. cit.*, p. 432.
[136] Burleigh and Wipperman, *op. cit.*, pp. 204–5.
[137] Noakes and Pridham, *op. cit.*, p. 419.
[138] Burleigh and Wipperman, *op. cit.*, p. 215.
[139] *Ibid.*, p. 215 and Freeman, *op. cit.*, p. 89.
[140] Noakes and Pridham, *op. cit.*, p. 441.
[141] *Ibid.*, pp. 442–3.
[142] Noakes and Pridham, *op. cit.*, p. 446.

Hitler but gained a momentum and totalitarian framework of its own through basic principles being understood and adopted across the stratums of society.[143] Simple physical regulations of school sport and Hitler Youth activities, with their limited potential for nonconformity were relied upon. The everyday routine of the child's day – homework, games, and youth group membership – became highly disciplined, competitive and politicized. Schools were however subject to constant interference from the *Hitler Jugend*, suggesting a power struggle with Von Schirach. Rust was also weak and not capable of providing effective control over education policy, allowing Hitler Youth regulations to contradict with education needs. But in effect this would have served Hitler's plans of indoctrination well. Competition between education authorities and Hitler Youth did not lesson the degree of attention towards children but guaranteed constant demands made of them from either direction, thus seemingly exemplifying their importance at each point of confrontation.

By 1933 all teachers could join the National Socialist League of Teachers (NSLB) and schoolchildren were taught only by those teachers who had accepted the tightening parameters of the Nazi curriculum. As the leader of the Nazi Teachers League stated: 'Those who have youth on their side control the future.'[144] Welch writes that the teaching profession from very early on was regarded by the NSDAP as a vanguard for their propaganda. In 1937 the Nazi Teachers League had 95 per cent membership.[145] Jewish teachers had been dismissed in 1935 following the Law for the restoration of the professional Civil Service.[146] The aims of the NSLB are evident in the following statement by one of its functionaries made in 1937:

> National Socialism is an ideology (Weltanschauung) whose claim to validity is total and does not wish to be subject to the random formation of opinion. The means of implementing this claim is through education ... It is being carried out with the same methods with which the movement has conquered the whole nation: indoctrination and propaganda.[147]

Children of non-Aryan origin attended German schools only by privilege. Even then, many were subject to discrimination and ridicule. They were frequently victimized by pupils and teachers and school was an exercise ground for a racial hatred. Aryan children were segregated even at an early age and at kindergarten Jewish children were often forbidden to play with Aryan children.[148] Ubiquitous Nazi propaganda told of the child's place in the German state. Intriguingly, the Nazis were capable of casually introducing the idea of child-sacrifice to children whilst drawing attention to their future as worthy citizens.[149]

---

[143]   Ian Kershaw, *Hitler, 1889–1936: Hubris* (London: Allen Lane, 1998).
[144]   Noakes and Pridham, *op. cit.*, p. 416.
[145]   Welch, *op. cit.*, p. 61.
[146]   Burleigh and Wipperman, *op. cit.*, p. 214.
[147]   Noakes and Pridham, *op. cit.*, p. 432.
[148]   Burleigh and Wipperman, *op. cit.*, p. 214.
[149]   Pine, *op. cit.*, pp. 22–7 and p. 23.

Recorded children's accounts show that many children shared a similarly simplistic perception of the war. They were aware that '[o]utside in the enemy's lands, the German soldier defended the homeland whilst the mothers starved themselves for the Fatherland and worried over the youngsters'.[150] Nazism was portrayed and understood in simple stories. According to Bernhard Rust, Minister of Education, the purpose of school textbooks was 'the ideological education of young German people, so as to develop them into fit members of the national community ... ready to serve and to sacrifice'. Education texts and teaching at best involved censorship, including reduction or abolition of religious education, and at worst blatant racial propaganda. Many textbooks and teaching aids were withdrawn and destroyed in 1933.[151] It took time to rewrite them and the curriculum was not easily replaced. From 1933 to 1937 there was an ad hoc reform of the curriculum. German, biology and history curricula were altered and new subjects introduced in colleges included genetics, racial theory, folklore, military studies and the study of the German borderlands. From 1938 education was reformed officially and textbooks produced. The German Central Institute of Education issued official guidelines for the teaching of history in secondary schools as follows:

> ... It is based on the natural bond of the child with his nation ... It will thereby awaken in the younger generation the sense of responsibility towards ancestors and grandchildren which will enable it to let its life be subsumed in eternal Germany ... the powerless and the insignificant have no history.[152]

The notion that the powerless have no history can be thought of as part of the unwitting societal preparation for the holocaust. The curriculum for boys and girls aged ten to fourteen began with a year studying Germanic Gods and Heroes, followed by a year studying 'Great Germans'. In their third year children were taught only of war over Germany and then progressed to a final year of study of Hitler and his co-fighters. At this stage the curriculum relied on an heroic interpretation of history, with tales of glory, honor and sacrifice, and war as a necessary and exciting part of the German history lesson. From the nature of the curriculum for fourteen- to eighteen-year-olds it is clear that older children were introduced to racial theory and German superiority as complementary explanations of Germany's present circumstance. A year of study on Germanness and German Achievement preceded a second year on the nation and its blood lineage, and for those who remained at school, a third and fourth year looking at contemporary questions about Germany and the world.[153] Wherever possible racial stereotypes of Jews were used in classroom examples and history textbooks showed considerable emphasis on blood lines, ancestry and

---

[150] *Deutschland-Berichte der Sozialdemokratischen Partei Deutschlands* reports cited in Housden, *op. cit.*, pp. 73–4.

[151] Burleigh and Wipperman, *op. cit.*, p. 212.

[152] Noakes and Pridham, p. 438.

[153] Housden, *op. cit.*, pp. 78–9.

patriotic history.[154] Noakes writes that in view of the racist and eugenicist core of Nazi ideology, biology inevitably acquired a new importance in the curriculum. An emphasis on society was intended to prepare them for what would be expected of them in choosing appropriate marriage partners, family size and if necessary, sterilization.[155] All subjects including mathematics could be vehicles of racial prejudice, for example through the racist settings in applied compound interest problems in which Jewish bankers featured as extortionists.[156] The following examples of propaganda were typical rather than exceptional. In both questions the opportunity cost of caring for the weak in society is clearly given:

(a) Question 95: the construction of a lunatic asylum costs 6 million RM. How many houses at 15,000 RM each could have been built for that amount?

Question 97: To keep a mentally ill person costs approx. 4RM per day, a cripple 5,50RM, a criminal 3,50RM. Many civil servants receive only 4RM per day, white-collar employees barely 3.50RM, unskilled workers not even 2RM per head for their families. a) Illustrate these figures with a diagram. According to conservative estimates, there are 300,000 mentally ill, epileptics etc., in care. b) How much do these people cost to keep in total, at a cost of 4RM per head? c) How many marriage loans at 1000RM each. ... could be granted from this money?[157]

Political messages also infiltrated early, informal education, making use of the simple story books, poems and illustrations, the innocent context of education at the mother's knee, and the proximity of a familial presence. Lisa Pine notes that there was strict censorship of the publishing industry and Nazi swastika flags and party slogans were added to many textbooks. Primers in the front of books showed Hitler with children or children saluting the Fuhrer.[158] The illustrations in very young children's books show that Nazi symbols were often used in conjunction with domestic themes in order to make them familiar and accessible to small children. Kindergarten coloring books were heavily propagandized, showing that the socialization of very young children was thought possible and important.[159] Illustrated children's story books and past-times clearly showed the difference between Aryans and Jews and one particular children's board game was called 'Get the Jews out'.[160] In a typical scene from a first reader textbook available in 1935, a small blonde girl speaks to Hitler with the words:

---

[154] Pine, *op. cit.*, p. 25.
[155] Noakes and Pridham, *op. cit.*, pp. 437–8.
[156] Fraser, *op. cit.*, p. 67.
[157] Burleigh and Wipperman, *op. cit.*, p. 154.
[158] Pine, *op. cit.*, p. 96.
[159] *Ibid.*, p. 23.
[160] Koonz, *op. cit.*, p. 220 see plate.

Mein Fuhrer: I know you well and love you like Father and Mother, I shall always obey you like Father and Mother, And when I grow up I shall help you like Father and Mother, And you will be proud of me like Father and Mother.[161]

For the little girl, lessons were soon to include how she too would help the Fuhrer through her potential motherhood. In *Mein Kampf*, Hitler stated that: 'The goal of female education must invariably be the future mother.'[162] In addition mothers were given the role of 'the first educator of children'.[163] Mothers were expected to instill in children an awareness of their responsibilities and an acceptance of their biological destiny.[164] Children of inferior races, for whom such education was not thought relevant, were instead subjected to exclusion and rejection or abuse by women teachers.[165] Illustrated children's books clearly show an idolization of the mother under headings such as 'heroes of everyday life'. Stories suggested that children were the key component of a family.[166]

In boy's literature there is evidence of changes in the views of what constituted manhood and masculinity. Heroism, particularly by men fighting together was popularized in children's stories. Nazi educationalists said that: 'if we wish to raise heroes then we will have to expose our children early enough to the concepts of war and heroism'.[167] Hitler Youth children aged between nine and twelve read vivid epics of WWI. One author in particular, Karl May, is credited with influencing the minds of many young readers and their parents before them, with adventure stories. His books encouraged youth to think of travel, conquest and manly adventure as natural extensions of boyhood. Many autobiographies of Nazi figures show that their future choices were in some cases determined by what they read and were inspired by.[168] The Nazi view of fairy stories was that they were 'a childhood means of education to a heroic view of the world and life'.[169]

The next section focuses on the youth movement and its militarization, and identifies how particular qualities of childhood and masculinity were bestowed with political capital. Welch neatly encapsulates: *Hitler Jugend's* purpose:

> to compulsorily 'involve' the 'national comrades' so completely that individuals were no longer left to themselves or ultimately left to think for themselves. Subordinating the rights of the individual to those of the 'community' entailed not only unconditional sacrifice but also the suspension of critical judgment.[170]

---

[161] Pine, *op. cit.*, p. 24.

[162] Adolf Hitler: *Mein Kampf*, cited in Burleigh and Wipperman, *op. cit.*, p. 349.

[163] Stephenson, *op. cit.*, p. 168.

[164] *Ibid.*, p. 170.

[165] *Ibid.*

[166] Pine, *op. cit.*, p. 25.

[167] Michael Rosen, *The Guardian*, Section 2, 16 October 1996, p. 15.

[168] Jurgen Reulecke, in Roseman, *op. cit.*, p. 98.

[169] Fest, *op. cit.*, p. 232.

[170] Welch, 2004 *op. cit.*, p. 237.

In an address to 80,000 Hitler Youth children at Nuremberg, Hitler exemplified the responsibility and role bestowed on youth 'You, my youth', he screamed hoarsely, 'never forget that one day you will rule the world'.[171] A more appealing prospect than being taught perhaps. Another famous statement by Adolf Hitler, made in 1933, reveals his confidence in a generation of children tasked with the realization of a Nazi future:

> When an opponent says: 'I will not come over to your side', I calmly say: 'Your child belongs to us already ... you will pass on.[172]

Just as he believed that children notionally 'belonged' to him, so he also prepared them for independence from their parents with a strategy to control and shape them physically. Through military training and a heavily prescribed if simple program of development, a generation of children experienced a significantly different upbringing from their parents and also shared in the esteemed qualities of the desired German race. The template of this process was the scouting and youth movements common to this age, and through assimilation of these, youth were harnessed with relative ease: an important military and political achievement in itself.

The importance attached to youth and to absolute control of the youth movement can be placed in historical context. The capture of 'a generation' – itself ultimately achieved with the youngest cohort of the population – had some precedent in Germany. The authors of a text on the 'phenomena of generations, argue that "generation" is, first and foremost, a word aspiring to catch social phenomena in its net rather than a clear-cut social reality for which we happen to have coined a term'.[173] Nevertheless there is evidence that the youth 'generation' in Germany were readily recognized by the Nazis as a distinct and particularly political cohort of the population, who should be tamed rather than left to their own devices. They were feared, and with good reason.

Roseman notes that from the 1770s onwards each pivotal shift in German politics was marked by youth mobilization and revolt.[174] Each generation of children experienced a radically different polity to their predecessors, yet their presence and mobilization remained constant. The 'projection "youth" in other words, remained so strong in Germany partly because the projection "nation" was so fragile'.[175] 'Youth' came to represent a vision of society in its own right. Instead of denoting merely a biological phase between childhood and adulthood (or between 'primary school and barracks'), it encapsulated a lifestyle independent of age. In the words of one historian: 'Youth was thus the new code-word for a renaissance, for the forging

---

[171]   Housden, *op. cit.*, p. 72.

[172]   Hitler in a celebrated speech of 6 November 1933, cited in David Welch, *The Third Reich: Politics and Propaganda* (London: Routledge, 1993), p. 63.

[173]   Roseman, *op. cit.*, p. 5.

[174]   *Ibid.*, p. 1.

[175]   *Ibid.*, p. 13.

of a new, more healthy world.'[176] From the turn of the twentieth century Germany experienced a very high degree of youth organization, through political, religious and sporting groups. By 1910 the state was active in 'youth-saving', improving youth welfare and behavior. The Weimar Republic authorities thought that a loyal and patriotic youth could be harnessed if both youth group identity and needs were recognized and supported in public. Crucially, by designing, disseminating and enforcing a new concept of adolescence through legislation, and by sponsoring youth organizations, the state hoped for an homogenized and indeed non-threatening youth generation.[177] 'The fantasy that youth might redeem the nation gained in attractiveness in response to what many saw as Germany's desperate, divided and beleaguered condition at home and abroad.'[178] Youth could as Roseman notes 'be the starting point for a fundamental recovery and revival in the spiritual, social and national-traditional (*volkisch*) life of the country'.[179]

But this hope was also to falter during the Weimar Republic. In short, rejection and youth-led revolt was more likely than youth-centered renewal. Despite state centralization of physical and intellectual education,[180] young people in the 1920s and 1930s faced unemployment, cuts in welfare provision, and increased pressure on their families. There was a sense of hopelessness and frustration amongst the young. Detlev Peukert writes: 'a self-styled "younger generation" declared war on a "senile" Republic that was unable to cater for its needs ...'.[181] Jurgen Reulecke suggests that this generation of youth also felt failed by their parents, and devoid of their childhood owing to the increased responsibilities and difficult conditions brought on by the war: '[c]heated out of their youth, unsettled by the turmoil of the post-war years ... they were eager to find new purpose, direction and followers'. It is significant that almost all Nazi leaders came from this 'front generation'.[182] This cohort of youth, too young to be sent to the front during WWI, actually generated the slogan the 'war is our parents'.[183] Their reaction is partly explained by the fact that youthful rebellion had often been perceived as working simultaneously against the father figure and the state. Nevertheless it was a powerful statement and could only lend itself to the Fuhrer's interpretation of fatherhood. The National Socialists provided a convenient platform for conflict between generations – attempting to replace the relationship between parent and child with a bond between child and party or regime. Organized youth groups or *Bunde*, deliberately represented themselves as apolitical, despite their uncooperative stance with state and society institutions.

---

[176] Jürgen Reulecke, 'The battle for the young: mobilising young people in Wilhelmine Germany', in Roseman, *op. cit.*, p. 97.

[177] Roseman, *op. cit.*, p. 24.

[178] *Ibid.*, p. 25.

[179] Jurgen Reulecke, *op. cit.*, p. 94.

[180] Detlev Peukert, *The Weimar Republic: The Crisis of Classical Modernity* (London: Allen Lane, 1991), p. 90.

[181] *Ibid.*, p. 94.

[182] Jurgen Reulecke, *o .cit.*, p. 104.

[183] *Ibid.*, p. 103.

Group activities however reflected a militarization of youth and the idealization of a soldierly existence, particularly 'the aestheticization of violent death'.[184] Historian, Joachim Fest argues that the Weimar state authorities, 'while concurring on what youth should *not* be and should not do, had never proclaimed clear educational goals nor a unitary image to which people were to conform; beyond that of promoting young people's physical, emotional and social 'fitness'. In contrast the Nazi state was to lay down explicitly the roles into which youth was to be molded: the German soldier and the German mother.[185] It was anticipated that Nazi Youth would rejuvenate the state, replenishing soldiers, whilst refreshing the ideology, and strengthening the young body politic. Existing youth groups were thus ideal targets for Nazi aims; not only did they naively judge their own behavior to be apolitical, they also willingly undertook military style activities and expressions of bravado as part of their group activities. Despite the militarized nature of learning, play and sport, youth remained largely content with what they considered to be easy forms education. Fest writes that youth 'naively interpreted as an appeal to a universal idealism what in fact served concrete aims of power politics'.[186] The enthusiasm generated by excited children was itself an advantageous resource for the regime to generate. A contemporary Sopade report of June 1934 commented that 'the constant stress on achievement and competition within the youth movement, (behind which lay the glorification of the heroic fighter) served to harness and channel young people's enthusiasm and project participation as a dynamic involvement'.[187] Children's zeal for playing and learning about war was not diminished by the dangers that war presented. Preparation for killing and the will to die for Germany formed a large part of Hitler Youth training. Nearly a million children participated in shooting competitions in 1938, and the youngest youth cohort the *pimpf* experienced weapons conditioning.[188] *Pimpf* were the cohort below *Jungvolk*, the ten- to fourteen-year-old group of the Hitler Youth. One official description of a child was given in relation to membership of Hitler Youth: '"child" describes the non-uniformed creature who has never participated in a group meeting or a route march'.[189] Such an identity marked the *pimpfe* as un-childlike. The uniform was a necessary part of this status.

Hitler Youth was intended to be a downward extension of the party regime. It was founded in 1922 as the Youth League of the NSDAP. The fastest developing group of this kind, its aim was total control over Germany's youth. The Law on Hitler Youth designated Hitler Youth as an educational institution equal in value to the home environment and schooling. In fact Hitler Youth gave itself the task of becoming the most important educational force in Nationalist Socialist Germany. In 1936 the law

---

[184]   Fest, *op. cit.*, p. 340.
[185]   Elizabeth Harvey, *Youth and the Welfare State in Weimar Germany* (Oxford: Clarendon Press, 1993), p. 297.
[186]   Fest, *op. cit.*, p. 349
[187]   Welch, *op. cit.*, p. 64.
[188]   Grunberger, *op. cit.*, p. 359.
[189]   *Ibid.*, p. 353.

deemed that 'the future of the German nation depends upon its youth and German youth must therefore be prepared for its future duties'.[190] In lectures to members there was no attempt to conceal the purpose of reproducing Nazi values:

> If, as the first task of the State in the service and for the welfare of its nationality we recognize the preservation, care and development of the best racial elements, it is natural that this care must not only extend to the birth of every little national and racial comrade, but that it must educate the young sapling to become a valuable link in the chain of future reproduction.[191]

The leaders of the youngest Hitler Youth branches were instructed to tell the children aged ten to fourteen, the following:

> With your vow and commitment you now become a bearer of German spirit and German honour. Every one, every single one now becomes the foundation for an eternal Reich of all Germans.
>
> … You, ten-year-old cub, and you lass, are not too young nor too small to practice obedience and discipline, to integrate yourself into the community and show yourself to be a comrade.[192]

Hitler Youth 'adopted' other youth organizations, often by coercive means and by April 1933 most youth organizations had been incorporated into it. Much of the pressure to join Hitler Youth was applied during school hours by school teachers although there was some resistance from the Catholic sector until 1934.[193] By 1934 it had 3.5 million members, and by 1936 more than six million, 95 per cent of ten-year-olds. Typically ten-year-olds attended its primer groups, the *Jungvolk* or *Jungmädel* before progressing to Hitler Youth or the League of German Maidens at age fourteen. At the age of fourteen those in the Hitler Youth for girls could assume a higher level of responsibility and attempt to influence other mothers and daughters. Dagmar Reese remarks that these girls were in a complex position of 'entanglement and responsibility'; not yet mature, yet able to perpetrate actions on behalf of the state's racist agenda.[194] By early 1939 Hitler Youth had a little over 7.25 million male and female members, aged between ten and eighteen. From December 1936 all German young people were required to be educated in the Hitler Youth, physically, intellectually and morally, and there was a noted increase in attendance at 'toughening up' camps.[195] Welch cites the example of the historian Stephen Roberts, writing in 1937 on the youth he had observed:

---

[190] Noakes and Pridham, *op. cit.*, p. 419.
[191] Burleigh and Wipperman, *op. cit.*, p. 202.
[192] Noakes and Pridham, *op. cit.*, p. 421.
[193] *Ibid.*, p. 417.
[194] von Saldern, *op. cit.*, p. 156.
[195] Freeman, *op. cit.*, p. 90.

To be outside Hitler's organization was the worst form of punishment. The resultant worship was too distressing. Their attitude of mind is absolutely uncritical. They do not see in Hitler a statesman with good and bad points; to them he is more than a demigod. ... It is this utter lack of any objective or critical attitude on the part of youth, even with the university students, that made me fear most for the future of Germany. They are nothing but vessels for State propaganda.[196]

Nazism was, according to Bessel, able to exploit 'emotions which already dominated the political arena and were a symptom of the transnational character of the period'.[197] As observed at the time, 'social despair, nationalistic romanticism and inter-generational hostility formed a classic compound'.[198] Nazi propaganda suggested a 'pioneer role' to youth: of spirited activities free from conservative or bourgeois links. Fest also suggests that the Nazis, as a party without a past, successfully appealed to youth who were also a group without a past.[199] In another significant way, children had no historical past to draw upon. Nazi recruitment drives in the 1930s were thus well attended by school children with no direct experience of war other than as a fantasy.[200] This may also explain why so much educational propaganda emphasized a generic, heroic German 'past': easily consumed yet unlikely to contradict or challenge youth's own agenda. Analysis featured in a contemporary *Sopade* report reflects the power inherent in their generation: 'it is the young men who bring home enthusiasm for the Nazis. Old men no longer make any impression ... the secret of National Socialism is the secret of its Youth'.[201] In the young generation, the regime found the population group that was the most malleable to its own purpose and one that returned the highest yield of self-sacrificing allegiance for the blandishment invested.[202]

The public face of Hitler Youth was one which emphasized community and partnership in the service of the entire German people. Nazi propaganda techniques channeled this community awareness towards a specific destiny: the birth of a new German Empire. Training sessions became more militaristic in character and a seed-bed for militarist aggression. One of the appeals of Hitler Youth was that it provided many opportunities for self-assertion.[203] Even children who did not enjoy its intense military drills and punishments remained compliant because of a desire to impress. Some were in the grip of military ambition and as one former member commented 'wanted to impress our sub-leaders with exemplary discipline, with our powers of

---

[196] Welch (2004), *op. cit.*, p. 231.
[197] Richard Bessel, 'The front generation and the politics of Weimar Germany', in Roseman, *op. cit.*, p. 220.
[198] *Ibid.*, p. 221.
[199] *Ibid.*
[200] Richard Bessel, *op. cit.*, p. 134.
[201] Welch (2004), *op. cit.*, p. 64.
[202] Grunberger *op. cit.*, p. 340.
[203] Freeman, *op. cit.*, p. 92.

endurance, with our military bearing'.[204] As Burleigh and Wipperman, note, *obiter dicta* such as "'[d]eath is only a departure for the sake of higher life', ill prepared teenage boys for their encounters with adult Allied soldiers in the rubble and ruins of Germany's cities'.[205] Perhaps not surprisingly children in such cities were quickly relocated to Hitler Youth camps.

Young people also followed the instructions given through Hitler Youth and concomitantly made demands of their parents that they also became good Nazis, by giving up Marxism, reactionism, and contact with the Jews for example.[206] The presence of uniformed Hitler Youth members in the classroom also 'compromised the authority of the teachers'.[207] Parents were controlled by having to visibly comply with the Nazis' detailed specifications, in effect made vulnerable by their children's everyday requirements. As one parent commented: '[o]ne cannot forbid the child to do what all children are doing, cannot refuse him the uniform that others have. One cannot ban it, that would be dangerous'.[208] By categorizing girls as part of 'youth', and by legally enforcing this categorization through to the remotest corners of the Reich, the Nazis also accelerated the process of liberating young women from the traditional bonds of the family.[209] One Nazi aim was to mobilize young women and exploit their productive and reproductive capacities by replacing patriarchal, religious, and social restrictions that had traditionally defined their womanhood and motherhood.[210] After 1936 membership of the *Bund Deutscher Mädchen* was compulsory and sport could occupy up to two thirds of the girls' time. It has been noted that: '[t]he BDM did not train girls in femininity, motherhood, or the polar roles of the old gender model, it was based on physical training, discipline, rationality and efficiency'.[211] A typical ideal was that girls should become 'politically conscious'. Girls were told of their duty of self care for the future of the nation. The primary goal of the organization then was to prepare girls for motherhood. [212]

The Nazis acceptance of young people as political actors was a narrow one based on their compliance and obedience in natural duties offered up for the state.[213] All regulated behavior in this totalitarian regime was thought of as political duty, and thus any attempt to avoid regulation was treated as a serious political threat. The economic and labor costs of the war created greater demand for youth employment

[204] Noakes and Pridham, *op. cit.*, p. 429.
[205] Burleigh and Wipperman, *op. cit.*, p. 218.
[206] Noakes and Pridham, *op. cit.*, p. 427.
[207] Burleigh and Wipperman, *op. cit.*, p. 215.
[208] Noakes and Pridham, *op. cit.*, p. 427.
[209] Dagmar Reese, 'The BDM generation: A female generation in transition from dictatorship to democracy', cited in Roseman, *op. cit.*, p. 236.
[210] Reese, *Ibid.*, p. 229.
[211] *Ibid.*, p. 237.
[212] See Lisa Pine, 'Creating Conformity: The Training of Girls in the *Bund Deutscher Mädel*', *European History Quarterly*, Vol. 33, No. 3, 2003, pp. 367–85.
[213] Burleigh and Wipperman, *op. cit.*, p. 236.

and also a greater need for discipline and control of this potentially disruptive age group.

One such working class youth resistance group, the *Edelweiss pirates*, received considerable notoriety. Motivated by intensive if not repressive conditions and increasing exposure to regulation, they successfully sought to control areas of cities as bandit units.[214] Such a backlash within Hitler Youth was in part a reaction to the intensity of their management and the maturity required of them. Children, it seems felt more acutely the attempts to manage their freedom. A former BDM leader for example recalled how the energy and high spirits in Hitler Youth was controlled to some degree by competition for all activities, from storytelling to sport. She writes that 'the idea of competition (behind which lay the glorification of the fighter and the heroic), often enough banished the element of meditation even from musical activities, and the playful development of the creative imagination, free of any purpose, was sadly stunted'.[215] The essence of childhood play was necessarily destroyed in this process of control. And perhaps, unrestrained by workplace and convention, more than any other cohort, children were exposed to repeated means of competition and performance:

> the nurturing aspect of adolescence was replaced by a wild activism and an increasing emphasis on combat and competition. Whereas older policy makers had hoped to achieve the goal of a healthy nation by a controlled mixture of sport and rest, the new movement demanded performance, struggle, victors and losers from every minute of the young person's day.[216]

Not surprisingly, all forms of uncontrolled youthfulness could be indicative of threatened order in society. Thus for sixteen-year-olds, dancing in an American jazz style placed them one step nearer to compulsorily sterilization and internment in a juvenile detention camp. As Burleigh and Wipperman note, the spread of rebellious cliques such as the 'swing' movement throughout Germany, illustrated that the Nazis had not been able to encompass and indoctrinate all young people. For the most part however, the Nazis were able to use youth as fully as they had used children although youth necessitated more surveillance and control. Youth's allegiance is most illustrated by the thousands of youths who volunteered for the frontline, knowing that death was certain. Roseman offers a reason for the volunteering of youth in the Nazi project. He writes:

> The fact that the Nazi movement was largely composed of the young, should not in itself surprise us; it does not prove that the movement's emergence was caused by a set of experiences peculiar to the young. It merely confirms that given a set of factors propitious to the rize of violent paramilitary politics, it was most likely to be the young who responded.[217]

---

[214] Housden, *op. cit.*, pp. 83–5.
[215] Noakes and Pridham, *op. cit.*, p. 423.
[216] Roseman *op. cit.*, pp. 30–31.
[217] *Ibid.*, p. 28.

Roseman writes that the new regime fundamentally altered the relationship between youth, the state and society. The young were in effect de-proletarianized especially through vocational training. It was accepted that youth did not have to be shielded from adult politics and could be actively politicized: the promulgation of Nazi racist and nationalist values was pursued at every level of youth activity.[218] The Law on the Hitler Youth proclaimed that: '[t]he future of the German nation depends upon its youth and therefore German youth must be prepared for its future duties'.[219] Roseman argues that this responsibility changed and reduced a whole generation's experience of late childhood and adolescence. The Nazis achieved generational mobilization without generational conflict, and youth were given the image of the youthful vanguard of the state.[220] The experience of young Germans after war also confirms the extent to which children were intrumentalized during the regime.

Youth no doubt played important roles on the home front. As the war intensified so too did the militarization of youth including the formation of a special Youth Battalion in 1943. After 1945 a whole generation of young people fell silent, no longer able to have faith in themselves, *the Volk*, or comprehend what they had helped to achieve. In addition their notion of a private existence was not stable or intact. Parents and the family were no longer either a refuge for youth or a source of opposition; they too were strained and silent, divided and changed.[221] Youth, described by one author as having experienced a form of pseudo-heroic idealism and passionate nationalism,[222] were unable to recover from their experiences in the war with the ease with which they had played a part. Their confusion is illustrated in the complaint made by members of Hitler Youth in 1944 who were 'good enough to become soldiers at fifteen or sixteen and get ourselves killed, but we're not allowed into cinemas to see "adult" films until we are eighteen'.[223] Germany had been on a 'child offensive', a situation which perhaps forms an important explanation of how the regime was sustained. Such young people were in between two worlds, of childhood and adulthood, and in each valuable roles were found.

Conclusion

What is now known as everyday history or *Alltagsgeschichte* history shows how high politics thrived and succeeded through the manipulation of the bland, innocuous, available, 'everyday' people and their domestic activities. Nazi history is a social history of the 'patterns of everyday life and subjective perceptions of "ordinary"

---

[218] *Ibid.*, p. 30.

[219] Burleigh and Wipperman, *op. cit.*, p. 229.

[220] Roseman, *op. cit.*, p. 31.

[221] *Ibid.*, see Introduction.

[222] Peter D. Stachura, *Nazi Youth in the Weimar Republic* (Oxford: Clio Books; 1975), p. 46.

[223] Grunberger, *op. cit.*, p. 348.

Germans far removed from the Reich Chancellery or the other halls of power'.[224] More recently, historical research has looked specifically at the social regulations in German life that predated the Nazi regime and continued after it. As Ian Kershaw comments, 'to an extent this challenges – and in some ways displaces – the traditional emphasis on the ideological, political, and criminal terroristic aspects of Nazism'.[225] The new eugenic paradigm as shown by the Detlev Peukert and also Claudia Koonz submerges anti-semitism under the desire for national eugenic renewal.[226] Peukert suggests that prior to the Nazi regime German civil society already possessed a hierarchical view of German life, evident in a justification for denying reproductive rights that it had supported since the nineteenth century.[227] Such interpretations of Nazi Germany focus on what might be called biological politics or the eugenics project and are uncomfortably placed with other interpretations of the era which primarily consider capitalism, fascism and anti-semitism.[228] Gisela Bock makes the point that the majority of Jews killed were women and children and that race policy was not gender neutral.[229] In any case it is evident that children were an important resource and form of instrumentality in life and in death.

What children thought, felt and did during the Third Reich is complex. Like many women, children could be victims and perpetrators at the same time.[230] It is not their capability in these roles *per se* that is of interest, it is the reasons they were given roles, represented aims and symbolized goals in the Nazi project. Children were politicized bodies in everyday Nazi life, partly due to the intensity of regulation in a racist totalitarian regime. But the concepts of childhood that allowed the ready manipulation of their political bodies, and the interdependence of the child's world with the political sphere, were not phenomena specific to this regime. This will be illustrated in the next chapter which looks at children as political bodies in Northern Ireland.

---

[224] Thomas Childers and Jane Caplan (eds), 'Introduction', in *Re-evaluating the Third Reich* (London: Holmes and Meier, 1993), p. 4.

[225] *Ibid.*, p. 5.

[226] *Ibid.*, p. 3.

[227] *Ibid.*, p. xiv.

[228] Childers and Caplan (eds), *op. cit.*, pp.xiii–xiv.

[229] Bock, *op. cit.*, p. 113.

[230] *Ibid.*, p.141.

Chapter 4

Children in Northern Ireland

Chapter 4 considers issues raised by the circumstances of children in Northern Ireland. It focuses on children's implicit and explicit participation in 'the troubles', through experiences of nationalization and militarization, in education, families and extra-curricula activities. It is often alleged that a political socialization of children is inevitable in a society tied strongly to historical events and historical narratives. Those which may significantly inform children (particularly through familial channels) are outlined here. Military roles children have adopted during the troubles are also considered. Finally the chapter looks at how constructs of children and their associated familial sphere can be intrumentalized for paramilitary practices. The chapter concludes with an analysis of initiatives based on the premise that children may be able to contribute to peace, itself an illustration that children are seen to be political bodies. Recognition of children as victims in the conflict has been hard earned despite, or perhaps because of, their ubiquitous political agency. The task of establishing the impact of the troubles is thus ongoing.

Politics

There are approximately 500,000 people under the age of nineteen in Northern Ireland,[1] a country which has experienced the longest period of concentrated civil disturbance in the Western world in modern times.[2] Children's politicization is central to the implicit and explicit maintenance of a sectarian divide and its violently upheld physical and political boundaries. Children's hearts and minds have been as valuable as adults in the struggles for identity, territory, justice and truth which characterize the troubles and the still 'troubled' peace process.

Two particular facets of the conflict have allowed for the propensity of children to acquire a political role or function. Firstly, the sectarian division of communities also divides and politicizes children's social institutions including schools, youth organizations and families. Secondly, Northern Ireland is characterized by a prominent nationalistic identification with, and attachment to, the past, in forms that are particularly conducive to children's assimilation and participation. Northern Irish children know 'their' history even if they claim not to know about politics. Ironically, the word 'politics' is of limited value in seeking views from participants,

---

[1]   Ed Cairns, *Caught in Crossfire: Children and the Northern Ireland Conflict* (Belfast: Appletree Press, 1987), p. 11.

[2]   *Ibid.*

...d with rhetoric and quagmire, though 'conflict', 'violence' and the ...nderstood and articulated politically.

...les' is a term originally coined by residents in Belfast. The term refers ...y years of propaganda, bullying, intimidation, gang-fighting, rioting, ...es and guerrilla warfare between Protestant and Catholic civilians, paramil...ry groups, Northern Irish security forces and the British army. In this period 3,600 deaths, over 40,000 injuries and the forced movement of large sectors of the population have taken place.[3] Though it usually refers to the escalation of paramilitary violence experienced since 1969, it may also describe the violent clashes in the 1920s, 1930s and 1950s. Paramilitary terrorist activity, it should be noted, extends to the British mainland and to Europe. In addition, both communities regularly remember and celebrate historic battles in pseudo-military parades unique to the area.

A comprehensive study of the 'cost of the troubles' shows the most frequent cause of death for children under the age of eighteen and those under the age of twenty-five to be shooting, followed by explosions. Figures compiled for all those under twenty-five, show that shooting and explosions have killed 1,186 people. But Smyth notes, 'the use of armoured vehicles, where the driver's vision of small objects is restricted, and where vehicles come under attack by stones and other missiles, requiring them to move fast in restricted spaces also constitutes a hazard to children in heavily militarised areas'. Strikingly there are no reliable figures for the numbers of children and young people who have been killed and injured in these ways.[4] Though the experiences of children in Northern Ireland vary widely, this chapter will illustrate some of the experiences of children closest to paramilitary activity and violence particularly in Belfast and Derry/Londonderry. However, the nature of the conflict is such that though not all of the population experiences violence directly, the everyday lives of most citizens contributes to the maintenance of hostilities and the culture of fear. Not least, it is often said that all who live in Northern Ireland have known friends or relatives who have been killed. The 'internalizing' of the enemy into civilian life through the covertness of terrorism also contributes to community-wide identification of blame and desire for retaliation. The 'patchwork' of residential areas associated with identities and paramilitarism necessarily makes for a geography of conflict: children's homes and families are part of the battleground. The parameters of conflict, and the parameters of analyzing the conflict are thus drawn wide.

---

[3]   Marie Smyth, *Half the Battle: Understanding the Impact of the Troubles on Children and Young People* (INCORE, University of Ulster: Derry Londonderry, 1998), see also Marie Therese Fay, Mike Morrissey and Marie Smyth, *Northern Ireland's Troubles: The Human Costs* (London: Pluto Press, 1999), p.199. See especially statistical material compiled by Martin Melaugh for the Conflict Archive on the Internet (CAIN) cain.ulst.ac.uk.

[4]   Marie Smyth (1998), *op. cit.*

The Past and Other Stories

The history of the troubles in Northern Ireland have given rise to an enormous amount of literature but few agreements over how to describe or categorize the contributory factors. John Darby describes the conflict as containing a tangle of six problems or themes: constitutional, social and economic inequality, cultural identity, security, religious difference and day-to-day relationships.[5] However, the themes are, in many hearts and minds, rooted in acts of discrimination which began many centuries ago. Particular episodes of Northern Irish political history are heavily and publicly drawn attention to in the present. For this reason, what is commonly thought of as 'politics' in conventional terms has until recently been to most Northern Irish people of secondary importance to 'history' in their lives. Accounts of the past are retained and made unusually resonant by political actors on both sides, not least for their implantation in the imagination of children. John Whyte has shown that children have shown little knowledge of politics and constitutional information in surveys, and they, like their parents, equate action such as voting as a display of loyalty not a means of change.[6] What we might identify as their political understanding is to them an everyday acknowledgement of historically continuous truths.

Particular dates of carnage, battles and glory, rebellion and protest, mark turning points in each 'side's' history, and these are easily imagined and described in a child's language. Historical scenes, rarely thought about amongst school children in the rest of the British Isles, are retained in popular reading and thinking material for each generation of children up to the present day. Begona Aretxaga observes that many narratives of Irish history have a particular emotive quality and are thus empowering politically. Historical narratives are thus political, in content and in delivery:

> In Northern Ireland, history is understood primarily in existential terms – as a predicament that gives meaning to people's lives, legitimising their politics and charging their actions with emotive power. This history is condensed in key events that, taken from Irish historical chronology have become part of the cultural consciousness of people.[7]

Characters and events employed in historical narratives, and the sensitivity attached to the recalling of such historical episodes also create Northern Irish conceptions of politics. The arrival of 'English' subjects onto 'Irish' soil particularly from the fifteenth century onwards marked the beginning of a hierarchy of British/English subjects over the Irish in terms of bestowed identity and socio-economic opportunity. The shaping of two communities, with different socio-economic and political status

[5]   John Darby, 'Conflict in Northern Ireland: A background essay', in Seamus Dunn (ed.), *Facets of the Conflict in Northern Ireland* (Houndmills: Macmillan Press, 1995), p. 21.

[6]   Ed Cairns and Tara Cairns, 'Children and Conflict: a Psychological Perspective', in Dunn (ed.) (1995), *op. cit.*, p. 100, and pp. 104–5.

[7]   Begona Aretxaga, 'Striking with Hunger: Cultural Meanings of Political Violence in Northern Ireland', in Kay B. Warren (ed.), *The Violence Within: Cultural and Political Opposition in Divided Nations* (Boulder: Westview Press, 1993), p. 224.

was crystallized by the Plantation of Ulster in 1609 by King James I, and the further confiscation of Catholic land by Oliver Cromwell. The 1690 Battle of the Boyne, in which the Irish Protestants sided with Protestant William of Orange, to defeat Catholic King James II and leave Ireland and Northern Ireland under Protestant rule, is celebrated annually in thousands of parades and other symbolic gestures of defiance in which Protestant children participate. The socio-economic consequences of dispossession were profound. Land inheritance was restricted to Protestants or forcibly fragmented amongst Catholic sons. Catholics were discriminated against and also subdued in Ireland through penal laws which prevented their right to a Catholic education or education abroad. Such practices were concretized in 1800 in the Act of Union, which united Britain and Ireland constitutionally. A school system was put in place that attempted to sustain this relationship, and created literate English-speaking children, newly divorced from 'backward' Irish language and culture. Catholic hardship was then further exacerbated by food shortages and poverty. During this period a quarter of the population emigrated and perhaps as many died. Despite such hardship, a group of intellectuals calling themselves 'Young Ireland', though ineffective in practice, attempted to forge a spirit of republicanism. This movement leant heavily on romantic imaginings of a national struggle. It appealed for a revival of Gaelic schools and traditions and, as its name suggests, it occupied a transient but still celebrated place in the formation of the Irish nation. Stories with significant elements of barbarism and heroism, of attempts to expel Catholics and massacre Protestants are publicly celebrated, committed to legend and playground rhyme, and pictured in many contemporary textbooks and street murals.[8] The Easter Rising of 1916 is an episode made familiar to many Catholic schoolchildren.

Celebrating and defining Irish culture was imperative in this political struggle. In Britain Irish representation was a source of public ridicule, especially in Victorian caricature. As is evident in political commentary and the popular press, humanized caricature or tropes of the Irish and English character diverged. The Irish represented themselves as upright, fair and gentle yeomen and women, of moral strength and resistance but were deemed 'racially inferior' by many British commentators to the point of being portrayed with smaller skulls.[9] In comic weeklies and cartoons the Catholic population were stereotyped as ugly and stupid, unevolved and ape-like. Ireland was thus characterized as incapable of ruling itself and still in need of British protection. Ireland was also personified as Hibernia – feminine, soft, delicate and dependent on British protection. Sisson demonstrates how 'ascribing a feminine sensibility to Irishness is double-edged'. On the one hand it fed into a pre-existing nationalist system of representation which allowed for an apposition between

---

[8]   For an overview of this history see, for example, John Whyte, *Interpreting Northern Ireland* (New York: Oxford University Press, 1990).

[9]   Rosemary Sales, *Women Divided, Gender, Religion and Politics in Northern Ireland* (London: Routledge, 1997), p. 61.

Irishness and femininity; on the other hand it reinscribed many imperial ideologies already in place about the susceptibility of the Irish for self-government.[10]

There are many different representations of the female form, as Sisson notes. The main point is that caricatures of the men debased real men and their politics. As real women entered politics however they were defeminized; caricatures of women instead served only to characterize or give agency to the imagined nation.

Such images and taunting were perhaps to have lasting implications given that the next 'generation' of republicans emerged as The Irish Republican Brotherhood in 1858. In short, the charge of femininity and weakness was answered with intense military resolve by an armed republican movement, which first battled for Irish Home Rule in 1858. Sinn Fein, the political party of the present-day IRA was founded in 1905. Republican, Patrick Pearse (1879–1916) also founded his own bi-lingual school, St Enda in 1908.[11] His pupils learnt the Irish language and read Gaelic literature. But much more than this, his intention was to re-masculinize Ireland. He considered the English educational system 'a murder machine' and in consequence children had been tamed. This new assertion of manly strength is perhaps reflected in the wording of The Declaration of the Irish Republic made in 1916:

> ... Having organised and trained her manhood through her secret revolutionary organisation, the Irish Republican Brotherhood, and through her open military organisations, the Irish Volunteers and the Irish Citizen Army, having patiently perfected her discipline, having resolutely waited for the right moment to reveal itself, she now seizes that moment, and supported by her exiled children in America and by gallant allies in Europe, but relying in the first on her own strength, she strikes in full confidence of victory.

These intentions were also fostered in the Nationalist youth organization, the Fianna Eireann, formed in 1909 by Constance Markievicz, a Sinn Fein MP, and the first woman elected to the British Parliament. It was encouraged by Baden Powell, and though looked 'innocent' enough it soon began to fulfill the military and patriotic intentions of nationalists. Remaining similar to boy scouts in terms of physical and military training, it also taught Irish history and language. Its aim was to revitalize Ireland and members swore allegiance to her independence. In its first handbook Markievicz implored 'the best and noblest of Ireland's children to win Freedom ... at the price ... of suffering and pain'. The best and brightest were thus by membership and definition boys. Markievcz revitalized the republican sister movement, the Daughters of Ireland which had also the strong backing of Erskine Childers T.D. When De Valera and these women proved unpopular their critics belittled them as the 'women and childer's party'.[12] Such mockery might reveal how female membership was thought of incomparable in political or nationalist worth, or might be a jealous aside at Childers' charms.

---

[10] Elaine Sisson, *Pearse's Patriots: St Enda's and the Cult of Boyhood* (Cork University Press, 2004).

[11] Sisson *op. cit.*, p. 12.

[12] Roger Sawyer, *We Are But Women: Women in Ireland's History* (London: Routl

Resistant to Home Rule, a number of unionist paramilitaries formed the UVF (Ulster Volunteer Force) in 1912. In 1919 the IRA began the Irish War of Independence, also known as the Anglo–Irish War, waged by men and women in Dublin and the southern counties. The British brought in 'black and tans', former soldiers selected on the grounds of their propensity for violence. In 1920 The Government of Ireland Act partitioned Northern Ireland and the Irish Free State. The 1921 Anglo–Irish Treaty established a Northern Ireland Parliament in Stormont and an autonomous Parliament in Dublin.

During the 1930s, however, membership of sectarian junior associations increased dramatically, though often in practice by 'adult' members. Early loyalist youth groups, such as the Protestant Tartan Gangs, later used as a recruitment base by the Ulster Defense Association and Ulster Volunteer Force, were given junior status in order to preserve their legality. In law at least, peaceful status was associated with the description 'junior'.[13] In practice, junior status offered a cloak to militarism. Children played a military part in republican and unionist confrontations throughout this period.

The Irish Free State comprised 26 of the 32 counties of Ireland and in 1948 declared itself the Republic of Ireland. Here was then a time of peace, if not contentment, until the Catholic civil rights movement sought to address the issue of discrimination, particularly in housing allocation, by demanding equality. The Catholic civil rights marches in 1968 led to confrontation, rioting and street violence in Derry/Londonderry and Belfast and British Army was sent in to quell the violence. Michael Taussig talks of images and histories generating our political consciousness and actions.[14] When violence increased in the early 1970s it has been argued that people 'turned instinctively to the only source of wisdom applicable to such circumstances – the inherited folk-memory of what had been done in the past, both good and bad'.[15] Bobby Sands, an imprisoned republican was barely eighteen yet thought it an obvious political strategy to educate fellow prisoners in the Gaelic language and sustain their political will with history lessons about domination. The latter were shouted to prisoners in other cells from his prison door.[16]

After the 1972 'Bloody Sunday Massacre', direct rule was imposed. There followed an escalation of violence between loyalist and republican paramilitary groups, British troops, Northern Irish security forces and police. Many became key targets of sectarian violence up to and during the recent cease-fire and peace settlement negotiations which began in 1994. Deeply entrenched bitterness and insecurity remains on both sides, and real and imagined discrimination. Both communities have written separate histories and literature, maintained separate

---

[13]   David Fitzpatrick, *The Two Irelands* (Oxford: Oxford University Press, 1998), p. 179.

[14]   Aretxaga, in Warren, *op. cit.*, p. 231.

[15]   A.T.Q. Stewart, *The Narrow Ground: Aspects of Ulster* (London: Faber and Faber, 1977), p. 114.

[16]   Aretxaga, in Warren, *op. cit.*, p. 231.

residential areas, schools and churches and engendered distinct political identities and at times almost racial stereotypes of the 'other'. Vivid constructions of heroes, demonization of the enemy, and polarization of good and bad, 'us' and the 'other', permeated Northern Ireland. Heroic myths, asserting sectarian histories and identities necessary to sustain a community under siege, were transmitted within families and by teachers during the troubles. Informal education was a recognized means with which to bolster nationalism.

Children, in particular are made aware of their otherness through their deliberate exposure to the history of the troubles. However one of the features of children's schooling in such a sectarian community is how little its divisiveness was acknowledged in formal circles.[17] Ninety-seven per cent of children in Northern Ireland spend much of their life in segregated schools despite the fact that they may not be so highly segregated in their own streets or even families. Segregation of education and prejudice in teaching have long been suspected of having key roles in sustaining the conflict.[18] It is typical however that school was not thought about as a 'political' institution. As Brazilian educationalist Paulo Friere has argued there is no such thing as neutral education. Education facilitates integration into the logic of the present, and conformity within, or becomes 'the practice of freedom'.[19] Schooling offers us one lens then with which to see political children.

Nationalization and 'the Other' in Education

The present-day segregation of education, and indeed the battle for children's minds, can be traced back to the 1820s when Catholic clergy were allowed to administer schools for Catholics excluded from state schools. This was a move perceived by Protestant authorities as a means of coexistence rather than a concession since Catholic children had become a source of disorder and needed to be accommodated. Once this power was given to the Church however it was unlikely to be relinquished.

In 1918 seventy-three Sinn Fein MPs were elected to the Dail in Dublin and Eoin MacNeill (1867–1945) became an influential Minister for Education. MacNeill revived the teaching of Irish history and literature and the Catholic school became a potential site of organized political subversion. He promoted Gaelic sport along with Douglas Hyde who began the Gaelic League for Athletics. He also promoted Irish surnames and the introduction of Irish teaching into primary schools. He succeeded in overt nationalist activity of this kind because his practices in education were largely perceived as they began, as 'non-political'.[20] Adults though, seemingly

---

[17]   Cairns (1987), *op. cit.*, pp. 119–20.

[18]   See for example articles in *The Northern Teacher* and *The British Journal of Religious Education*.

[19]   Mark Patrick Hederman, 'Paolo Freire's Pedagogy of the Oppressed', in *The Crane Bag: Latin American Issue*, Vol. 6, No. 2, 1982, p. 58.

[20]   Michael Laffan, *The Resurrection of Ireland: The Sinn Fein Party, 1916–1923* (Cambridge University Press, 1999).

chose to think in Irish but speak in English as the Dail's retention of English in business and in schooling demonstrates.

The creation of the separate entity of Northern Ireland in 1921, however, led to the provision of separate schools for Catholic and Protestant children. Lord Londonderry's 1923 Education Act had intended that Catholic and Protestant children were schooled together without religious instruction, but considerable opposition from the churches resulted in the segregation of schools from the 1930s onwards.[21] Schools maintained moral high ground over their role, but ultimately by default engendered distinct curricula and the promotion of Irish and British values which became signals of dissent and nationalism, and allegiance to the Union respectively. Most Protestant children were not taught the development of republicanism or the history of Irish nationalism and references to Irishness were replaced with illustrations of Britishness.[22]

The school system has remained almost entirely divided. At present Northern Ireland's compulsory education includes all children between the ages of four or five and sixteen and a large body of literature has been produced on the potential societal impact of the school systems, questioning whether division in education contributes further to social conflict. Much of the proposed new curriculum represents the resolution of a 'peace' issue, recognized in all 'subjects' and not privileged solely through religious or national labels. Lifestyle, values and personal development infuse what may be characterized as a cutting edge, curious person's curriculum. However, many educationalists argue that schools are a contributory factor to the conflict, through their institutionalized segregation and the culture of the 'other' that this represents or fosters.[23] Two basic hypotheses have been advanced about the effect of segregated schooling.[24]

The first, termed the cultural hypothesis looks at the cultural disparity of education. Here, it has been noted that there has been relatively little research on the presence of a politicized 'school ethos' or nationalized 'hidden curriculum' in school teaching. John Darby and Seamus Dunn suggest that 'the earlier research had reached the classroom door, but had not entered. The difficulty of examining the teaching of controversial subjects alongside the teacher has proved too great'.[25] This inability to get in the classroom, to monitor what is said, illustrates how effectively education can evade close scrutiny, perhaps a consequence of protracted non-political status but highly political agency. Segregation of schoolchildren is seemingly condoned by

---

[21]   Leslie Caul, *Schools Under Scrutiny: The Case of Northern Ireland* (London: Macmillan, 1993), p. 131.

[22]   *Ibid.*

[23]   Dunn, S., Darby, J. and Mullan, K., *Schools Together?* (Coleraine: Centre for the Study of Conflict, 1984).

[24]   Darby J. and Dunn S., 'Segregated Schools: The Research Evidence', in Osbourne R.D., Cormack, R.J., and Miller, R.L. (eds), *Education and Policy in Northern Ireland* (Belfast: Policy Research Institute, 1987).

[25]   *Ibid.*, p. 88.

the school, which is acting in *loco parentis*. The school is in a powerful position to act as a further conduit for children's political socialization.

It has been argued that children's perception of differences between the communities can be concretized, unwittingly or intentionally by the school's material teaching environment. A school's religious or political identity can be made highly visible through daily rituals and teaching aids. Even the green uniform of Catholic primary school children, may indicate to Protestant teachers a political message.[26] Dominic Murray's survey of the casual literature, books and stimuli found in Protestant and Catholic schools found a sharp difference in the content of material. Texts and images in Protestant schools were mostly either of a Biblical nature or about British history and London. Literature in Catholic schools reflected an interest in Irish history and Rome. Similarly, he observed that during informal conversations, teachers and pupils willingly shared understandings of their sectarian counterparts and five-year-olds demonstrated perceptions of sectarian stereotypes.[27] Difference in the two school systems is particularly evident in the teaching and availability of sport, Irish, and music. The inclusion of Irish language has until recently been equated with Irish nationalism and therefore not available or taught to Protestants.[28] Murray talks of the alternative 'three R's' to which children are subject: religion, ritual and rivalry.[29] Catholic children continue to play Gaelic team sports, but cricket, hockey and rugby are generally avoided as symbolically British.[30]

The school may also foster children's articulation and communication of political norms and values, particularly to each other. In 1968 researchers found that Catholic school children's favorite subject in school drama classes was the Easter Rising of 1916. In Catholic school playgrounds, the British soldier has featured prominently. Four years prior to their arrival the British soldier had become a popular antihero or demon figure particularly amongst children who held IRA men in high regard.[31]

A notable contributory cultural factor to some children's politicization has been the type of history teaching that they have received. Prominent terrorists have cited the school, and nationalistic tones of history books as prompting their first interest in joining the paramilitary or doing something for the cause.[32] The absence of a common history syllabus in the education system until 1990 may have allowed the development of a hidden political agenda. During the 1960s history textbooks in Protestant schools for example notably emphasized the Protestants' arrival amongst a hostile and backward people, the constant need for vigilance, and the siege of

[26] Dominic Murray, 'Identity: a covert pedagogy in Northern Irish schools', *Irish Educational Studies*, Vol. 5, No. 2, 1985, pp. 190–93.

[27] Dominic Murray, 'Rituals and symbols as contributors to the culture of Northern Ireland primary schools', *Irish Educational Studies*, Vol. 3, No. 2, 1983.

[28] Caul, *op. cit.*, p. 130.

[29] Dominic Murray (1985), *op. cit.*, pp. 182–97.

[30] Cairns (1987), *op. cit.*, p. 124.

[31] Morris Fraser, *Children in Conflict* (Harmondsworth: Penguin, 1973), p. 143.

[32] Ed Cairns, *Children and Political Violence* (London: Blackwell, 1996), p. 127.

Derry.[33] The following extract, taken from a textbook used in the 1960s in a Catholic school, is typical in its identification of Ireland in the context of her struggle:

> Ireland is only a small country but her strength is based on things spiritual, and because of her long fight for freedom and justice and her loyalty to the Christian traditions, she holds an honoured place amongst the nations.[34]

However, this example and others are too firmly of the past. Since the 1970s discontent over prejudice in teaching materials has been significantly lessened and little reported. Also, as the authors of contemporary studies on the role of history learning and teaching in such a divided society report, 'home-history' is perhaps still as significant as school curricula:

> ... young people's historical perspective in Northern Ireland is considerably influenced by what they see and hear in their families and communities and that this history is often partisan and politically motivated. It also demonstrates that they recognize that school history has a different, more objective, function, providing them with a multi-perspective view of past events. What is less clear is how these informal and formal aspects of their learning play out in practice. Our previous work indicates that some students as their school careers progress become adapt at selecting aspects of their school learning in Irish history to support their growing political assimilation to the values of their communities. However, this study suggests that students are conscious of the uses and abuses to which history is put and, whatever their backgrounds, are keen to study history formally in a way that sheds light on the contemporary situation. Perhaps, what is required are initiatives to enable them to confront the interface between past and present and to clarify for them why they, too, are likely to see the past through the lens of their own background.[35]

The second hypothesis regarding the effect of segregated schools, is termed the social hypothesis, and suggests that the fact of separation is what matters. This view holds that regardless of similarities in curriculum, segregated schooling initiates children into the conflict by emphasizing and validating group differences and hostilities, encouraging mutual ignorance and, perhaps more importantly, mutual suspicion.[36] The school is essentially a closed environment where potent sentiments expressed between children can ramify their notions of religious difference and physical bullying and peer pressure can reinforce concepts of identity. Children aged eleven for example have been pressured at school by others to join the Junior Orange League, join in anti-Catholic games and not to speak to Catholics. They may be discouraged

---

[33] Magee, J, 'The Teaching of Irish History in Irish Schools', *The Northern Teacher*, Vol. 10, No. 1, 1970.

[34] Cairns (1987), *op. cit.*, p. 128.

[35] Barton, K.C., and McCully, A.W., 'Learning History and Inheriting the Past: The Interaction of School and Community Perspectives in Northern Ireland', (2005), *International Journal of Historical Learning, Teaching and Research*, Vol. 5, No. 1.

[36] William G. Cunningham, *Conflict Theory and Conflict in Northern Ireland*, M.Litt Thesis, University of Auckland, 1998, http://cain.ulst.ac.uk/conflict/cunningham.html.

with taunts such as 'Fenian lover'.[37] The term itself has embarrassing connotations when applied to potential childhood friendships which are often guardedly defended as innocent at this age. Children beyond ten years can 'tell' religious identity through the individual's home, school, name, looks and accent. They are aware of themselves and 'other' before they can articulate political and historical contexts.[38] A number of writers concerned with reconciliation have also looked at the process described as Social Identity Theory[39] to explain how the sectarian divide is maintained in education. The school is the largest 'group' that children identify with, and the concretizing of a group and peer identity is a core stage in their political socialization. Research and efforts into school contact schemes and integrated education suggest that the school's contribution to society is not disputed. However, an admission that education for peace is possible is also in effect a stark admission that education has been part of the problem,[40] and that concomitantly both education and children are political issues.

In an attempt to address the problems associated with segregated schooling, the Department of Education for Northern Ireland, reviewed texts and examination syllabuses and in particular approaches in history teaching. Changes were made to the education system in The Education Reform Order of 1989 and have produced much analysis.[41] Education for Mutual Understanding (EMU) and Cultural Heritage became compulsory 'baskets' of subjects to be taught in the curriculum. Education for Mutual Understanding includes personal development, subject development and participation in contact schemes. Many of the changes were due to longstanding education research programs and curricular initiatives such as the 'Schools Curriculum Project', begun in Queen's University of Belfast in 1973, and the 'Schools Cultural Studies Project', developed in the New University of Ulster in 1974. Inter-school links and contact programs for primary and post-primary schools are also arranged through the Cross Community Contact Scheme. Today initiatives regarding joint schooling often cause the surprised reaction from pupils that 'they' are just like 'us'. Children have been shown to assume that 'they' are different, even in some visible way.

In 1969, Catholic parents who sent their children to a state school were threatened with refusal of communion by the bishop.[42] Integrated education was perceived as an attack on the Catholic religion. The All Children Together movement set up by parents, aimed to promote desegregated schools and contributed to the opening of Lagan College as a mixed school in 1981.[43] However, even though there is a

---

[37]   Fraser, *op. cit.*, p. 143.

[38]   Cairns (1987), *op. cit.*, p. 113.

[39]   H. Tajfel, *Human Groups and Social Categories* (Cambridge: Cambridge University Press, 1981).

[40]   Seamus Dunn, 'The role of education in the Northern Ireland conflict', *Oxford Review of Education,,* Vol. 12, No. 3, 1986, pp. 234–6.

[41]   See Caul, *op. cit.*

[42]   Fraser, *op. cit.*, p. 40.

[43]   Cairns (1987), *op. cit.*, p. 140.

significant proportion of children that have mixed parents in Northern Ireland
– almost 10 per cent of marriages were mixed between 1978 and 1982 – there
are only enough places for 3 per cent of children to go to mixed schools.[44] The
lack of progress towards integrated schooling is in part due to the moral content
of the existing curricula being thought adequately ameliorative. Religious authority
figures such as the Bishop of Northern Ireland have claimed that Northern Ireland
Catholic schools provide valuable stability and normality and are not in themselves
divisive.[45] The Catholic Church has since remained opposed to integrated schools,
often providing theologically based deterrents to parents. A recent initiative to unite
two teacher training colleges was opposed by the Church and 'pressure was exerted
on schoolchildren to get parents signatures opposing it'.[46] The sensitivity of Catholic
clergy is well illustrated by their efforts to influence children's opinion.

It has been suggested by some observers that the contact thesis that underpins
integrated educational approaches does not necessarily address why children's
expectations of each other are different in the first place.[47] Although young people
will reconcile their differences face to face, this itself may not be a sufficient basis
for eradicating prejudice or resentment felt across the community and acted out in
group behavior. Tajfel explains that 'intergroup' behavior like this is resistant to
change. It is not only polarized but dictated by group identity, as distinguished from
the identity of individuals.[48] Individual characteristics may be changeable but group
behavior and recognition cannot be altered from within the group. Children may
meet across the divide, and hope may be invested in them as the future generation,
but these children also belong to communities where the difference will remain
evident in daily intergroup behavior particularly through military activities and
family ties. School is however only one source of education. Children may become
socialized to political violence through their proximity to, and participation in, the
paramilitary organizations which operate in their communities. Belfast psychologist
Morris Fraser writing in the 1970s argued persuasively that there are no civilians in
Ulster because children and their parents are themselves the combatants.[49]

---

[44]   Colin Irwin, 'Social Conflict and the failure of education policies in two deeply
divided societies: Northern Ireland and Israel', in Hastings Donnan and Graham McFarlane
(eds), *Social Anthropology and Public Policy in Northern Ireland* (Aldershot, Hants: Avebury,
1997), p. 99.

[45]   Cairns (1996), *op. cit.*, p. 82.

[46]   Sally Belfrage, *The Crack, a Belfast Year* (Grafton, 1998), p. 20.

[47]   Miles Hewstone and Robert Brown, 'Contact is not enough', in *Contact and Conflict
in Intergroup Encounters* (Oxford: Blackwell, 1986), p. 27.

[48]   Tajfel, *op. cit.*

[49]   Fraser, *op. cit.*, p. 8.

Militarization: Youth Wings and Riots

The militarization of children in Northern Ireland can be shown as a cumulative process which begins with their acceptance of violence as a political tool and ends with their mobilization. Anti-army attitudes amongst Catholic children were common before open warfare began, and studies show Catholic schoolchildren exhibited fear and demonization in their play and everyday activities.[50] The Irish Republican Army (IRA) has played no small part in constructing the British soldier as the cult hate figure on which children have focused their play and political values.[51] For many young children, therefore, the antihero they might usually have confronted within the confines of play or the television, could sometimes be found patrolling on the doorstep.[52] Such children also played at riots, before 1971,[53] and their popular songs and games clearly express violent animosity. Researchers who listened to children talking to each other within communities heard the following chants for example:

What shall we do with the Para bastards?
Early in the morning
Kill shoot burn the soldiers (repeat)
Kill shoot burn the bastards
Early in the morning

If you hate the British soldiers clap your hands.[54]

It has also been argued that children educate and police each other within their own private conversations and encounters. The mother of one seven-year-old explained how he was the wrong religion for playing in the park: he 'gets stones thrown at him, and can only play outside our door'.[55] Children may be approached by child-gangs and asked to demonstrate their political allegiance to the Crown by kissing a Union Jack for example. As noted in Chapter 1, such horizontal peer learning, or peer pressure and peer influence is only now getting recognition in child development studies.

Children in groups together can suggest many things, not least an unsettling coalescence of energy and confidence. Writing in 1973, Fraser noted that gangs in Belfast were not only bigger and younger than elsewhere in Northern Ireland, but approved of by some adults.[56] Child gangs contribute to a culture of fear by their very presence especially amongst other children. They are also potentially involved

---

[50] *Ibid.*, p. 140.
[51] *Ibid.*, p. 56.
[52] *Ibid.*, p. 139.
[53] Cairns (1987), *op. cit.*, p. 31.
[54] James Hewitt, *Flashpoints in the Irish Question* (East Sussex: Wayland, 1986), p. 62.
[55] *Ibid.*, p. 55.
[56] Fraser, *op. cit.*, p. 139.

in youth wings of paramilitary groups. It has been argued that children's disruptive energy was focused on 'the troubles' and channeled by youth wings of paramilitary organizations.[57] Analysts have also argued that conformity with parents and the paramilitary causes ironically distracted children from 'normal' youthful rebellion.[58] Intergenerational difference was subsumed under the societal reproduction of sectarian values. To not be involved in 1973 was to be 'the odd one out'. Michael McLoughlin, former chairman of Dungannon council in County Tyrone said of sectarian gang fighting in 1990:

> these young people have learned all their politics, their attitudes to society, growing up in segregated schools, segregated housing estates and segregated youth clubs. They never meet, they're never met. I don't expect them to be any different to what they are. There are entrenched attitudes on both sides, I don't expect that to change overnight.[59]

In the absence of men and particularly fathers in the community and families (through covert activity, fear or death), children can transfer their loyalty to the brotherhood within gangs and youth movements. In these groups some children find strength and identity through common purpose, make sense of their situation and are further able to actively play a role in the troubles.[60] Such gangs present a half-way experience for children. They can publicly posture or covertly behave like adults, particularly in a quasi-military fashion. In a contemporary analysis of children from West Belfast, a psychiatrist commented that through violent participation, often initiated amongst themselves, children learnt that violence achieved results.[61] Injuring a soldier and hijacking a bus gained praise and had heroic implications within a gang, thus enabling boys in particular to benefit socially from political violence.[62] The children were noted as disciplined, even ritualistic in their attacks. Through membership of youth groups such as the Junior Auxiliary of the Catholic Serviceman's Association or Junior UDA, children experienced further 'character building' and adult-like discipline and rules.[63] Their arrest and interrogation may even sometimes be intentional on their part. For arrest, (being equated with non-minor status in the eyes of the law) also serves to concretize their involvement with the paramilitaries and may later serve as 'the seminal experiences that demarcate political maturity' in the eyes of their leaders.[64] For many boys, 'politics' and/or their sense of participation, is also equated with action, sacrifice and loyalty. Children joined the republican

---

[57]   Rona M. Fields, *A Society on the Run: A Psychology of Northern Ireland* (Harmondsworth: Penguin, 1973), pp. 134–5.

[58]   Ed Cairns and Tara Cairns, in Whyte, *op. cit.*, p. 103.

[59]   Sean O' Neill, *Northern Ireland* (East Sussex: Wayland, 1991), p. 20.

[60]   Fraser, *op. cit.*, p. 129.

[61]   Fields, *op. cit.*, p. 101.

[62]   *Ibid.*, p. 103.

[63]   *Ibid.*, pp. 134–5.

[64]   Allen Feldman, *Formations of Violence: The Narrative of the Body and Political Terror in Northern Ireland* (Chicago: University of Chicago Press, 1991), p. 97.

youth movement: Fianna Eireann, for example, long before the onset of violent activity. Eighty per cent of Catholic children have fathers, uncles and brothers in the republican movement, making republicanism a hereditary tradition.[65] Protestant children are also members of paramilitary youth movements though not to the same extent as Catholics. However, their militarization is effectively demonstrated through association with the Orange Order and its Junior Lodge, and particularly its military style parades. The Orange Order founded in the 1790s precedes the organized republican movement considerably.[66] Once secret, it has been a prominent feature of life in many Protestant families. Protestant boys, potentially also members of the youth wing of the UVF, the Young Citizens Volunteers, the Ulster Young Militants or the Apprentice Boys of Derry, join their fathers in 'pseudo-military' displays throughout the parading season.[67] All sectors of the community on both sides of the divide are made particularly aware of its aims and militant nature. The parades have existed since 1690, were legalized in 1872 and since the 1970s have taken on a strongly militaristic nature. Over 3,500 take place each year, though the numbers of members are diminishing.[68] Orangemen and loyalists stage arguably aggressive displays, walking en masse with their children across divided residential areas which often prompts rioting.[69] The Orangemen's marches visually illustrate the restrained force and traditional symbolism of historical conquest. For young boys of four or five a parade can be a celebrated first public association with the Orange Order. Women or younger girls are kept to the sidelines.[70] Participation is usually male and the paraders mimic aggressive postures. The routes of the marches may be perceived as statements of territorial claims. Most celebrated of all is the 12th of July Parade, a commemoration of the victory 300 years ago of the Protestant William of Orange over the Catholic James II. Children at the 1999 12th of July Parade, waved flags and babies wore bibs reading 'Born to walk the Garvaghy Road', referring to the Parade's most contested route.[71] The closing of the Garvaghy Road prior to this particular parade had led to 130 loyalist arson attacks, one of which killed three Catholic children.[72]

Fraser describes the Orange Order as a potent force of education and organized politics.[73] Boys may join aged eight, and mostly participate between the ages of eight

---

[65]   *Ibid.*, p. 97.

[66]   *Ibid.*, p. 287.

[67]   Neil Jarman, *Material Conflict: Parades and Visual Displays in Northern Ireland* (Oxford: Bergman, 1997a), p. 217.

[68]   *Ibid.*, p. 67.

[69]   Bryan Dominic and Neil Jarman, 'Parading tradition, protesting triumphalism: utilising anthropology in public policy', in Hastings Donnan and Graham McFarlane (eds), *op. cit.*, p. 214.

[70]   Jarman (1997a), *op. cit.*, pp. 118–19.

[71]   Fionnula O'Connor, 'Tonight's the Night', *The Independent on Sunday*, 11 July 1999, p. 13.

[72]   John Mullin, 'Loyalists target Catholic families', *The Guardian*, 13 July 1993, p. 3.

[73]   Fraser, *op. cit.*, p. 49.

and twelve. Arguably the Order and its activities are an education in themselves, described as 'the major agency for the introduction to Protestant children of cross-cultural myths, fears and hatreds, and for the sanctioning of verbal and physical aggression'.[74] The chants and rhymes associated with this movement are essentially composed of violent and bloody episodes of Irish history. Here the boundaries between formal and informal education blur. Images and stories told between children on the street mix with their street politics. A typical Orange loyalist song known to Protestant children in the 1970s begins:

> *I was born under the Union Jack,*
> *I was born under the Union Jack*
> *Do you know where Hell is?*
> *Hell is up the Falls*
> *Kill all the Popeheads, and we'll guard Derry's walls.*[75]

Parading can be seen in the context of the importance and centrality of history in the minds of young and old alike. Neil Jarman quotes Peter Lowenthal in saying that: 'Ireland does not lie in the past; rather Ireland's history, lies in the present'.[76] He argues that historical and mythical figures anchor identities and play an important role. Parading is an illustration of traditional repetition of social memory, relied upon to stimulate loyalism and nationalism.[77] In short a hierarchy is confirmed in the street, in a format perhaps particularly conducive for younger people to become involved in and enjoy.[78] Parades and marches are vivid, colorful, and loud.

Jarman comments that:

> parades take on the aspect of a slow moving chaotic cartoon, with no obvious beginning or end to its story, but with constant variations on the theme of individual and collective faith, betrayal, sacrifice, resistance and victims, endlessly repeated and connected together.[79]

Approximately 300 nationalist parades take place compared to 2,500 loyalist events.[80] By contrast the Catholic marches, for example those of The Ancient Order of Hibernians are less militaristic in tone and often have women and children included at the front. Republican parades are noted as being less aggressive in display, quieter, and with less uniformed presence. They celebrate and direct attention towards five causes: the United Irishmen Rising of 1798, the Easter Rising of 1916, 'Bloody

---

[74]   *Ibid.*
[75]   *Ibid.*
[76]   Jarman (1997a) *op. cit.*, p. 1.
[77]   *Ibid.*, p. 9.
[78]   *Ibid.*, p. 26.
[79]   *Ibid.*, p. 17.
[80]   Bryan and Jarman, *op. cit.*, p. 213.

Sunday', internment in 1971 and the hunger strikers of 1981.[81] Parading typically illustrates the intensity of sectarian feeling.

Children have however played a more significant role as militarized bodies than mere parading, through their actual involvement in political violence, including paramilitary activities, guerrilla-warfare and terrorism. Studies have shown that in trouble spots across the world young people usually make up a significant percentage of liberation and national groups.[82] Northern Ireland has been no exception. Young people below the age of eighteen were a prominent cohort of covert paramilitary organizations in the early 1970s, and the majority of actors at the flashpoints of the troubles have been young male Catholics.[83] Children's membership of the youth gangs and organizations enabled their swift incorporation into paramilitary activity as youths and later as adults. The Irish Republican Army was revived after 1969 and its youth organizations provided the platform for its future direction. Distinct generations of members in the IRA Army Council include those active in the 1940s as young volunteers, those who orchestrated the campaign years of 1952 to 1962, and those who first participated between 1969 and 1972.[84] Many members were in their early teens when they joined at the height of the violence. The IRA has remained very successful in attracting pre-adolescent children into its youth groups. Fianna Eireann, the largest junior branch of the IRA organized weekly meetings and a scout-type uniform and the Fianna cub section was available for seven- to eleven-year-olds. Such groups taught up to a hundred boys at a time about guerrilla techniques, fighting the army and use of firearms. Members wore black berets for official occasions such as funerals, and green berets for field work.[85]

The fact that children were also not eligible for arrest made their participation in riots and demonstrations particularly valuable. Young children acted as deterrents or shields and occupied the front line causing soldiers to delay their fire, or encroach further and become drawn into range of other weapons.[86] Psychologist Morris Fraser writes that these children were especially able to accept roles in these riskier areas of street confrontation:

[c]hildren, with limited death concepts, unable with immaturity to anticipate all the risks of their actions, have accepted this role without hesitation ... . Children run up to within a few yards of a soldier with an aimed high velocity rifle and lob a petrol bag over the sandbags with a nonchalance few adults could imitate.[87]

The majority of rioters have been aged between fifteen and twenty-four, though many children aged between five and fifteen who participated as stone throwers were

---

[81]   *Ibid.*, pp. 136–7.
[82]   Cairns (1996), *op. cit.*, p. 116.
[83]   *Ibid.*, p. 27.
[84]   John Bowyer Bell, *IRA Tactics and Targets* (Poolbeg Press, 1997), pp. 15–19.
[85]   Fraser, *op. cit.*, pp. 12–13.
[86]   Fraser, *op. cit.*, p. 58.
[87]   Fraser, *op. cit.*, p. 153.

as accurate and powerful as their adult counterparts.[88] At the height of the troubles, boys aged between twelve and sixteen typically used wires to stop jeeps while younger boys banged bin-lids to alert others. Their whistles distracted police into ambushes, they made petrol bombs, nail and paint bombs, directed traffic, created road blocks and burned vehicles. The youngest children were used to send messages or gather up ammunition.[89] The youth wing of the IRA also marked territory and invoked sentiments of nationalism by painting murals of political symbols and historical scenes, sometimes referring to the Palestine Liberation Organization.[90] In psychologist Morris Fraser's many interviews with young boys he found that typically children of eight-and-a-half could explain how to make petrol bombs and Junior Orange Lodge members casually stated that all Catholics should be killed or burned.[91] Fraser claimed that Ulster children at the time, were used as never before in guerrilla warfare and that their training also began early.[92] As a leader of a youth organization in one of Belfast's mixed areas he regularly witnessed the acts of children, noting that they often overstepped boundaries of respectability towards the dead. He argues that it is a more powerful act for children to stone a jeep, stone the driver, and then stone the ambulance carrying the dead body, than for an adult to pilot a military aircraft.[93] As will be seen in the next chapter, this has resonance with Southern Africa where children's violent acts have been encouraged because they appear to demonstrate indifference to, or greater capacity for, horrific behavior.

During 1969 British media images and accounts of the civil rights riots in Belfast and Londonderry vividly portrayed these youths and children fighting.[94] London-based reporters represented and described children as innocent victims in an adult conflict. Fraser argues that in most media reportage of the troubles, 'rioting' and 'civil rights disturbances' were under-descriptions of the urban guerrilla-warfare that took place.[95] The term 'rioting' implied confined and spontaneous fighting rather than organized battles against the army. Children's participation at every level of street fighting, often at the forefront, is thus similarly misinterpreted as accidental rather than organized and deliberate.[96] Child stone-throwers and petrol bombers in the front line attracted a great deal of front-page coverage and shocked comment. The Daily Mirror reported in August 1972: 'it is profoundly tragic that the children of Ulster can no longer be called the innocents'.[97] And Newsweek commented that '[t]he brawling children of Ulster ... have passed prematurely from the innocent

---

[88]   Cairns (1996) *op. cit.*, p. 111.
[89]   *Ibid.*, p. 18.
[90]   O'Neill, *op. cit.*, p. 27.
[91]   Fraser, *op. cit.*, pp. 16–17.
[92]   *Ibid.*, p. 9. See also *Cost of the Troubles Study*, *op. cit.*
[93]   *Ibid.*, p. 8.
[94]   Cairns (1987), *op. cit.*, p. 12.
[95]   Fraser, *op. cit.*, pp. 19–21.
[96]   *Ibid.*
[97]   Fraser, *op. cit.*, p. 22.

games of childhood to the deadly serious business of street warfare.'[98] Throughout
the media reporting of 'the troubles' children were described as having lost childhood
and innocence. Reporters made sense of children in battle by comparing them to an
idealized normal child:

> [H]e was no bigger than my own six year old. He ... teetered to a halt three yards from the
> soldiers. The street was a perilous carpet of stones, broken bottles and jagged metal. The
> soldiers ... watched as he swung his arm in the glare of a burning single decker bus ... The
> half brick fell harmlessly at the feet of a battle weary corporal. The kid retreated picking
> up another rock ... He trotted back to his pals. Nine-year-olds, 12-year-olds, 14-year-olds.
> The little ones are assembling the piles of ammunition. The big ones are hurling it.[99]

The majority of accounts suggest that these children became 'premature adults'
given that they grew up and played alongside armed soldiers, lost family members
to terrorism, witnessed chaos, and felt fear in their everyday activities. It can also be
argued that such narratives about children implicitly serve to illustrate a perceived
lack of control or desperation, when in actual fact the use of children is illustrative
of the depth of social involvement in the conflict, not societal demise.

Psychologist Ed Cairns believes that children such as these are participating
in violence and 'acts of destruction that impact on power relations in society'.[100]
They too may comprehend the political value of this violence. Of the children who
have attracted the attention of researchers in medical science, especially as agents
of physical violence, research has shown that from the age of five they can explain
the difference between violent crime and political violence. They condone political
violence, recognizing it as self defense of their community, but condemn on moral
grounds violence or crime for any other purpose.[101] Psychiatrists have sought solace
in the fact that children are able to make a distinction of any kind, believing that this
rationalizing is a healthier response to violence than delinquency or confusion. But
the greater lesson is perhaps that children know they are capable of participating in
political conflict. Children engaged in, and prepared for, such acts of destruction
may be desired to do so, however, not because of their political understanding but
because their qualities and capabilities are different from those held by adults. A
directive to IRA members makes this clear:

> Youngsters and older children are ideal material for the work of planting bombs and
> rigging booby-traps ... They attract less attention and suspicion than adults, are sensitive
> to rewards, and ask no questions. If captured by the British army or security officers they
> are unable to give any information about their employer ... More gelignite nail-bombs and
> petrol bombs must be readily available.[102]

---

98 *Newsweek*, 19 April 1971, p. 22.
99 *The Daily Express*, 9 February 1971, p. 19.
100 Cairns (1996), *op. cit.*, pp. 10–11.
101 Ed Cairns and Tara Cairns, in Whyte, *op. cit.*, pp. 98–9.
102 Fraser, *op. cit.*, pp. 56–8.

The directive continues: 'British Army patrols can be lured into ambushes more easily when children, youngsters and women are the bait.'[103] In this case it is clear how it is thought that children and women can succeed in terrorist activity: their 'civilian' and 'feminized' status deceives the enemy. This is only possible because of the assumptions already in place of their non-political or non-combatant status; assumptions made because of a myriad of 'natural' qualities assigned to women and children. This in turn enables them to be used as a human shield to cover the political actions of others nearby. Children who have been killed in the fighting are publicly described by paramilitary organizations as heroes rather than victims. Their participation in the cause colors the local death notices. For example, the death of a thirteen-year-old member of the Junior IRA, shot by the British Army, was marked by the following words pinned up on walls:

> In this supreme hour the Irish nation must, by the readiness of its children to sacrifice themselves for the common good, prove itself worthy of the august destiny to which it is called ... Dear Ireland, take him to thy breast this soldier who died for thee; within thy bosom let him rest among the martyrs sanctified.[104]

Attention is drawn to the child's death, but it is framed in the context of sacrifice for a 'mother nation', therefore making the sacrifice also above question from the mothers of the nation. The final section of the chapter will look further at the construction of a passive maternal and child sphere that accompanies such military tactics and targets.

Nationalization: Soft Tactics and Soft Targets

Constructs of protected children and their associated familial sphere are evident in discourses of nationalization in Northern Ireland and have become a rationale for paramilitary practices, particularly for nationalists. In this context, protecting children and using the construct of the maternal sphere (though not ascribing them with a nationalist role), may be described as 'soft' tactics. The term 'soft', is used in the terrorist context of 'soft target', to essentialize the concept of unarmed civilians especially women and children. Inclusive in this terrorist appropriation of the construct of softness, is both its valuation and denigration – what is to be targeted is what should be most protected. The notional distancing of children and mothers, from a political and military sphere which seemingly protects them rather than is them, also makes them valuable in themselves, and hence also valued as 'soft targets' by the enemy. This is also explored later on in the section. Finally there will be a discussion of how tentative steps towards peace have also been taken using children – practices that might be described as 'soft options'.

---

[103]   *Ibid.*, pp. 57–8.
[104]   *Ibid.*, p. 148.

Soft Tactics

The image of the subordinate or helpless mother provides an inherent moral argument for male, armed aggression or protection of the mother from state domination.[105] Within Catholic representations of nationality, the notion of protecting 'Mother Ireland' may be invoked. For Catholics, the meek submissive figure of Mary, the Virgin Mother, or 'Queen of Ireland', has combined in nationalist mythology with a noble female personification of Ireland, to provide a potent, ambiguous and complex symbol in the struggle against British imperialism. As has been argued: 'The overall effect is to reproduce a highly conservative, highly sentimental, even patriarchal, image of "Mother Ireland" which is detached from political activist and feminist alike'.[106] The familiar sphere is particularly invoked in Irish identity within Catholic communities through 'Eire' the historic Irish female and mother figure.[107]

Lynda Edgerton writes that: 'Irish nationalists developed a discourse of nationality in which the masculinity of the people was underwritten by the idealization of traditional motherhood within the symbolic terrain of nationalist culture; the rural home'.[108] Roman Catholicism emphasizes the strength of the father and the gentleness of the mother, and associated school curricula material illustrates that a woman's place is in the home using traditional stereotypes.[109] Begona Aretzaga has observed in particular the display of maternal and protective images, in public and highly militarized localities and contexts. In the Catholic Falls Road, a huge mural of a protective 'Madonna and Child' look down over the street, thereby adding to the exposure of Catholic girls to the model of the pure Virgin Mary.[110] Many murals show the suffering of mothers and sons and imply martyrdom.[111] Street images about the conflict are also polarized between violent men and their anguished statements, and passive mothers who sacrifice their sons. This passive representation, says Aretzaga, is inaccurate. Women and mothers have played a part almost inversely proportional to their recognition. She writes: 'precisely because of their anomalous and subversive character within established definitions of the political, the politics of nationalist women has been eclipsed in the accounts of the conflict'.[112] Their politics is seen as

---

[105] Lynda Edgerton, 'Public Protest, Domestic Acquiescence: Women in Northern Ireland', in Rosemary Ridd and Helen Callaway (eds), *Caught Up In Conflict, Women's Responses to Political Strife* (Basingstoke: Macmillan, 1986), p. 70.

[106] Valerie Morgan and Grace Fraser, 'Women and the Northern Ireland conflict: experiences and responses', in Dunn, Seamus, (ed.), *Facets of the Conflict in Northern Ireland, op. cit.*, p. 82.

[107] Fields, *op. cit.*, pp. 56–7.

[108] Begona Aretxaga, *Shattering Silence: Women Nationalism and Political Subjectivity in Northern Ireland* (Princeton: Princeton University Press, 1997), p. 150.

[109] Egerton, *op. cit.*, p. 62.

[110] *Ibid.*

[111] Aretzaga (1997), *op. cit.*, p. 47.

[112] *Ibid.*, p. 4.

irrelevant or marginal. She makes the case that 'gender is used as a symbolic terrain wherein to formulate arguments of domination and resistance'.[113]

Studies have suggested that despite the sectarian divide, families at the height of the troubles differed very little with regard to gendered and socio-economic roles of family members. Working-class women in both communities employed similar gender stereotypes, notably that the growing boy 'learns that men are men, and boys are men'.[114] With high male unemployment and women as providers it is argued that men have allowed paramilitary involvement to fulfill their need for protective and strong behavior, thus further equating protection with machismo and masculinity.[115] Popular resistance is by contrast regarded as a feminized inside – of homes and families, women and children. Men may be largely absent from the familial sphere, as military targets and targeters involved in the particularly masculine experience of nationalism.[116] The perception of a sphere of popular resistance in the home merely serves to give more kudos to nationalist paramilitary activity – the equal of the British Army or RUC presence. The subordination of women as victims or lesser perpetrators also occurs within Protestant ideology through the equating of women with mothers, though Protestant society does not have an equivalent dominant symbolism of the mother/Madonna and child.[117] Older Protestants have however exhibited a fear of Catholic families 'swallowing up their sons and breeding uncontrollably': the higher Catholic birth-rate having at times incited Protestant riots in Catholic areas.[118]

For most Catholic young girls and women their sense of belonging in the community is fulfilled by having a baby as early as practicable. Rona Fields argues that the pressure to have children and provide is an example of how 'women in Ireland are compelled into fragmenting themselves – to becoming either bodies for breeding, feeding and martyrdom, or spirits with intellectual resources and vocation but bound by vows of chastity and obedience'.[119]

Women who have children are thus soon socialized into the strong maternal role of keeping the family together and as the role is so demanding they have little opportunity to think critically about the situation.[120] Lynda Egerton observes how it is often the mother who has the heavy responsibility of trying to bring up a family in a situation similar to a war environment. At the same time, Northern Ireland appears under the veneer of a 'normal state in a liberal democratic country'.[121] The difficulties are compounded by the fact that husbands are the main victims of death, imprisonment, maiming and disabling. It is notable that the majority of children in Northern Ireland, who have undergone counseling have proved themselves to be

---

[113]   *Ibid.*, p. 150.
[114]   Fraser, *op. cit.*, p. 37.
[115]   *Ibid.*, p. 38.
[116]   Feldman, *op. cit.*, p. 96.
[117]   Fields, *op. cit.*, p. 155.
[118]   Liam de Paor, *Divider Ulster* (Harmondsworth: Penguin, 1970), p. 129.
[119]   Fields, *op. cit.*, pp. 161–2.
[120]   Edgerton, *op. cit.*, p. 61.
[121]   *Ibid.*, p. 77.

seemingly unaffected by the troubles, provided that their family is able to provide information, emotional support and justification for their circumstances.[122] Despite this, mothers and children are identified within the nationalist cause rather than as agents of it.

Eithne McLoughlin describes Northern Irish society as matrifocal with an emphasis on the mother's role of sacrifice and maintenance of the family beyond childhood years: 'women see their mothers and daughters more often than men see their parents or children'.[123] The 'strong woman', the mother and the family are important constructions of everyday life in Northern Irish society, particularly amongst Catholics, yet there is little study of their role in the conflict. McLoughlin points out that though it is a sphere to which attention is drawn and valued, it remains distinctly subordinate to the male sphere. She writes that: 'comfortable ideas about cheery families supporting their members from evil without is an idealization rather than an analysis of the nature of family life in Northern Ireland'.[124] Women have been accepted as guardians of the family, transmitters of cultural values to the next generation and the eternal sufferers for Mother Ireland.[125] In particular it is assumed that mothers will rear sons who will devote themselves to the cause.[126] Mothers can be actively involved in transmitting and preserving nationalist aims and may also resort to violence themselves. Family loyalty and family paramilitary connections influence children from an early age. The mother of three sons who were killed in action in the IRA had 'encouraged their sense of Irishness and read them bedtime stories which reflected Irish history'.[127] Minds may be influenced by more subtle political identities presented in the familial sphere.[128] Though the family and home may be revered as a site and reproducer of violence, yet it is also perceived as non-political. 'Politics' becomes a subject which is not or cannot be spoken about in the home, even though it infuses everyday life. Women and children through their embodiment of protection, are thus further ramified as non-political and non-threatening. However, childlike or soft qualities can be politically useful per se; they can lead to the strategic use of the 'soft' sphere for military practices, as well as be constructed and appropriated in nationalism. Importantly, bestowed childlike qualities have enabled children, women and the female elderly to associate with or act as perpetrators in terrorist activity, and remain above suspicion. In this case what is seen also determines what is not seen.

Children's presence can signify peaceful intent and by extension a non-violent or protected sphere. During a family shopping trip in Northern Ireland, children may be

---

[122] Eithne McLoughlin, 'Women and the family in Northern Ireland: a review', *Women's Studies International Forum*, Vol. 1, No. 4 (1992), p. 554, and Cairns (1987), *op. cit.*, pp. 50–64.

[123] McLoughlin, *op. cit.*, pp. 556, 561, see also Hastings and McFarlane, *op. cit.*

[124] *Ibid.*, p. 555.

[125] Sales, *op. cit.*, p. 62.

[126] *Ibid.*, p. 68.

[127] Cairns (1996), *op. cit.*, p. 126.

[128] *Ibid.*, p. 153.

left behind in the parked car, not for their own safety but as a visual demonstration that the car itself is not a threat and does not contain a bomb.[129] The concept of child as innocent is retained in this example of peaceful signaling. By comparison the young street fighter necessarily loses this construction of childhood through his political participation. Reversing traditional etiquette, young girls have been known to walk their boyfriends home because on their own, boys risk being lifted by the army. Suspicion is averted by the presence of the young female and a familial relationship between them may also indicate pacifity or diverted attention.[130] A sixty-year-old mother and son can walk a heavily patrolled street with guns concealed underneath her cardigan and about his person because [s]he 'outsmarts a far more powerful enemy through her intimate knowledge of the locality and manipulation of the soldier's filial respect for elderly women'.[131] It was not until 1972 that very young children were bag-and-body searched on entering a store,[132] and the army regularly searched schoolchildren's bags, as well as prams, knowing that they could contain gelignite.[133] The troubles can be seen then to take place in, and create, a highly gendered environment in which children have both active masculine roles and a perceived passive presence, may fight alongside men, and yet conceptually remain in the sphere of mother and family.

Soft Targets

The separation of children and mothers from a political and military sphere, and the attention drawn towards their protection and their embodiment of nationalism also makes them valuable in themselves, and hence also valued as 'soft targets' by the enemy. To place the apparently protected and separate mother and child under direct or arbitrary threat is a key terrorist tactic; this also serves to demonstrate the other side's vulnerability. Children and female family members are thus a particularly high category of 'soft targets'; they meet the terrorist description of individuals who are not armed and not openly involved, but carry weight as victims.

'Soft targets' may be victims of bomb attacks, random doorstep or house shootings. The man or most active member is killed, but the attack is anticipated to frighten other men's dependents. In the words of one terrorist: 'the wife is going to demand that he gets out when one of his mates gets whacked ... they can't cope with it in the home.'[134] Mark Urban, however has noted the power to intimidate through the assassination of women in the home. Mothers can be shot in bed, in front of the

---

[129] Cairns (1987), *op. cit.*, p. 23.

[130] Egerton, *op. cit.*, p. 65; see also Lorainne Dowler (1998), 'And They Think I'm Just a Nice Old Lady: Women and War in Belfast, Northern Ireland', *Gender, Place and Culture,* Vol. 5, No. 2.

[131] Aretzaga (1997), *op. cit.*, p. 38.

[132] Cairns (1987), *op. cit.*, p. 23.

[133] Fraser, *op. cit.*, p. 57.

[134] Feldman, *op. cit.*, p. 74.

children.[135] In 1977, 62 per cent of casualties were civilian non-combatants, and the majority of these injuries and deaths occurred in Belfast or Londonderry.[136] Between 1969 and 1973, over 15,000 families moved from their homes.[137] The killing of children can be a significant and symbolic indicator of aggression, as in the petrol bombing of the three boys under ten in July 1998.

Many thousands of children are still attacked and maimed each year. The charity Childline, for example, recently reported that it received 5,000 calls each week from the Province.[138] However, the balance between tragedy and strategy is a fine one. The killing of children may be tactically avoided to prevent allegations of barbarity. An INLA terrorist describes the potential disruptive power of the family or children in the context of an assassination attempt:

> The provies nine times out of ten will bang him as he's getting out of his car and bang him when he's getting into his car or put a bomb into it. But then you have to see does he drive the kids to school and allow for that. That would scrub a car bomb right there and then. If that doesn't work, you're going to knock the door which is harder to do. Because if you knock the door and he doesn't answer, you're going to have to go into his house looking for him with his family all mixed in. If you hurt any of them you count the operation as a loss. The political impact is just wiped out because now its just 'criminals terrorising families,' never mind what or who your man is.[139]

Home or the family is one of the key sites of political intimidation, resistance and socialization. For many terrorists family commitment and loyalty may play an important part in the continuation of the armed struggle. In some cases children's deaths become the turning point in a search for peace. The death of three children including a baby of four weeks prompted the biggest popular peace movement in 1976.[140]

Soft Options

Street battles and terrorism within communities also confuse the categorization of protector and protected.[141] With the disappearance of men into covert operations which place home and family under attack, the role of the mother as a provider of stability and safety has increased. Edgerton argues that it is this threat to motherhood and the family that has prompted women's involvement in the struggle particularly

---

[135] Mark Urban, *Big Boys' Rules, the SAS and the Secret Struggle against the IRA* (London: Faber and Faber, 1992), p. 187.

[136] Darby, J., *Conflict in Northern Ireland: The Development of a Polarised Community* (Gill and Macmillan: Dublin, 1976), p. 237.

[137] Cairns (1987), *op. cit.*, p. 48.

[138] See Internet site: 'www.childline.org.uk'.

[139] Feldman, *op. cit.*, p. 74.

[140] Cairns, (1996) *op. cit.*, p. 47.

[141] Egerton, *op. cit.*, p. 67.

for peace.[142] In one notable example in 1970, despite a strict curfew imposed by the army on the Lower Falls Road, 3,000 women pushed prams with food to those who could not feed their children. They were able to force the British Army to turn a blind eye in confusion and embarrassment.[143] Mothers and children together created a powerful yet infantilized and feminized construct. The connotations assigned to this advancing civilian sphere of mothers and babies also overrode the capacity of the army to act. It is noticeable that attempts to find peace in Northern Ireland have often begun with reference to children.

Children's deaths prompted the formation of 'The Peace Women'; later, more accurately, it was termed the 'Peace People'. Its founders (Mairead Corrigan and Betty Williams) were awarded the Nobel peace prize, and achieved a great deal of publicity.[144] The non-sectarian 'Woman's Coalition' was founded in 1996 by two women who questioned the machismo and militantism on both sides. These women represented those who saw themselves as a civic space poised between the formal realism of politics and the domestic arena, and found their political voice in a consultative 'civic' forum.[145] Recently women activists have been able to make space for peace by identifying their potential roles and challenging their limited control at home. They argue that '[w]omen are far more tolerant ... . Bringing up children has a lot to do with it. It means you have to listen to all their tantrums and take both sides.'[146] Through such talks for peace, by women and mothers, the distinction between formal and informal politics has been further broken down.

One of the difficulties in promoting peace has been this delineation between political and non-political spheres which are thought of as separable, though they are mutually inclusive. To avoid talking politics at home as many families claim,[147] is an example of a political strategy itself. In a society described by Ed Cairns as having two versions of everything including the truth, little can be viewed as non-political or without a sectarian significance or at least involving a degradation of the 'other'.[148] Despite the condition of peace, the charity Childline, whose interest is all children, had to move into costly city center premises in Belfast to avoid accusations of sectarianism. As Monica McWilliams noted, the millions of pounds put into community relations projects has had to exclude all services with sectarian provision such as playgroups. It is not surprising therefore, that peaceful change has been initiated in one of the most politically benign areas of popular culture, namely the children's holiday.

In 1975 the Community Relations Commission and the Department of Community Relations were abolished. In their place the Department of Education in Northern

---

[142] *Ibid.*, p. 86.

[143] Aretxaga, *op. cit.*, pp. 58–9.

[144] Jennifer Harris, 'How Ireland's women won the war for peace', *Women's Journal,* August 1998, pp. 60–63.

[145] *Ibid.*, p. 33.

[146] *Ibid.*, p. 30.

[147] Murray (1985), *op. cit.*, also Cairns (1987), *op. cit.*

[148] Cairns (1987), *op. cit.*, p. 15.

Ireland assumed responsibility for grant-aided community relations holidays, for large groups of children preferably of both communities. In 1988 for example, 6,000 children took part.[149] The contact requirement of such schemes is not always made clear in the arrangements and guidelines. The description of the holiday as available to both communities may be the only indicator that children may be closely integrated. The accompanying literature to be read by host and child families states firmly that there is to be no political agenda although they hope to help each child to have some impact on the way people relate to one another in Northern Ireland.[150] Reports of one of the largest programs, Project Children, suggest that slightly secretive methods were used to attract sectarian communities with little reference to the reconciliation theme. Protestant children for example did not know that they were staying with an American Catholic family.[151] Post-holiday reports show that both Protestant and Catholic children were extremely surprised when they did meet at how similar they were. Parents also requested more opportunities to meet each other in the context of children's holidays.[152] Criticism has been that these holidays cannot help the pressure from families on children's return.[153] They may have to appear to have gone back to more traditional thinking on returning home. In addition these encounters are often taking place outside the contentious environment and only for a short time.

It is interesting that there has been no substantial report into the success of the holidays. This could illustrate the difficulty in following political values back into the home amidst the fear of sectarian reprisals or it could suggest that there is not much change anticipated from schemes. These schemes which operate in many communities, youth clubs and schools, also fulfill a role for adults who want to improve the lives of children (or be seen to be doing so). Small beginnings towards peace it seems are more easily gestured with small children. With regard to the 1990s peace process it seems that when change did occur it was through adults, not through children or generational change. In the present political system only adults have the capacity to make peace although recourse to children, as was shown in Chapter One, is perhaps a part of the symbolism of conciliatory gestures. Children are frequently the subject of impassioned pleas by politicians and peace promoters. Mo Mowlam, former Minister of State for Northern Ireland, explained in 1998 that it was thinking of the children, who 'had known nothing else' that kept her going through the deadlocked negotiations which finally gave way to the Good Friday Agreement.[154] The recent initiatives and reports generated by the peace process have however drawn attention to the lack of policy and policy culture through which

---

[149] Karen Trew, 'Evaluating the impact of contact schemes for Catholic and Protestant children' in Harbison, J.I. (ed.), *Growing Up in Northern Ireland* (Belfast: Stranmillis College, 1989), p. 133.

[150] Dominic Murray, *The Chance of a Lifetime: An Evaluation of Project Children* (Centre for the Study of Conflict: University of Ulster, 1993), p. 16.

[151] *Ibid.*, p. 27.

[152] *Ibid.*, p. 28.

[153] Trew, *op. cit.*, p. 137.

[154] ITV *News at Ten*, 29 January 1998.

children's experiences may be adequately dealt with in the forthcoming frameworks for reconciliation and inter/intra community re-building.[155] The conception of children as non political has played no small part in this policy gap. Children remain caught up in the troubles in far greater numbers than have been addressed since the cease-fires, primarily in punishment shootings by paramilitary groups.[156] The continuation of violence by children is also to some extent placing a focus on children as agents of change within their communities. The question of their 'political participation' is also raised too, but ironically with interpretations of 'their political' capacity being narrowly drawn.

In a recent report Connolly and Healy have shown how 'children are already demonstrating some awareness of the events around them at the age of three and this awareness grows significantly over the next few years. Moreover, by the age of six, the findings suggest that around a third of children in Northern Ireland already see themselves as belonging to one of the two main communities and just under one in six are making sectarian statements'.[157] They too highlight the limitations of strategies not also oriented towards the family and local community. Of three-year-olds they note:

> While they may not know what these things represent as yet, they are clearly developing and internalising a set of predispositions to prefer certain events and symbols over others. Within this, the power of the local area – the specific field of relations within which these young children are located – is also quite apparent in the way that it tends to feed and shape this emerging ethnic habitus. The painted kerbstones, the flags, murals, Celtic and Rangers shirts and Orange Marches represent just some of the cultural symbols and events that characterize the young children's local areas and which they are now beginning to recognize and assimilate into their sub-conscious.[158]

Conclusion

This chapter has attempted to substantiate the arguments advanced in the previous case, that of Nazi Germany, by showing how children can play a central role as nationalized and militarized bodies in conflict. Children's political socialization in Northern Ireland has been shown to be facilitated by their community upbringing and by the sectarian nature of the conflict. Sectarianism divides and politicizes social institutions, especially schools, making children constantly aware of sectarian

---

[155] Fay *et al.*, *op cit.*, p. 199.
[156] Liam Kennedy, *They Shoot Children Don't They? An Analysis of the Age and Gender of Victims of Paramilitary 'Punishments' in Northern Ireland*, Report prepared for the Northern Ireland Committee against terror and the Northern Ireland Affairs Committee of the House of Commons, 2001, http://cain.ulst.ac.uk/issues/violence/docs/kennedy01a.htm.
[157] Paul Connolly and Julie Healy (2004), *Children and the Conflict in Northern Ireland: The Experiences and Perspectives of 3–11 Year Olds* (Belfast: Office of the First Minister and Deputy First Minister).
[158] *Ibid.*

values and boundaries. Children in Northern Ireland are also particularly exposed to a re-living of history, and daily nationalistic identification with the past. Such a construction of political values in almost cartoon format, on walls, in their schools and in stories told within families, is easily assimilated by children. The absorption of nationalist sentiment in this way can be seen to aid their assimilation into various militarized roles. Throughout the duration of the troubles it is likely that children's participation is far greater than has been accounted for. They have been shown to be 'socially competent in the ways they appropriate racist discourse from the ages of five and six'. And by the ages of seven and eight are 'able to talk extremely confidently and knowledgeably about their own experiences and attitudes towards others'.[159]

As was shown in Chapter Three on Nazi Germany, familial and informal activities can transmit political ideas to children. Terrorism in Northern Ireland can be seen as depending on the informal and political spheres, and the concept of 'soft' targets. The familial sphere has a specific importance. Though mothers and children of Ireland are identified in nationalist sentiment as iconographic victims and beneficiaries of the conflict, they also function as a shield for political activity. This notional separation from the conflict also makes children and the construct of the child a valuable political currency and apparent political refuge; ultimately they can become a target of terrorist activity themselves.

In Nazi Germany, the private and political spheres were detached conceptually, though they were interdependent in practice. In both cases studies, the construct of a child can be seen as fluid, though always accompanied by a historically continuous, trans-cultural image of the innocent child, in whom nationalism is embodied. As Chapter 1 illustrated, children, and their capabilities, are constructed as well as being biologically natural. A particular construct of child, the protected innocent, can be seen as embodying the nationalist cause par excellence for militarized practices. Their alleged non-role and non-political status has been also shown to create their role and political presence, and give them greater capacity for playing a military role. Children's contribution to a conflict may be deduced from its corollary: their expected contribution to peace even in the face of adult intransigence. In Northern Ireland peace initiatives centered on children have problematized the meaning of 'political' within the community, a term which until recently has been conflated with 'historical' and detached from the domestic sphere. The relationships between constructs of 'the political' and children's politicization will be further explored in Chapter 6; but before that the final case study looks at children's politicization in apartheid South Africa and in Mozambique's Civil War.

---

[159] Paul Connolly, 'The Development of Young Children's Ethnic Identities: Implications for Early Years Practices', in Carol Vincent (ed.), *Social Justice, Education and Identity*, (Routledge, 2003), p. 180.

Chapter 5

Children in South Africa and Mozambique

This final case study seeks to provide further evidence of children's nationalization and militarization. Attention is turned to Mozambique and South Africa, with an examination of Mozambican, Afrikaner and African children as political bodies. Consistent with the other two case studies, nationalization and militarization are the organising themes in each exploration of children's political roles. In each context, education is identified as a crucial site of nationalization and political socialization – 'the social techniques by which a dominant caste serves to preserve its power'.[1] The maternal and familial sphere is considered within discourses of South African nationalism. The attempted destruction of the family in Mozambique's civil war and her struggle against South African backed militia, is examined as a practice of de-nationalization. An analysis of children's military roles completes each section, namely as soldiers in Mozambique, militarized Afrikaners, and members of the resistance movement in South African townships. Finally, the chapter addresses the role children may be playing in the development of the new democratic South Africa.

Mozambique: Nationalization and Education

Demographically, Mozambique can be described as a young country. In 1992 over 40 per cent of the population were under fourteen years of age.[2] Mozambique, typical of most African states, has a young, impoverished and recently decolonized population. It can also be said that young Mozambicans share a social memory dominated by conflict, namely the 'the long war of independence' which lasted from 1964 to 1974. This devastating conflict has been described as 'never really one war, or even two but a collage of the region's distraught face'.[3] The fight for independence gave rise to the formation of the resistance movement, Frelimo, founded in 1962, in order to resist Portuguese rule which lasted until 1975. It is estimated however that since 1980 over 500,000 civilians have died in Mozambique as a direct or indirect result of the struggle against the underground army, Renamo. This section begins with practices established

---

[1]   Leonard Thompson and Andrew Prior, *South African Politics* (London: Yale University Press, 1982), p. 108.

[2]   Derrick Knight, *Mozambique: Caught in the Trap* (Christian Aid, 1988), p. 57.

[3]   Hillary Andersson, *Mozambique: A War Against the People* (London: Macmillan, 1992), p. 77.

in the wake of independence from Portuguese colonial rule, when Frelimo first prioritized and implemented their education policies.

The previous colonial system of education had left 97 per cent of the population illiterate and by independence only 1 per cent of black Mozambicans had been educated to the point of being classed as *assimilados*, meaning in Portuguese terms that they had 'social and economic intelligence and good manners'. Soon after gaining independence and prior to the threat of the resistance force, Renamo, the Mozambican state had recognized that education as a social institution played a vital role in the internal security of their state. Firstly, education could counter the population's frustration of heightened expectation and limited socio-economic potential in the light of the recently ruined infrastructure of the country. Secondly, education could be used to promote democracy and mobilize people's politics. Most Mozambicans had not had access to education that could develop these potentials and had only experienced rudimentary education from the Churches, with a consuming and restrictive emphasis on religion.

The popularity of Frelimo has been attributed to the expansion of the new 'people's education' into rural areas, and the associated health and literacy campaigns which were particularly aimed at girls.[4] Frelimo viewed education as the easiest means of creating opportunities for self-improvement within the population and placed a great deal of attention on the education system reforms of 1974 to 1979.[5] Education provision was also developed as a means of nationalization and its first ideological role was to serve as an alternative to the colonial model. In the liberated zones, and after independence, class consciousness became a core issue of education policy.[6] Satisfying the pent-up demand for mass basic education became fundamental to the legitimacy of the state. The then Minister of Education, Grace Simbine, addressed young teachers during the program for national reconstruction, telling them, '[t]he people need you, and you must make the transformation from knowledge previously gained, to that knowledge that serves the interest of the great Mozambican family'.[7] The state also recognized that the heightened expectations of education could be potentially disruptive, if not fulfilled.[8]

Primarily though, education was viewed as a means of fostering national unity, skills, and newly consolidated political and social values. Teaching was characterized by a vocational curricula; it included Political and Social Studies, a democratic approach and the encouragement of girls to attend school.[9] The major reforms made

---

[4]   *Ibid.*, p. 12.

[5]   *Ibid.*, p. 91.

[6]   Anton Johnston, 'The Mozambican State and Education', in *Education and Social Transition in the Third World*, Martin Carnoy and Joel Samoff (Princeton New Jersey: Princeton University Press, 1990), p. 291.

[7]   Chris Searle, 'Classrooms of freewill', *New Internationalist*, August 1977, p. 9.

[8]   Johnston, *op. cit.*, pp. 309–10.

[9]   Sarah Graham-Brown, 'Battling for Survival: War, Debt and Education in Mozambique Nicaragua and Sudan', in *Education in the Developing World: Conflict and Crisis* (London and New York: Longman), p. 117.

in 1983 were severely disrupted by the continued conflict and by 1985 there had been a significant drop in standards and resources. Schools were closed down or destroyed by the Mozambican Resistance movement. Children and their education were specifically targeted by Renamo in recognition of Frelimo's evident success in attaining political support and societal stability through its management of the school system.

Renamo's original members were 'dissident Portuguese colonials, security police and anti-Frelimo fugitives', given cover and cohesion by Rhodesia's Central Intelligence Organization who were already monitoring Zimbabwean rebel forces in Mozambique.[10] On losing its role following Zimbabwean independence, it came under the influence and control of the South African military intelligence services, and in 1980 began working as a fake liberation movement to remove Frelimo.[11] Renamo made education a primary military target. Firstly, their intense military activity prevented primary school children from attending schools. They also sought out and destroyed schools and equipment, attacked teachers, and reversed the progress made in the education system.[12] Children who experienced this kind of setback also lost hope in their future and became similarly dispirited with their country. By 1986 the state was under World Bank management and the subsequent spending restrictions prevented further investment in education.[13]

Mozambique De-nationalization: The Family

In addition to disrupting education, Renamo's secondary aim was to destroy the rural economy and create instability within communities. It achieved this by directing its intimidation and force against the family. At this time 84 per cent of the population were rural workers. The mother in particular was identified as a target because she was most likely to have sole responsibility for the home and children's upbringing. Her death or disappearance constituted a critical disruption to the rest of the family and also the community.[14] The family was recognized as the unit around which social cohesion depended and thus became the primary military target in addition to health services which were also valuable. It is worth noting that in this society and in Northern Ireland the family acted as, and was seen as, an agent of conflict or lynchpin of stability accordingly. In African society the family had an additional significance: persons without families may be regarded as outcasts, as women without husbands are often regarded as unrespectable or whores. Renamo child conscripts who were forced to commit atrocities on family members also became permanent family and community outcasts, though they were often 'repatriated' into the official army. The

---

[10] Derrick Knight, *op. cit.*, p. 28.

[11] Oliver Furley, 'Child soldiers in Africa', in Oliver Furley (ed.), *Conflict in Africa* (London: Tauris, 1995), p. 29.

[12] Andersson, *op. cit.*, p. 88.

[13] Graham-Brown, *op. cit.*, p. 122.

[14] Andersson, *op. cit.*, pp. 80–81.

use of the family as a means of destabilization of a state is of interest here. In a US State Department report it was recorded how Renamo forces invaded rural areas and maintained territorial control by breaking down families to varying degrees. They demanded food and sexual favors from females, divided the family into working mothers and working children living apart, then destroyed their crops.[15]

In Mozambican/African society the extended family and mother provide emotional support and understanding and also teach many daily skills for survival. The family can be a self-contained survival unit, unlike Western families which are generally smaller and more able to make use of training and support readily available in other institutions. The family was recognized by Renamo as the keystone of African society,[16] and therefore a constituent part of security in a broad or deep sense. It was therefore a target in itself. It is interesting that Renamo believed that they could in a sense destroy the family through killing the child. Many Mozambican children were killed in order to reduce the morale of fighting parents.[17] The child came to resemble an essential symbol of society and was thus an important target for militia and terrorists. The infanticide that became a common practice in the civil wars of Mozambique and Rwanda can also be recognized as a strategic move – a rationalized attempt to locate the Achilles' heel of a society.

The South African objectives in Mozambique, of which Renamo was one instrument, were to destabilize the country and make it appear incapable of governing itself. It was hoped that instability would lead to economic and trade problems and facilitate the dominance of South Africa. Renamo founder, Ken Flower, said in defense of such practices that: 'it is a war, and in war all things are allowed'. But later he wondered if he had created a 'monster beyond control'.[18] Renamo was unlike other 'liberation movements', has yet to 'liberate' anyone and is only known to destroy.[19] In this sense its practices were a clear indication of perceptions of how to destroy national identity and national security within a state, and by negation therefore indicates how nationalization was perceived to operate at the levels of the family and school. Renamo sought to destabilize the country and disrupt society through killing and fear. UNICEF estimated that half a million children died as a result, and possibly 850,000 unarmed civilians have been murdered so far. Women and children were killed in as great if not greater numbers than men.[20] In a population of only 12.6 million, this is a significant proportion.[21]

Children who survived attacks, had by no means necessarily escaped Renamo. For example, children who survived a village massacre of their parents might then be further traumatized by tortuous tasks such as placing a piece of a relative in the

---

[15]   *Ibid.*, p. 62.

[16]   *Ibid.*, pp. 100–101.

[17]   Carolyn Hamilton, 'Children in armed conflict – New moves for an old problem', *The Journal of Child Law*, Vol. 7, No. 1, 1995, p. 46.

[18]   Andersson, *op. cit.*, pp. 46–7.

[19]   Knight, *op. cit.*

[20]   *Ibid.*, pp. 65–6.

[21]   Joseph Hanlon, 'From Marx to the mixed economy', *South*, December 1984, p. 25.

village water supply.[22] Such 'torture' served to alienate them from their community particularly in kinship and as future workers, and cripple them emotionally. The effects of violence on children are greatly mitigated by the presence of parents and family, especially the mother. In Mozambique, the strain experienced by mothers and the threat to their own lives rendered parental support particularly difficult or impossible.[23] Isolation and emotional pain experienced by children separated from their family were recognized by Renamo as the ideal mental conditioning for the life of a nasty, brutish and short-lived child soldier. Psychologists and psychiatrists have noted the extreme damage done to children's minds and concentration in Mozambique, especially by trauma. Mozambican children have been shown to invest their entire hope for the future in whether their nation can cope. Through this sense of personal insecurity, identification with a group, particularly a resistance group may become a crucial vehicle for self-preservation and make children newly aware of a political rather than personal concept of security.[24]

Militarization and Child Soldiers

The use of child soldiers is however the most common way that Frelimo and Renamo have relied on (perceived) children's vulnerability and their employment to achieve their aims. For boys in particular the military can offer comradeship and closeness and can seem attractive by its structure and support which are based closely on the kinship of the family and order of the school. Abandoned boys are easy prey for recruitment into the military.[25]

Some children were made to attack or kill their family members as a means of further bonding them with Renamo. They were first dehumanized by witnessing a close relative or friend being hacked to death or sexually abused at close range. Drugs, witchcraft, isolation, exhaustion, starvation, and discipline were used as learning aids. In a typical report, a boy first watched his parents' decapitation, and then, after his attention was caught in fear, he was taught to assemble assault weapons.[26] The more horrific the acts committed, the greater the social stigma they would experience and more dependent they would become on Renamo. As they lost moral direction and increased in dependency, the psychological burden was often deliberately induced through torture training and participation in massacres. If they disobeyed they were likely to be killed. Despite some Renamo fighting units being were made up entirely of children the attacks were often recorded in army reports as being committed by men.[27] Children were perhaps as effective as men, but to avoid

---

[22] Andersson, *op. cit.*, pp. 102–4.

[23] Ed. Cairns, *Children and Political Violence* (London: Blackwell, 1996), p. 169.

[24] *Ibid.*, p. 186, see also Cole P. Dodge and Magne Raundalen, *Reaching Children in War: Sudan, Uganda and Mozambique* (Bergen, Norway: Sigma Forlag, 1991).

[25] See Alex Vines, *Renamo: Terrorism in Mozambique* (London: James Currey, 1991).

[26] Andersson, *op. cit.*, pp. 59–60.

[27] Vines, *op.cit.*, pp. 33–4.

describing them as children would seem to be evidence that they were valued by Renamo for their particular capabilities and not their child status.

It has been reported that Renamo's child combatants appeared undisciplined, on drugs, in trauma and generally deprived. Some were tortured until they lost their spirit, and then rewarded for killing. They were 'programmed to feel little fear or revulsion for such actions, and thereby carry out these attacks with greater enthusiasm and brutality than adults would'.[28] Child soldiers were also given different tasks from adults. Many Renamo children were taught to shoot indiscriminately in the dark. They are described as having made awesome soldiers, because of their 'accurate' (i.e. accurately indiscriminate) and complicit actions after being given drugs.[29] The Save the Children co-ordinator in Mozambique reported that 'child soldiers are effective because they are easy to organize and don't ask questions'. Renamo leaders admit to using boy soldiers as young as nine, and later reported that 'they had the hardest job really, they were often the first to go forward when we attacked a village'. Those who did not follow orders or failed in some way, would be killed by one of the soldiers, or to prove their loyalty to Renamo, by one of the boys in front of the whole group.[30] 'During wartime the Renamo child soldier was something of an aristocrat', said the head of UNICEF's emergency section in Mozambique.[31]

Though practices of Renamo reached new heights of barbarism in their attempts to destabilize the family using dead, and deadly children, it is worth noting that children were also forcibly recruited into the Marxist Frelimo movement and the Portuguese army during the long war of independence (1964–74), though not in the same numbers or in such calculated ways. Later, a substantial portion of youth and children, unable to find work and seemingly unwanted by the new Marxist government, were readily available for military activity and a new source of allegiance in Renamo.[32] However, the number of youths and children in this guerrilla movement, from age six up to sixteen, cannot be solely attributed to an overall increase in volunteers when fighting intensified in the late 1980s. Renamo placed great emphasis on the recruitment of children (through enticement with food and shelter) but particularly with kidnapping. Many recruits were taken at gunpoint. Between 1978 and 1987 the average age of their recruits fell from twenty-five to 16.93 years.[33] Renamo recruited child soldiers because they were easier to control and prevent from escaping. Up to a hundred children at a time could be taken from a school from the ages of six to sixteen, using brutal methods of enforcement.[34]

[28]   *Ibid.*, p. 32.
[29]   John Fleming, 'Children in bondage: Young soldiers, labourers, and sex workers', *Sunday Independent*, Johannesburg, 13 August 1995, reproduced in *World Press Review*, January 1996, p. 9.
[30]   *Ibid.*, p. 10.
[31]   *Ibid.*
[32]   Vines, *op. cit.*, p. 34.
[33]   Andersson, *op. cit.*, pp. 59–60.
[34]   See *New African*, February 1993, p. 32.

In Mozambique as in much of Africa there is no historical record, or social memory of child soldiers being used prior to their recruitment in the first anti-colonial battles, for example by the Belgians. It is thought that the technique of using child soldiers was originally a colonial practice, or that it was initiated through South African support of the guerrilla movement.[35] Renamo achieved its principal aims through the targeting of civilians, especially children and the family, as a result of their embodiment of national security, and then through attacking their principal means of nationalization, the school. The use of children and the extremities of violence that children participated in broke norms or rules of civilian non-participation and this itself would have served as a strong indication of instability in Mozambique. Any open acknowledgement of the effectiveness of Renamo's policies by the state, and the consequences for civilians merely served to further illustrate that the state was not in control. Children's participation in violence does not mean that their political understanding has changed or been imposed.[36] A military identity and role may be their means of personal survival. Although they made a marked contribution to the effectiveness of this anti-Communist guerrilla movement, their role and their absence from official histories constitutes a screaming silence.[37]

Although the civil war ended in 1992 the children involved did not necessarily have the ability to re-enter their communities and start again. It was not until 1994 that they were helped to return home. Psychological re-entry was even more difficult. Renamo did not admit to being responsible for many of the children in its camps and many were too traumatized to adapt to a new life. Many resented being treated like children again: the norm of violence had been deeply inculcated, and they had become accustomed to exercising the power of life and death without constraint or consequences. Post-war rehabilitation has often been restricted to these boy soldiers at the expense of other victims. In addition there has been the need for children's roles to be kept secret after the war, since their past roles if later exposed would not be tolerated by their communities. There was a high level decision by aid agencies not to publish pictures of child soldier's faces, and the media were asked not to publish their full names or other details which could identify them as former soldiers.[38] Children too try to compartmentalize their past so as to minimize future condemnation.[39] Many children have been damaged and the solutions to their recovery will necessarily be long term projects. By 1989 an estimated 250,000 children had been orphaned or abducted by Renamo, and some 1.5 million children had physical stunting from malnutrition and its associated mental problems and limited brain development.[40] The main consequence of the conflict which 'ended' in

---

[35] *Ibid.*

[36] Cairns *op. cit.*, p. 110.

[37] Andersson, *op. cit.*, p. 43.

[38] Oliver Furley, *Child Soldiers and Youths in African Conflicts: International Reactions* (African Studies Centre Occasional Papers Series, No. 1, 1995), p. 28.

[39] *Ibid.*, p. 27.

[40] Andersson, *op. cit.*, pp. 100–101.

1992 is the highest infant mortality rate in the world: 325 out of every thousand. And for those that survive, a life expectancy of forty-five years[41] and a future of painful memories.

The next part of the chapter turns to the experiences of children in neighboring South Africa. It considers Afrikaner children and African children separately, for the purpose of further clarifying, by comparison, the political roles they embodied. The section begins with an analysis of practices of Afrikaner nationalization and militarization in the familial sphere, in the education system and in the military institutions provided for children. The section will then move on analyze children's role in African nationalization and 'military' mobilization.

Afrikaner Nationalization: The Family

Through its establishment of apartheid in South Africa after 1948 the National Party engaged in the division, categorization and regulation of all social institutions. To be effective, this had to include all elements of society in order to sustain the myth that through separate provision for communities they could each maintain a separate identity and viable existence. The practices of the South African Defense Force (SADF) including the 'systematic militarization of the polity' provoked organized violence by black Africans which were typically described in minimalist terms as 'unrest, fighting, rioting, terrorism' and not war or conflict.[42] It was a situation of tight control but considerable fear and uncertainty. The popular perception amongst whites was however that a war was going on, and that it could readily disintegrate into a Namibian-type guerrilla war.[43] The ANC made it clear that it was fighting a low level civil war even though the level of fighting was not continuous, and declared that it would observe human rights efforts to not injure civilians.[44] During the most violent time of the 1980s the SADF used the concept of 'total strategy' and the *Umkhonto we Sizwe* or 'Spear of the Nation', the armed wing of the ANC, used the term 'people's war' to describe the conflict.

In using the term 'total strategy', the Afrikaners alluded to the threat felt by the whole of society including the family: it was to counter a perceived 'total onslaught'. The stable, strong Afrikaner family and protected Afrikaner child were often the focus of attention when the nation was under threat. Mothers and children were publicly invoked as key symbols of national strength. The specific literary concept

---

[41]   *Ibid.*, p. 87.

[42]   A 'crisis' was publicly denied. See 'South Africa,' *New Internationalist*, No. 47 January 1977, p. 4.

[43]   Kenneth W. Grundy, *The Militarisation of South African Politics* (Oxford: Oxford University Press, 1986), pp. 59 and 114.

[44]   Jacklyn Cock, *Women and War in South Africa* (London: Open Letters, 1992), pp. 4–5.

and iconographic image 'Mothers of the nation' was a readily available construct.[45] Isabel Hofmeyr notes a concern earlier in the century at the decay of the Afrikaner family and the need to socialize the young in nationalist values. This was to be achieved by harnessing femininity and motherhood through the notion of selfless giving for one's children, and hence the survival of the volk as a whole. In popular literature mundane tasks such as care of the house were linked with the survival of children and care of the *volk*. Afrikaner nationalism was thus 'sedimented beneath the identities of woman and mother, and was exposed at key points of conflict throughout the century'.[46]

Afrikaners asserted national identity and illustrated racial strength using the home front; motherhood was synonymous with femininity.[47] The concept of motherhood was invoked by Afrikaner nationalists, through remembrance of Boer mothers and children killed in 1902. The 26,370 women and children who died in British concentration camps became iconographic emblems of suffering in the nationalist cause, enshrined in Afrikaner and English literature and the teaching of history. It remains a sensitive part of Afrikaner national memory.[48] During the 1920s and 1930s mothers were once again encouraged to present their homes and families as a 'powerhouse of domestic ethnic mobilization'.[49] As historians are beginning to discover, idealized motherhood was a central construct within Afrikaner nationalism. Groups such as the Afrikaans Christian Women's Organization (ACVV) publicly warned against inadequate childcare or 'dangerous motherhood' which could endanger the volk.[50] The construct of an ideal family unit was thus readily understood as a constituent part of the struggle against what was later termed the 'total onslaught'; home and family were encouraged to be mobilized against the outside threat. A 1978 Nationalist Party pamphlet, 'Women as silent soldiers' echoed Hitler's views and stated that '[a] woman's most important task is the educational

---

[45]   Shula Marks and Stanley Trapido, 'The Politics of Race Class and Nationalism' in Shula Marks and Stanley Trapido (eds), *The Politics of Race, Class and Nationalism in Twentieth Century South Africa* (Harlow: Longman, 1987), p. 23.

[46]   Cherryl Walker, 'Building a Nation from Words: Afrikaans Language Literature and Ethnic Identity, 1902–1924' in C. Walker (ed.), *Women and Resistance in Southern Africa to 1945* (London: James Currey, 1990), p. 113.

[47]   Cock, *op. cit.*, p. 49.

[48]   Edmund King, 'Afrikaner Education', *International Review of Education*, Vol. 25, 1979, p. 488.

[49]   Deborah Gaitskell and Elaine Unterhalter, 'Mothers of the Nation: A Comparative Analysis of Nation, Race and Motherhood in Afrikaner Nationalism and the ANC', in Nira Yuval-Davis and Floya Anthias (eds), *Woman-Nation-State* (London: Macmillan, 1989), pp. 61–3.

[50]   Marijke du Toct, '"Dangerous motherhood": Maternity Care and the Gendered Construction of Afrikaner Identity, 1904–1939', in Valerie Fildes, Lara Marks and Hilary Marland (eds), *Women and Children First: International and Infant Welfare 1870–1945* (London: Routledge, 1992), p. 215.

task. A child develops pride in his cultural assets, his language, his nation and his country largely through his mother's guidance'.[51]

The ideology of the volksmoeder, namely her heroism in times of national crisis, was thus assimilated into popular culture. Though this idealization was distinctly different from real conditions, the image remained a powerful one, serving perhaps the interests of the statesmen who designed and fostered the image as much as it improved women's morale.[52] As in Nazi Germany, the Afrikaners attached a particular importance to family, domesticity and child-rearing in the white community and 'although not official policy, the raising of the white birth rate had an important place in the strategy to maintain white racial supremacy'.[53] However in practice women were very much thought to be the weaker sex, in need of protection. This perception can be seen to have contributed to the cult of militarization and masculinity, which was to be the mainstay of Afrikaner nationalism.[54]

Leonard Bloom problematizes how groupings such as the family are presented as cohesive, and publicly addressed as a commonly understood unit. Such constructions may be present in the political discourse, and thus the social imagination of the people, but they may not be present in practice.[55] Linzi Manicom argues that the idealization of the family and assumptions of its 'natural' qualities are inevitably political because the family is a politically contested term and as a social unit is historically fluid and socially complex, infused with gender assumptions about roles themselves supported by and supporting broader binaries/categories of society.[56] She cites Nicholas Rose that the state is not the locus of all social power, but is a complex set of agencies which are involved to different extents in projects for the regulation of social and economic life whose origins, inspirations and power often come from elsewhere. She writes:

> The state in South African History should be understood not merely in terms of state policy that reflects patriarchal and racist ideology but rather as organised by gender (and race) difference and subordination in its very formation.[57]

The valued motherly and domestic private sphere can be seen to play a similar role as that recognized in Nazi Germany, namely, that mothers and wives and the institution of the family made a vital contribution to the apartheid state by incidentally preserving the illusion of normality or love in an environment of hatred. Dirk Coetzee, South

---

[51]   Gaitskell and Unterhalter, *op. cit.*, pp. 65–6.

[52]   Elsabe Brink, 'Man-made women: gender, class and the ideology of the *volksmoeder*', in C. Walker, *op. cit.*, p. 281.

[53]   Cock, *op. cit.*, p. 104.

[54]   *Ibid.*, p. 29.

[55]   Leonard Bloom, *Identity and Ethnic Relations in Africa* (Aldershot: Ashgate, 1998), p. 119.

[56]   Linzi Manicom, 'Rethinking State and Gender in South African History', *Journal of African History*, Vol. 33, No. 3, 1992, pp. 441–65.

[57]   *Ibid.*, p. 457.

African Police captain with responsibility for death squads was able to declare: 'I did it for volk and vaderland, for my wife and children and father and mother'.[58] His actions seem sanctioned because of this association with dependants in his family thus he makes them causal. All soldiers are 'normal', but recourse to associations of families and children; and especially emphasis on their protection and innocence reveals that they are thought of as a separate sphere.[59] Mothers and children could both be used to shield dehumanizing behavior. In addition, recourse to them could affirm humanitarian and moral virtues, thus strengthening and rationalizing means of nationalism and militarism.

The reverse of this is that the breakdown of families can be used as a powerful signifier of diminishing state control. The divided family, lone mother and lost child are invoked to express a particular relationship of power and domination, as was illustrated in targeted mothers and families in Mozambique and the request for strong stable families made by Afrikaner nationalists.[60] 'Total onslaught' was portrayed as being directed at the Afrikaner family, with the perceived aim of the disintegration of the state.[61] This too is reminiscent of Nazi Germany; the role of the family is especially invoked as an extra resource in times of national crisis.

Bloom endorses Erica Burman's argument that to understand control in South Africa we have to examine how power is transmitted in the basic units of society.[62] Other writers have used a Gramscian observation to illustrate the legitimizing effect of the 'civilian' sphere, once it is appropriated within a totalitarian agenda. Educationalists argue that:

> The institutions of civil society, ranging from education, religion and the family, to the microstructures of the practices of everyday life, contribute to the production of meanings and values, which in turn produce, direct and maintain the 'spontaneous' consent of the various social strata of society to that same status quo.[63]

The employment of black domestic servants in white homes invariably meant that young white children were aware at an early age that blacks, though 'inside' the home were also 'outside'/different/and inferior to themselves.[64] Teachers, thinkers and church leaders were able to question the apartheid system but not meaningfully oppose it without the high risk of becoming traitors. It was said that 'in one sense the National Party is more than a party. It deems itself to be the only legitimate

---

58   Cock, *op. cit.*, p. 23.

59   *Ibid.*, pp. 55–6.

60   Manicom, *op. cit.*, p. 459.

61   Cock *op. cit.*, p. 115.

62   Bloom, *op. cit.*, pp. 132–7.

63   Volker Wedekind, Cassius Libisi, Ken Harley and John Gultig, 'Political Change, Social Integration and Curriculum: A South African Case Study', *Journal of Curriculum Studies*, Vol, 28, No. 4, p. 431, citing Holub R., *Antonio Gramsci: Beyond Marxism and Postmodernism* (London: Routledge, 1992), p. 7.

64   Thompson and Prior, *op. cit.*, p. 109.

political home for an Afrikaner'. Therefore there was a 'promotion of Afrikaner self-consciousness in every sphere of human activity'.[65]

Leonard Bloom suggests that children first identify with meaningful others within the family and school and then later let those significant others direct their educational, social and cultural learning. The importance of children's peers in cementing their political identity has been suggested in research on Northern Ireland, which was drawn attention to in Chapter Four. In Northern Ireland, identity within the community was distinctly polarized, leading to an environment where children could not help but find their perception of an 'other' seemingly affirmed in everyday life. Apartheid in South Africa can be seen to have achieved the same effect on white children. Their segregation informed their political understanding, and the holistic experience consolidated their opinion. This was particularly so in education.

Afrikaner Nationalization: Education

One Africanist has commented that '[a]partheid South Africa may be unique in the way it deliberately planned for the educational underdevelopment of the human potential of its majority population and articulated its objectives'.[66] African education was dealt with by the Department of Education and Training, and white education by the Department of National Education. Prior to the 1967 Education Acts, which allowed for administration from the provinces, nationalist politicians were determined that education remain centrally controlled, and for arguably highly potential reasons in the following words:

> [E]verything loses its meaning when the spirit of the nation is killed. Our schools must be able to make ... [the children] proud of this their only fatherland which the creator has given them. Therefore our education must be national ... fostering a love for those things which are one's own; ... love for their flag, their freedom and their national anthem must be impressed upon them daily. To the child these things must be beautiful and precious.[67]

These sentiments echo those expressed in different national contexts in the previous two chapters. South African education had been an issue of 'national' concern from colonial times. Leonard Thompson and Andrew Prior suggest that Afrikaner mythology was a central element of education that served the present by its distortion of the past.[68] In this respect South Africa shares Northern Ireland's experience of history as a social memory which infuses the present and is particularly suitable for socializing children. Historical mythologies when exposed, may explain origins of social structures in which people still operate, and how behavior is shaped by ideas

---

[65]   *Ibid.*, pp. 170–71.

[66]   Jakes Gerwel, 'Education in South Africa: means and ends' in Jack E. Spence (ed.), *Change in South Africa* (London: RIIA:Pinter, 1994), p. 84.

[67]   Thompson and Prior, *op. cit.*, p. 112.

[68]   *Ibid.*, p. 33.

of the past. Nazi Germany deliberately created a romantic history of Germany for its youth, in order to reinvent a different future for them.

The manipulation of the curriculum to suit racist ideology is a further example of how power is invested in the medium of education. Stephen Ball describes Africa as a laboratory for racist educational practices and points to the political legacy created by the way South Africans were told about their past. In the early part of the century South African school children were told a great deal about Britain particularly British heroism and battles and heroes, basically an overview of the benefits of Britain.[69] The colonial curriculum was later used as a means of establishing and perpetuating political inequalities amongst races. Historians assert that such 'school knowledge' is a political assertion. In the words of James Mangan:

> It attempts to establish the parameters of acceptable knowledge, impose ideological boundaries, determine the range of permissible interpretations, point the way to action – and, both overtly and covertly, create images of self belief and self-doubt.[70]

History was a cornerstone of Afrikaner Christian National Education. A history of Western civilization, and of whites in South Africa was taught to all racial groups and was widely used to legitimize the government's values. African people were stereotyped and their history distorted or ignored.[71] In summary, Christian National Education, based on Afrikaner exclusivity, underpinned and significantly perpetuated apartheid and politicized and militarized whites. For South African whites, the constant rationalization of apartheid as acceptable was fostered in schools through myths of Afrikaner nationalism and black African inferiority. In education policy and public speeches, the need for an uneducated workforce achieved through specific education management, underlay the rationale for not only separate education systems but considerable economic disparity.

Even in the last quarter of the twentieth century, South Africa has sought social control through education material. John Laurence has revealed how the majority of publicity material on South Africa used in numerous books, brochures, journals, glossy covers of magazines and also BBC material has included a 'false history' of South Africa, in order to legitimize apartheid by distorting the place of the African. During the 1970s for example, special education kits for American and British schools were produced about South Africa, putting forward the idea that the Bantu and whites arrived on the southern part of the continent at the same time, rather than the view that the colonists displaced Bantu peoples. Many British and American

---

[69]   Stephen Ball, 'Imperialism, social control and the colonial curriculum in Africa', *Journal of Curriculum Studies*, No. 25, 1983, pp. 237–63.

[70]   J.A. Mangan, 'Images for confident control', in J.A. Mangan (ed.), *The Imperial Curriculum: Racial Images and Education in the British Colonial Experience* (London: Routledge, 1993), pp. 16–17.

[71]   Brian Bunting, *The Rise of the South African Reich* (Harmondsworth: Penguin, 1964), pp. 201–2.

schools may not have realized the nature of the information being used.[72] What is of interest is the perceived need, on the part of the apartheid regime to produce such propaganda for children overseas; it is another illustration of the presentation of historical myths as part of the militarization of education. It reveals recognition of the latent military power in Afrikaner children's bodies and minds.

Afrikaner Militarization

In this discussion of South Africa the term 'political violence' rather than conflict will be used, meaning 'acts of physical destruction that impinge on power relations in a society'.[73] This part of the study will look at the Afrikaner militarization of society which was such a prominent feature of the political violence that took place. 'Militarization' refers to the 'social process that involves mobilization of resources for war and expansion of the power and influence of the military as a social institution'.[74] There was a concentrated attempt to socialize Afrikaner white male youth into a rigidly masculine and militarized body. Boys in white communities were encouraged to become involved in military activity; they were told that one of the benefits of this was that they could 'look like men'.[75] Their role was portrayed as increasingly urgent and was compounded by the government's appeals for an increase in the size of white families to off-set the ratio of 'nine blacks to each white'.[76] In South Africa, the age distribution is younger than the international average, and it was expected that 60 per cent of the population would be under the age of twenty by the year 2000.[77] Thus the white community's perception of itself as a minority race surrounded by a rapidly expanding black Africa contributed to its sense of insecurity.

From 1976, white sixteen-year-olds had to register for paramilitary training in the South African Defense Force (SADF) school cadet system. They were expected to develop a sense of responsibility and love for country and national flag, instilled in civil defense and good citizenship training.[78] The Cape Education Department Cadet Training Manuals refer to the effectiveness of Nazi recruits in terms of their physical fitness, and stated that young people were under particular threat from revolutionary attack. In 1972 the Youth Preparedness Programme began in Transvaal schools. A compulsory subject, it included military preparedness, discipline and patriotism, outdoor activities, veld schools, and general indoctrination. The educational

---

[72]   John Laurence, *Race Propaganda and South Africa* (London: Victor Gollancz, 1979), p. 91.

[73]   Jacklyn Cock, *op. cit.*, p. 4.

[74]   *Ibid.*, p. 25.

[75]   Cairns, *op. cit.*, p. 123.

[76]   Ursula J.Van Beek (ed.), *South Africa and Poland in Transition: A Comparative Perspective* (Pretoria: Human Sciences Research Council, 1995), p. 116.

[77]   *Ibid.*, p. 142.

[78]   Cock, *op. cit.*, pp. 68–9; see also P. Frankel, *Pretorias Praetorians: Civil–Military Relations in South Africa* (Cambridge: Cambridge University Press, 1984).

environment was in effect militarized.[79] Experience in the youth wing of the National Party, Nasionale Jeugbond, for example, was particularly associated with later extremism evidenced in South African Members of Parliament. Pressure was placed on young men not to be 'mommy's little boys' in the words of the Minister of Defense, and the Defense Force promoted itself as engaged in 'making a man of boys'.[80] A degree of socialization was thus imposed by the conflating of manhood, masculinity and militarization. During 1973, war games and war toys were popularized and made familial and acceptable, advertised as 'the family games of the future'. This may have been a deliberate attempt at 'family' socialization.[81]

During the 1980s the SADF became increasingly involved in shaping the South African education system. The subject of 'Youth Preparedness' was added to the education system's curriculum and the syllabus and textbooks inculcated a militaristic attitude and indoctrination in apartheid. Pupils also had a code of honor in which they stated that they would swear allegiance to the volk. Thompson and Prior argues that for the whites, the family church and school provided the same socialization process by segregation and theories of racial superiority; there was no opportunity for a different experience.[82] Schools were the key instrument of socialization; they were thought of at the time as 'the vehicle by which modern society transmits its most important values to young people'.[83] The corollary of Afrikaner education was that by design, its implicit subject (the African or 'Bantu' child) was also politicized. This next section will turn to the politicization of African children, as victims of and also instruments against apartheid. The section begins with the nationalization of Africans which occurred through the apartheid system of appropriation and manipulation of their education.

African Nationalization: Education

The 1995 Education White Paper titled 'Education and Training in a Democratic South Africa: First Steps to Develop a New System', stated that:

> In the post-World War II period, the struggle for equal educational rights and equal citizenship became completely identified, because the denial of equal educational rights constituted a direct attack on the human dignity and life chances of the vast majority of South Africa's peoples. As a result, schools, colleges and universities became part of the arena of political mobilization and confrontation with the security forces.[84]

'The National Party government, over a forty-year period, blatantly used education policy as an instrument for social control, designed to maintain white supremacy

---

[79]   *Ibid.*, pp. 68–9.
[80]   *Ibid.*, pp. 70–71.
[81]   *Ibid.*, p. 73.
[82]   Thompson and Prior, *op. cit.*, p. 112.
[83]   Grundy *op. cit.*, p. 58.
[84]   *Ibid.*, p. 39.

at the expense of black aspirations to benefit from the fruits of modernization.'[85] In 1948 the Nationalist Party renewed debate as to whether blacks were to be part of a common Westernized society or were to be segregated. By 1949 they had appointed a Commission on Native Education and its subsequent report (the Eiselen Commission's Report in 1951) became the basis of Bantu education legislation introduced in 1953. The report made clear reference to what were seen as blacks' inherent racial qualities, and their distinctive characteristics and aptitude.[86] Much of this analysis was informed by the same racist thinking which influenced some European philosophy, in particular Nazi theory. That the blacks were considered naturally underdeveloped was overtly articulated in education policies. Bantu education, contributed to the socio-economic freezing of millions of blacks who were unable to learn and develop educational skills in the sparse, tri-lingual, underdeveloped schools made available to them.

The Minister of Bantu Education said in 1959 that 'the Bantu must be so educated that they do not want to become imitators (of the Whites), but they will want to remain essentially Bantu'. The report was severely criticized by various proponents of race relations.[87] Dr M'Tikulu, a prominent African educationalist, argued that, 'Africans seek for integration into the democratic structure and institutions of the country' and the most effective way of achieving this was through education.[88] Dr Verwoerd had stated in the 1950s that education was only designed to produce workers for laboring jobs.[89] In effect this meant very little education. Much of this education was taking place in huts with no facilities, appropriate to the blacks' 'potential', and thus drew further attention to the superiority of Afrikaner Christian National Education. As the blacks were undereducated and their employment opportunities limited, so the whites' racist and selective values seemed validated and the notion of difference heightened. In 1965 the Bantu Education Department said that in order to realize the ideal of self-supporting Bantu communities, a place of honor continues to be given in the school to everything of value in the Bantu culture, so that the Bantu may thereby retain his identity. The 1966 Report said that its task was by means of the school and the products of the school, to lead the various Bantu nations to independence and self-reliance. [90]

One private independent group of Afrikaners did however criticize Bantu education as short sighted and flawed, arguing that 'because education is not merely a science and an art, but also a social force with a vital bearing on the social, moral and economic welfare of the country' the negative consequences would be felt by

85   Jack Spence, *op. cit.*, p. 12.
86   Horrell, *op. cit.*, p. 4.
87   *Ibid.*, p. 5.
88   *Ibid.*, p. 6.
89   Khotsio Seatlholo, 'Black schools in uproar', *South*, December 1980, p. 18.
90   Muriel Horrell, *Bantu Education to 1968* (Johannesburg: South African Institute of Race Relations, 1968), pp. 6–7.

whites.[91] This was however a minority opinion that perhaps could not compete with fearful and ignorant hearts and minds. One Afrikaner academic argued that progress towards equity was being made and the number of Bantu pupils completing basic education had increased by 38 per cent from 1959 to 1962 although certain groups were still 'relatively backward, owing to different levels of civilization'.[92] He neglected to mention that eleven times more Rand per capita was spent on white education.[93]

It was perhaps not considered by such academics and ministers that the repression of education might stimulate retaliation. Since education allows for mass congregation of youth – the most active cohort of society – it is not surprising that it also became the starting point for a movement of popular resistance during the 1970s. Education was turned into a window of opportunity to politicize and mobilize the majority of the politically active from the townships. This disruption created in effect greater gains for the oppressed group. The disruption of the official school system allowed the development of 'peoples education' which provided an opportunity to further politicize young people, emphasize the liberation struggle[94] and equip them for revolt.[95] Education reform became a means of expressing resistance and organizing mobilization. Children's sense of legitimacy was enhanced by the self-worth and esteem gained from such mobilization. The ensuing 1976 riots focused on the 'language issue' or the government's insistence on Afrikaans as the teaching medium. A leader of the Soweto pupils in 1976 and 1977, commented that:

> twenty years ago when Bantu Education was introduced, our fathers said: 'Half a loaf is better than no loaf', but we say: 'Half a gram of poison is just as killing as the whole gram'. Thus we strongly refuse to swallow this type of education that is designed to make us slaves in the country of our birth.[96]

Although the budget for Bantu education was increased almost tenfold between 1972 and 1980, this did not mean that the quality of education altered. Misleading facts and figures were presented which did not illustrate crucial qualitative inequalities. The same standard was expected and provided for in exam setting, as for whites for example, but the quality of teaching for blacks was inferior, leading to mass boycotts by children in 1980. The school boycotts of the 1980s also stimulated parents to form various civic rights organizations such as the National Education Crisis Committee in 1985.[97] Education was not officially classed by Afrikaners as a political issue though in 1985 per capita spending on education was as follows: 293.86 Rand was

---

[91]   *Education for South Africa: The 1961 Education Panel First Report* (Johannesburg: Witwatersrand University Press, 1963), p. xiv.
[92]   *Ibid.*, p. 70.
[93]   Laurence, *op. cit.*, p. 126.
[94]   Cairns, *op. cit.*, p. 128.
[95]   *Ibid.*, p. 81.
[96]   Seatlholo, *op. cit.*, p. 18.
[97]   Graham-Brown, *op. cit.*

spent on each African child and 2,746.00 Rand on each white child.[98] A year later Dr. Viljoen asked that education could be 'depoliticized'. Like many Afrikaners he could not understand that for as long as the racially based disparity in funding existed, the situation would always be 'political' and protests would continue. Emergency rule across South Africa was imposed on 12 June 1986 in order to suppress the civil rights protests against education and housing. During 1985 and 1986 the SADF was unable to end the school boycott and over 12,000 children were arrested and detained without trial.[99]

Members of COSAS (The Congress of South African Students) were targeted by police who were constantly active in and around schools. The SADF were often armed and stationed outside classrooms, regularly disrupting lessons. By 1989 up to a million school pupils were involved in boycotting and made significant progress in arresting the progress of apartheid and prompting reform. Education was classed as an area for political reform with some difficulty. In 1991 the democratic movement had to persuade the South African government that education should be discussed alongside political and constitutional issues. Very little was achieved until a National Education and Training Forum began in 1992. Black school children and students used the communal experience of oppression in education as a springboard of political resistance and not a means of change in itself.[100] However educational reform and people's education can be seen as a 'microcosm of the "macro" struggle for the achievement of democracy'.[101] As Linda Chisholm and Bruce Fuller note:

> The interconnectedness of the collective struggle against an oppressive education and the apartheid system, or of education and politics, meant that schools were not conceived as neutral space to which to return once the struggle was over, or as somehow insulated from it, but manifested the most fundamental social relations found in society. [102]

African Militarization

It is worth noting however that black African families could not mobilize the home or invoke the protection of the core family in the same way as the Afrikaners.[103] The black African family was more likely to have been fragmented through pressures of poverty and apartheid and so nationalist mobilization was initiated instead in the

[98]   *Subverting Apartheid: Education, Information and Culture under Emergency Rule* (London: IDAF Publications, 1989), p. 38.
[99]   *Ibid.*, p. 6.
[100]   Aslam Fataar, 'Access to schooling in a post apartheid South Africa: linking concept to context', *International Review of Education*, Vol. 43, No. 4, 1997, p. 340.
[101]   Linda Chisholm and Bruce Fuller, 'Remember people's education? Shifting alliances, state-building and South Africa's narrowing policy agenda', *Journal of Education Policy*, 1996, Vol. 11, No. 6, pp.700–701.
[102]   *Ibid.*, p. 702.
[103]   Unterhalter, *op. cit.*, p. 63.

only communal areas – the school, workplace and streets. South Africa is dominated by its youth and being a young country, its black population were readily mobilized and readily met with political violence against them. As in Northern Ireland, the street became their battleground. After the Sharpeville massacre of 1960 it was noted that young people were no longer 'beholden to adult leadership' and activated themselves into the leading resistance and youth organizations of the 1970s and 1980s.[104] Studies have shown that in terms of political development, peer groups are more important amongst black students than parents, especially compared to white, colored and Indian groups.[105] The Black Consciousness movements inspired youth initiatives to generate mass mobilization, putting children in the front-line with the aim of making South Africa visibly ungovernable. One culmination of this political violence was the allegedly indiscriminate murders of Afrikaans-speaking white families which took place from 1986 onwards.[106]

Peter Mokabo, former president of SAYCO (South African Youth Congress) noted that the youth were mobile, and as a group critical, and politically active.[107] The term youth is used typically to indicate young people between the ages of fifteen and twenty-four years. Black 'youth' however included younger children from twelve years and adults into their early thirties. The age of twelve is typically the age of majority for black Africans. This extended age range of youth is often found within 'junior' wings of paramilitary groups. Youth had its own historically founded associations of resistance against authority and an accompanying negative public image particularly in the minds of whites. Studies of stereotypes of black youth in South Africa reveal that they were perceived as violent, politically committed to a cause and often involved in political unrest.[108] In particular they were assumed to be assimilated into youth gangs and organizations such as SAYCO and the African National Congress Youth League. Such fear of black youth and children made them potentially volatile participants in organized protests and particularly over education and boycotts.

The United Democratic Front (UDF) a particularly significant organization for youth and schools, was launched in 1983 with half its members taken from the Congress of South African Students (COSAS). It was banned in 1985 and replaced by SAYCO, launched in March 1987 under the slogans, 'Freedom or Death – Victory is Certain' and 'Roar, young lions, roar'.[109] SAYCO had a membership of more than two million, with many more regional youth congresses affiliated to it. It followed the Freedom Charter of the ANC and its self-declared aim was:

---

[104] Kotze, *op. cit.*, p. 126.
[105] *Ibid.*, p. 130.
[106] *Ibid.*, p. 126.
[107] *Ibid.*, p. 118.
[108] *Ibid.*
[109] *Ibid.*, p. 128.

to politicise and unite the youth; to channel the militancy and creativity of the youth to the advantage of the entire national and class struggle; to strive for free, non-racial, democratic and compulsory education; and, to organise the unemployed youth for the struggle.[110]

During the 1970s and 1980s children in Soweto fought against the Police force and South African Defense Force respectively, in similar ways to children in Northern Ireland, by stone throwing and rioting within an organized command structure. The price they paid was however comparably higher since their younger status did not prevent then being fired upon. Between 1970 and 1986 up to 1,000 children were shot dead, and reports show that 55 per cent of them were shot in the back.[111] In the Soweto riots which began on 16 June 1976, 10,000 students and young children were involved in disruption which lasted a year. Security forces officially shot dead twenty-five Soweto students and thus helped foster a new generation of militants.[112] In late 1977 renewed protests began in Cape Town over the 'language of oppression' – Afrikaans – which was used throughout the educational system. Peaceful protest marches were broken up as police attacked schools. Schools became 'laboratories and fortresses of resistance, providing raw political education to the pupils passing through them and deeply influencing the youths outside'.[113] The tension within black schools and the school culture of repression and resistance was itself responsible for children's recognition of their potentially political bodies. Hundreds of children were killed and several hundred thousand imprisoned between 1984 and 1986.[114] The youngest armed fighters, 'The Young Lions', caused considerable disruption through rioting and street fighting and hence effectively gained world attention. There is now a memorial in Cape Town – to all the children – with a tree planted by President Clinton when he visited South Africa in 1998.

Psychologists have shown that such children can be aware of the political significance of violent acts at an early age. Psychologists working in South Africa believe that children have political knowledge and their political ideas are fundamental to their psychological response to violence.[115] Archbishop Desmond Tutu described them as 'a new breed of children. They believe they are going to die ... and the frightening thing is that they actually don't care.'[116] They may have a different or partial political knowledge compared to adults but it is still significant. After the riots, some children left to train with the 'MK Umkhonto we Sizwe' ('Spear of the Nation') or armed wing of ANC which had members as young as ten years old and

---

[110] *Ibid.*

[111] 'Apartheid's Violence against children', IDAF 1988 Fact Paper on South Africa, No. 15, p. 7.

[112] Cairns, *op. cit.*, p. 113.

[113] Cock, *op. cit.*, p. 219 citing Johnson S. (ed), *South Africa: No Turning Back* (London: Macmillan, 1992).

[114] 'South Africa', *New Internationalist*, No. 47, January 1977.

[115] Cairns, *op. cit.*, p. 109.

[116] *Ibid.*, p. 223.

many between the ages of twelve and sixteen. They became active in patrolling the townships in groups of 100 or 200.[117] The 'Young Lions' led very different lives to their counterparts; the white 'boys on the border'. Dan Motsisi, a black youth leader, said that for these armed boys 'soldiers meant only tear gas to them, policemen only enemy targets. There was such a great contrast with the young whites, still playing with toys and pestering their mothers for pop-corn and ice-cream.'[118] He perhaps underestimated the degree of military education that was taking place in between their ice-cream eating. Amongst black African children, therefore, there was very much a perception that they were politically motivated and useful in an adult world.

Leonard Bloom comments that such children's military response was in proportion with the violence they were subjected too. Apartheid was a violent ideology and the children who suffered under it responded assertively and passionately using similar means.[119] As Jack Spence has noted, the riots involving young people were the most violent to take place in South African history.[120] The presence of uncontrolled children or youth, and the international attention may have been a contributory factor in exacerbating the pressure for change. However, the initial trigger for children's violence may have been the level of individual insecurity brought by apartheid which led them to act and identify en masse in the first place. Social psychologist and psychoanalyst Leonard Bloom has looked at emotional defenses against power, and how individuals go about protecting their 'self' through collective identification and in particular ethnic collective identification. Citing Edward Said, Bloom argues that the most negative feature of apartheid was that it 'allowed people to believe that they were only mainly, exclusively white or black'.[121] This he argues hindered the emotional development of children whose attention was necessarily focused on this difference, at the expense of finding self worth in other respects. The notion of self worth, often bestowed by families, is central in surviving conflict situations.

It is, Bloom suggests, difficult to reverse emotional identification with an ethnic group and children go on to perpetuate myths of ethnicity which still need to be addressed and dispelled. This he predicted would evade even the Truth and Reconciliation Committee's attempts to reunite the country.[122] Myths of identity have helped to cultivate oppression in addition to the effects of poverty. In addition he argues that each generation is hindered by a 'deeply entrenched authoritarianism that permeates South Africa's social and political relationships. Leaders are seen as "fathers" and their followers in the main as disappointed children'.[123] Bloom argues that this has also created in effect adult 'children' of apartheid. Authoritarianism

---

[117]   *Ibid.*

[118]   *Ibid.*, p. 218.

[119]   Bloom, *op. cit.*, p. 129.

[120]   Spence, *op. cit.*

[121]   Bloom, *op. cit.*, p. 119 citing Edward Said, *Culture and the New Imperialism.*

[122]   *Ibid.*, pp. xiii and xiv.

[123]   *Ibid.*, p. 122.

and apartheid have enforced an infantilized status and identity upon the population. Adults, for whom survival has been more important than education, and for whom ethnicity has been their primary identification, remain emotionally impoverished and highly dependent.[124] As one school teacher noted recently:

> ... 'We still feel very much inferior to whites ... Sometimes when you do something perfectly they call you umlumgu (white man) as if a white man is capable of doing only good things' or 'I get angry with myself when my child's invited to his "white friend" and we feel honoured!'[125]

New South Africa: Nationalization

With regard to history education in the new South Africa, reformists and educationalists suggest that history teaching can play a part in nation-building and citizenship. Balance was not given to historical interpretations, and both white and black pupils were exposed to mythologized ideological bias and supposedly factual history. As Peter Kallaway commented 'the political assumptions and ideology of the ruling groups reached into the very classrooms of the new generation'. South African history has been taught in the context of political domination and conservation, versus resistance or critique, at all times.[126]

Present policies underway in the new South Africa include the 'Africanizing' of the curriculum and allowing pupils a greater awareness of African history and leaders. The report of the Curriculum Group of the National Education Policy Investigation stated that 'the curriculum is not a neutral or technical account of what schools teach; it is a contextual and historical settlement which involves political and economic considerations as well as competing interests'.[127] An alternative history curriculum could allow for the redress of past wrongs and restore the history of the oppressed people as part of the common heritage.

Problematically, distortions in the history of the continent are still unquestioned, partly because of the authoritarian and unquestioning culture in the teaching profession, which renders revisionist history dependent on the rewriting of textbooks for guidance, rather than critical re-evaluation.[128]

> Many of these schools have been unable to redirect their energies and remain dysfunctional. Within a curriculum context, the internalisation of the 'official narrative' has been thorough

---

[124] *Ibid.*, pp. 132–7.

[125] Gail Weldon, 'Post-Apartheid South Africa, Education and Society', *International Journal of Historical Learning, Teaching and Research*, Vol. 5, No. 1, 2005

[126] Peter Kallaway, 'History Education in a Democratic South Africa', *Teaching History*, No. 78, January 1995, p. 13.

[127] *Ibid.*, p. 15.

[128] Wedekind *et al.*, *op. cit.*, p. 422.

and many teachers struggle to deal with interpretations and alternative points of view. They often do not have the confidence to challenge that narrative.[129]

Black education as a site of political contest and political strategy has been little researched and is a pressing issue of post apartheid reform. There is new emphasis on textbook provision for blacks, more critical revisionist history and the racial content and organization of education is recognized by all parties as being in need of revision.[130] New objectives and values mean that there will be significant dismantling of the structure and resources in education as well as rolling curriculum development. Reforms have coalesced in a framework for action named Curriculum 2005. Its aims include 'confronting the challenge of the past and moving beyond the legacy of apartheid' and 'the challenge of the future and developing a curriculum that will provide a platform for the knowledge, skills and values for innovation and growth, and cultural creativity and tolerance for an African Renaissance'.[131]

> However, little attention has been paid to the attitudes and values of teachers which will impact on implementation. All South Africans who lived under apartheid have been conditioned in varying degrees to the attitudes and the prejudices of the apartheid society. If we are to embrace this values-driven curriculum and develop in learners a respect for human dignity, equality and social justice, then teachers need to develop these same values first and use them to transform their classrooms and teaching.[132]

> In South Africa, young people, the first generation, do not want to learn about apartheid and parents tend not to discuss it. Learning about apartheid inevitably means confronting the racism that is being submerged by the consumer culture that currently prevails. Not engaging in or creating a collective memory makes it easier to 'deny' the past with much less guilt and enables many young people to avoid choices other than those of consumerism. [133]

Although education is a vital part of democratization and state-building, the education process is only one part of social transition, including social transition into a 'secure' condition. In Mozambique and South Africa it can be shown that education is transformative only under certain social and political conditions. It can reproduce a social order, crystallize existing ideas, manipulate and propagandize the vulnerable, but it cannot on its own transform society unless the rest of society also has the possibility of change.[134] However for black South Africans and Mozambicans the

---

[129] Weldon, *op. cit.*

[130] Jacqueline Dean and Robert Sieborger, 'After Apartheid: The Outlook for History', *Teaching History*, No. 79, April, 1995, pp. 32–8.

[131] South African Curriculum for the Twenty First Century: Report of the Review Committee on Curriculum 2005, Presented to the Minister of Education, Professor Kader Asmal, Pretoria, 31 May 2000.

[132] Weldon, *op. cit.*

[133] Weldon, *op. cit.*

[134] Harold Wolpe and Elaine Unterhalter, 'Reproduction Reform and Transformation: Approaches to the Analysis of Education in South Africa', in Elaine Unterhalter *et al.* (eds),

educational process became an epicenter and vehicle of political mobilization. The long term goals of reformed education in South Africa and Mozambique have not yet been achieved. Laurence cites an imprisoned black man who stated simply that 'violence means suffering and death', and 'apartheid means suffering and death'.[135] Apartheid's influence on the health and education policies employed in South Africa, may also be seen as imposed violence, continuing today in the form of widespread disease, death, malnutrition and its associated arrested mental development and high infant mortality rate.[136]

A recent publication on the transformation of Southern Africa emphasizes that the political stability of the region is tied to the future of these children.[137] Children under fifteen make up the majority of the population of most Southern African states and the future is therefore in the 'hands' of children who are still not secure, whose environment is still in social transition even after a political settlement has been reached. In a sense they are the citizens that best illustrate the condition of a state, not just in their roles as soldiers and nationalists. According to Pinda Samao, '[t]he way a country treats its children is one of the sharpest reflections of its true character'.[138] In Angola, for example, more than half of the population are children, and the thirty-four-year history of physical and spiritual destruction has left four million children in need, and one million displaced.[139] Of the half a million dead almost two thirds were young children. Because of the psychological impact of war on children, through direct trauma or witnessing of events, their rehabilitation and empowerment may be difficult to achieve. This may be a critical issue in Angola, Mozambique and South Africa if the countries are to retain stability and move forward, particularly as a region.[140] Child mortality in Angola and Mozambique is amongst the highest in the world, due to military expenditure and destabilization policies exacerbated by South African support of rebel groups.[141]

Apartheid Education and Popular Struggles (London: Research on Education in South Africa, 1991); see also, Francine de Clerq, 'Policy Intervention and Powershifts: An Evaluation of South Africa's Education Restructuring Policies', *Journal of Education Policy*, Vol. 12, No. 3.

   [135]   Laurence, *op. cit.*, p. 123.

   [136]   *Ibid.*, pp. 122–5.

   [137]   *Transcending the Legacy: Children in the New Southern Africa* (AEI/SARDC/ UNICEF: Amsterdam, Harare, Nairobi, August 1995).

   [138]   *Apartheid's Violence Against Children,* IDAF Fact Paper on South Africa, No. 15, 1988, p. 7.

   [139]   Pinda Simao, 'Education in Angola in the Post-Apartheid Era: Overcoming Physical and Spiritual Destruction', in *Transcending the Legacy, op. cit.*, p. 61.

   [140]   Lucienga Muianga, 'Rehabilitation and empowerment of the victims of war and violence in Southern Africa' and R.H. Thomas, 'Rehabilitation and empowerment of children in difficult circumstances: the experience of Mozambique', in *Transcending the Legacy, op. cit.*, p. 161.

   [141]   Jeff Balch, Phyllis Johnson and Richard Morgan, 'Apartheid and Destabilisation in Southern Africa: The legacy for Children and the Challenges Ahead', in *Transcending the*

These children, their suffering, and their involvement in conflict has attracted a great deal of attention in the West through the media, and attempts to legislate for them in international law. War photographer Stuart Freedman argues that the particular publicity surrounding African child soldiers merely aids passivity in the West because they are rendered incomprehensible in the way they are presented. They are interesting because they seem out of place. How they do fit in and what they are doing and whether they are poor or political is generally not of interest. Such attention often does not explore the reasons behind their militarization. It also shows a David against Goliath; a 'good story' wherein armed children are presented as emblems of underdog outrage or hopeless victims.[142] This could also be based on the myth of innocence and the lack of understanding about how children are politically mobilized.

Ed Cairns also suggests that the domination of medical literature on children in Africa has left the impression that children are passive victims of political violence.[143] He claims that there has been very little research into children and war and much of it assumes a 'universal decontextualised model of child development' and does not engage with different realities of social constructs of the child across different cultures.[144] Most of the emphasis is on coping and stress and the psychological measures of participation and not socialization. Media editorials and medical research, and their publicized accounts of suffering children do little more than show a tragedy taking place, they do not look to see how it is able to occur.

Conflict in Africa is often attributed to a fight for shares of a shrinking pie of economic resources, in which individuals intent on protecting patterns of distribution and control harness whatever support they can from other states.[145] South Africa remains a deeply divided state and recent revisionist history of South Africa argues that the 'mineral revolution' requiring cheap labor after the 1880s to fuel industrialization, capitalism and ultimately white supremacy, created the circumstances of apartheid.[146] However the role of the child, notably in practices of nationalization and militarization, undoubtedly makes a contribution to understanding Southern Africa, even within more structural theories of capitalism and race. The impact of black children's repression may yet explain the current violent crime wave sweeping the townships of South Africa. Apartheid is not official policy but it remains institutionalized through poverty and in many hearts and minds less tolerant and much younger than the former president Nelson Mandela. The childhood legacies of apartheid will be kept alive in South Africa for a long time to come.

Legacy, op. cit., pp. 1 and 7.

[142] 'Children who kill: Photographs by Stuart Freedman, words by Blake Morrison', *The Independent on Sunday*, 7 October 1998, pp. 20–27.

[143] Cairns, *op. cit.*, p. 179.

[144] *Ibid.*, pp. 165–6.

[145] Oliver Furley, 'Introduction: Africa: The habit of conflict', in Oliver Furley, *Conflict in Africa* (London: Taurus, 1995), pp. 4–5.

[146] Nigel Worden, *The Making of Modern South Africa: Conquest, Segregation and Apartheid* (Oxford: Blackwell 1995).

The previous three chapters examined children's politicization, nationalization and militarization, in three very different historical settings. The sixth chapter will explore some of the theoretical dimensions of the material and arguments presented so far.

Chapter 6

Containment, Interdependence and Infant Power

Containment

The thesis has so far shown how concepts and practices have constructed children as political bodies and therefore as appropriate subjects for study in International Relations. The first two chapters illustrated the multiplicity and flexibility of concepts and constructs of the child, and the containment of their political representation. Case studies explored children's bodies in practices of political socialization, nationalization and militarization. This chapter is the theoretical heart of the thesis, and attempts to further explore the concepts and theories which underpin the constructed politicization of children already introduced. This final chapter comprises three sections using the themes introduced at the beginning of the book. These are:

- the containment of the political and the containment of the child
- the interdependence of child's world and the political world
- infant power.

These themes will be shown to underpin the nationalization and militarization of children's bodies evidenced in the empirical material used so far. Key International Relations texts which shed light on the relationship between constructs of the political and children's politicization will be drawn upon throughout the analysis. This chapter begins with two important moves. First, there is an exploration of how children's political agency may be achieved under the guise of their non-political status. Second, it exposes how theoretical assumptions about what constitutes the political in International Relations significantly contributes to the underplaying of children's politicization and also aids the construction and mobilization of the child as a political body. Together this discussion reveals some limitations of the discipline as a result of conceptual containment.

Contemporary and traditional International Relations theory can shed light on how the concept of the political is contained, and how children are apparently depoliticized. Critical security studies, feminism and theories of deconstruction/postmodernism in International Relations for example share the project of questioning how the human subject is politically constructed. Children's roles in conflict and security measures remain represented as exceptional to and therefore only of marginal interest to the main body of literature in International Relations, the main focus of which remains security. Children are generally found in the literature of International Relations in only a limited number of 'political' contexts, especially as victims and child soldiers. Children may be thought of as naturally and typically resident in a non-political sphere, namely of the innocent, weak and vulnerable, in families and houses, schools and workplaces. Outside this sphere, the 'political' defines and realizes itself. Newsworthy children are however 'found' within the political sphere: their childhood is simultaneously presented as 'lost'. Child soldiers are seen as a political anomaly because they are holding military power, and child victims attract attention as the ultimate essentialized civilians in need of humanitarian and/or political assistance. This too is symptomatic of the containment of the concept of the child as unpolitical. I argue that the 'political' and the 'child' are constructed so that they appear to be mutually exclusive or contained. The conceptual separation of child and the political makes it possible for the child to be specifically brought in to the political when necessary. A common example is as an emotive *raison d'être* of security practices, when a state is under threat.

The power of the infant, and the interdependence of the everyday child's world and political practices are not accounted for in traditional International Relations. Political socialization in Northern Ireland is maintained in the everyday sphere of the family, on the streets and inside the home. The sectarian divide is both performed and exacerbated by the perception of separate political and non-political spheres. Informal and formal spheres are brought together through politicized education, militarized youth movements and children's military roles. The media can also be seen to reflect a conceptual separation of informal and political spheres, in their reporting of children which renders their participation as exceptionally political rather than recognizing that such children are already politicized. Media reportage during the most active years of the troubles demonstrated the impact of conflict on civilians by showing the 'innocents' resorting to performing military roles. Children made headlines and symbolized the essence of the conflict for British reporters – revealing the senseless nature of sectarian violence. Children's presence and participation was reported as unnatural though its illumination further obscured the everyday politicization and nationalization of children's minds and bodies in other spheres. Almost all media accounts tell of 'military' children who lose their childhood, playing a zero sum game where the political or military sphere gains extra bodies at the expense of children's childhood. Children have also traditionally remained outside the parameters of military analysis, despite their intensive use. Denial of their activities and their place in historical record contributes to their continued invisibility as a political force in their own right. International Relations contributes to this invisibility by its focus on relations between states, defined narrowly as the business of governments, and marginalizing internal matters as a result of seeing the international as an autonomous sphere. Traditional International Relations assumes that state actions do not make civilians/children insecure and that internal matters do not significantly contribute to international affairs.

In Northern Ireland and South Africa the extent of the fighting in civilian areas, and the participation of youth and children has been played down by observers in the media and in academia. Minimalist terms were used in the media to describe the actions of the ANC, and the power of the youth resistance movement, despite the militarization of the white social institutions as if prepared for civil war. In Belfast and Derry/Londonderry, 'riots' and unrest' were terms used in descriptions of intense conflict, thus reducing the everyday civilian/military participation to temporary acts of frustration or spontaneous crime; as if anarchic rather than organized resistance.[1] The roles played by children in each case-study cannot be adequately conceptualized as civilian or military. It is therefore worth looking in more detail at how these spheres are constructed and separated in International Relations.

The domestic politics/international relations divide in International Relations remains the principal justification for the existence of a separate discipline and thus retains a crucial symbolic importance. International Relations is the product of the separation 'between the public sphere of politics (and economics) and the private sphere of families, domestic labor and reproduction',[2] which has been sustained in political philosophy and exhibited in almost all current texts on politics and security. As Charlotte Hooper explains, 'International Relations then symbolically forms a wholly masculine sphere of war and diplomacy, at the furthest conceptual extreme from the domestic sphere of families, women and reproduction in the private/public/ international divides of modernity'.[3]

Children in International Relations are, however, present in the political and the private sphere as the cases demonstrate. Their presence is constituted in what we think of as 'us' and 'what we perceive as threats to "us"'.[4] Ken Booth talks of the need to reinvent International Relations, by 're-examining basic concepts; opening up what has been dehumanised; degendering what has been gendered; celebrating confusion rather than certainty; and listening carefully to the subject's "screaming silences"'.[5] Cynthia Enloe validates this disruption in her observation that '[n]o individual or social group finds themselves on the "margins" of any web of relationships without some other individual or group having accumulated enough power to create the "centre" somewhere else'.[6] She attributes the discipline of International Relations

---

[1]   Morris Fraser, *Children in Conflict* (Harmondsworth: Penguin, 1973), p. 58.

[2]   Charlotte Hooper, 'Masculinities, International Relations and the Gender variable: A cost-benefit analysis for sympathetic gender sceptics', Department of Politics, University of Bristol, July 1997, unpublished paper, p. 26.

[3]   J. Anne Tickner, *Gender in International Relations: Feminist Perspectives on Achieving Global Security* (New York: Columbia University Press, 1992), p. 30.

[4]   Marysia Zalewski and Cynthia Enloe, 'Questions about Identity in International Relations', in Ken Booth and Steve Smith (eds), *International Relations Theory Today* (Oxford: Polity Press, 1995), p. 284.

[5]   Ken Booth, 'Dare not to Know: International Relations Theory versus the Future,' in Ken Booth and Steve Smith (eds), *op. cit.*, p. 330.

[6]   Cynthia Enloe, 'Margins, silences and bottom rungs: how to overcome the underestimation of power in the study of international relations', in Smith, Booth and Zalewski

with some of this power, writing that 'in International Relations, the *raison d'être* for studying international politics is explanation, cause and effect'.[7] She points out that by definition, those who are marginalized, silenced and on the bottom rungs 'are precisely those who lack what it takes to have a meaningful impact on the course of those particular events that together cause certain regional or world patterns to take the shape they do'.[8] Children, then, are denied causality, and by extension a place in the political and so in International Relations.

It is the categorization of such social groups as non-political which is particularly disabling, and as the politicization of children's bodies shows, incorrect. As Joan Scott writes, '[a]ny unitary concept rests on – contains – repressed or neglected material and so is unstable, not unified'.[9] Earlier chapters have shown constructs of children which are used to downplay their political power. In particular the idea that children are naturally unpolitical serves to deter further analysis of them. International Relations 'presumes a priori that margins, silences and bottom rungs are so naturally marginal, silent and far from power that exactly how they are kept there could not possibly be of interest to the reasoning, reasonable explainer'.[10] International Relations and its component subjects engaged in a search for explanations of power has only recently recognized that it too contests and contains power as a discourse.[11]

> If, in Clausewitzian terms, war is the extension of politics, can we speak of politics being extended through the arms of an eleven-year-old? The question isn't rhetorical: What, exactly, does this say about the nature of power? Of force? And of political participation? No state code in the world today recognizes a child as an adult political actor. So what politics are forged in the conveyance of war through nonpolitical actors, through underage soldiers?...[12]

Thinking about how we selectively lose and find children in our thinking about International Relations is possible owing to significant re-evaluating of the discipline over the last fifteen years, particularly with the opening up and deepening of security studies and gender sensitive analysis.[13] The discourse of traditional state-led security

---

(eds), *International Theory: Positivism and Beyond* (Cambridge: Cambridge University Press, 1996) p. 186.

[7]   *Ibid.*, p. 188.

[8]   *Ibid.*

[9]   Joan Scott, quoted in Jean Bethke Elshtain, *Power Trips and Other Journeys: Essays in Feminism as Civic Discourse* (London: University of Wisconsin Press, 1990), p. xviii.

[10]   Enloe (1996), *op. cit.*, p. 188.

[11]   See R.B.J. Walker, *Inside Outside: International Relations as Political Theory* (Cambridge: Cambridge University Press, 1990), and Mark Hoffman, 'Critical Theory and the International Politics Debate', *Millennium: Journal of International Studies*, Vol. 16, No. 2, 1987, pp. 231–49.

[12]   Carolyn Nordstrom, *Shadows of War: Violence, Power, and International Profiteering in the Twenty-First Century* (University of California Press, 2004) p. 76.

[13]   Jane Flax, cited by Christine Sylvester, 'The contributions of feminist theory to international relations', in Smith, Booth and Zalewski (eds), *op. cit.*, p. 257.

analysis for example, is particularly depersonalized: 'no children are ever born and nobody ever dies. There are states, and they are what is'.[14] The sphere of the child and per se the family and mother has been most silenced in International Relations which conceptualizes itself as distanced from these referents. This does not however mean that they are not thought about within the discipline. The concept of security at the heart of International Relations may be understood as ultimately the pursuit of security provided by states on behalf of their people. Children may be implicitly and explicitly referred to in justifications for security practices. What may be less evident is how the language of security is already contained, as if it is distanced from, and ultimately protecting and not using, children. One of the tasks of critical security studies then, is to recognize children's presence in concepts and practices of security and insecurity. In doing so it has also to reveal and tackle the mechanism of gendering which is employed all too effectively in marking out worthwhile subjects for analysis and securing, and thus invisibilizing and depoliticizing these same children. Not all children are invisible in International Relations literature, although references to them are sparse.

The construct of an ideal child is commonly employed in propaganda and security discourse as an iconographic symbol of what is being protected. It inevitably dissociates security practices from their human consequences. Carol Cohn's analysis of American National Security discourse shows how it 'shapes expectations, interpretations and fixes boundaries' and 'skews what is discussed and what is thought about'. Weapons may be spoken of only in the 'most clinical and abstract terms, leaving no room to imagine a seven-year-old boy with his flesh melting away, or a toddler with her skin hanging off in strips.'[15] She continues:

> what gets left out then is the emotional, the concrete, the particular, the human bodies and their vulnerability, human lives and their subjectivity – all of which are marked as feminine in the binary dichotomies of gender discourse.[16]

What gets left out is what is deemed politically uncomfortable in favor of the comfortably political.

Critical Security theorists, feminists and postmodernists have questioned and problematized the state and the pursuit of national security as secure concepts in International Relations. Traditional approaches do not recognize and cannot explain the relationship between children, the state and war which is clearly expounded in the empirical evidence, on these terms. The direction of thought is that of states in relation to other states, leaving threat construction within and by the state largely unexplored. Recognizing the state's dependency on children might thus be seen to open up a Pandora's box in security studies. Spike Peterson points out that although

---

[14]   Jean Bethke Elshtain, cited in J. Anne Tickner, *op. cit.*, p. 42.

[15]   Carol Cohn, 'War, Wimps and Women: Talking Gender and Thinking War', in M. Cooke and A. Woolacott (eds), *Gendering War Talk* (Princeton: Princeton University Press, 1993), p. 232.

[16]   *Ibid.*

threats to the security of mankind from an increasing diversity of areas are being recognized, the state as prime referent, actor and contributor of security remains and continues to effectively delimit the extent of our analysis about security.[17] Theories of deconstruction are able to expose the partiality of security as it has been conceptualized thus far. The militarization of children, exposed in all the cases explored in earlier, would also suggest that security practices do not 'protect' children. Their use or their presence may also render them as protectors as it may also render them unprotected. According to Spike Peterson:

> the dichotomies of protector–protected, direct–indirect violence, war and peace are inter-woven; denying them as oppositional dichotomies means recognising the complexity of (inter)dependence, the interrelationship of oppressions and the uncertainty of security.[18]

In recognizing this relationship, feminist approaches and Critical Security Studies in effect remove the simplicities of security discourse, expose hierarchical binaries, and resort to a less popular position intellectually, claiming that the theories they critique are a manifestation of the problems they seek to address.[19] Theory can be a manifestation of practice, and not theorizing children can mask their use in practice. Children are thus a manifestation of power in International Relations which is yet to be fully located and unveiled. As Enloe writes: 'omitting a myriad strands of power amounts to exaggerating the simplicity of the entire political system'.[20]

Steve Smith has shown how the 'ways in which International thought has been categorized, has created privileged, that is to say primary and dominant understandings and interpretations'. He makes it clear that 'a discipline's silences are often its most significant feature'.[21] 'The dominant strain in international theory has been one which sees ethics as applicable to the kind of community that international society cannot be.' So, he continues: 'it has tended to be a discourse accepting of, and complicit in, the creation and recreation of International practices that threaten, discipline and do violence to others'.[22] Thinking truthfully often means engaging not with the thrilling, but with the downright nasty.[23] Similarly 'all reification can be said to be 'a forgetting', and as Richard Wyn Jones suggests, it is surely right that we

---

[17]   V. Spike Peterson, *Gendered States Feminist (Re)Visions of International Relations Theory* (Boulder: Lynne Rienner, 1992).

[18]   *Ibid.*, p. 56.

[19]   Richard Wyn Jones, 'Travel without maps: thinking about security after the cold war', Richard Wyn Jones and M. Jane Davis (eds), *Security after the Cold War* (Brookfield, VT: Edward Elgar, 1996), p. 198.

[20]   Enloe (1996), *op. cit.*, p. 188.

[21]   Steve Smith, 'The Self-Images of a discipline: A Genealogy of International Relations', in Ken Booth and Steve Smith (eds), *International Relations Theory Today* (Cambridge: Polity Press, 1995) p. 2.

[22]   *Ibid.*, p.3.

[23]   *Ibid.*, p. xii.

'worry more about what lies beyond security studies' artificial borders – that which has been forgotten – than about any loss of focus or intellectual coherence.[24]

As the case studies illustrate, children's politicization takes place off the pages of a guide to politics. To look at political children requires an engagement with other spaces, other people, other disciplines and an understanding of International Relations' emergence as an exclusive set of knowledge assumptions about the 'international'. As Smith explains: '[i]nternational theory is but one aspect of a much wider range of social, political ethical and economic theory and these are aspects of International theory'.[25] He argues that an autonomous theory of International Politics has been the central thrust of the discipline. Thus the discipline of International Relations is firmly implicated in the question of how children and the private sphere are so invisibly politicized and ineffectively secured. The third debate in International Relations offers the most promising way into the child's world and its containment within the discipline. As Marysia Zalewski explains:

> [T]hose who hover in and around the post modernist camp would claim that the epistemologies and methodologies of modernism do not provide us with neutral or indeed innocent tools to learn about the world, but instead only provide us with the means to produce meaning in the world.[26]

In the academic debates of the last decade 'international relations as a discipline is accused of being reactionary, theoretically naive, male biased, gender insensitive and generally ill equipped even to start thinking about the problems of the contemporary world politics in any more than a superficial way'.[27] For postmodern theory, a core concern is how to 'destabilize the forms and practices associated with state sovereignty in order to allow ethical relations between self and other, insiders and outsiders, to develop'.[28] Postmodern discourses and practices suggest that the concept of threat is premised more on difference.[29] Such theories show a supplementary relationship between the 'containment of domestic and foreign others, which helps to constitute political identity'.[30] Containment of the political and the child, is at once personal, political and international, domestic and foreign. In the same way, intellectual containment is practiced as political containment and vice versa.

---

[24]   Richard Wyn Jones, *op. cit.*, p. 208.

[25]   Smith, *op. cit.*, p. 9.

[26]   Marysia Zalewski, 'All these theories yet the bodies keep piling up', in Smith, Booth and Zalewski (eds), *International Theory: Positivism and Beyond* (Cambridge: Cambridge University Press, 1996), p. 351.

[27]   Marysia Zalewski, 'Well what is the feminist perspective on Bosnia?', *International Affairs* Vol. 71, No. 2, 1995, p. 340.

[28]   Richard Devetak, 'Postmodernism', in Scott Burchill and Andrew Linklater (eds), *Theories of International Relations* (London: St. Martin's Press, 1996), p. 206.

[29]   *Ibid.*, p. 198.

[30]   *Ibid.*

How security is operationalized and justified also depends on contained constructs. The expansion of the security studies referent is not a sole solution to the containment of the concept of security, for the concept of containment is Janus faced in that it patrols and looks within as well as towards.[31] For example, Elaine Tyler May provides a detailed account of how the US policy of 'containment' was also administered in comprehensive detail down to the domestic and personal everyday lives of American families. Parameters of correct political behavior were clearly drawn well within the domestic sphere.[32] Traditional concepts of state security are similarly patrolled. They do not make reference to embodiments of security within society, as would be expected from a discipline that is primarily concerned with the position of the state in the anarchical sovereign system. Ken Booth and Peter Vale describe South Africa as the most distressed and insecure region in contemporary world politics. Such a state was made insecure from within, further destabilized and vulnerable through the traditional military security practices which reinforced a sense of threat and insecurity. In their words, apartheid was 'neither natural, nor inheritable, nor commonsensical, but its power was such that many people came to believe it was, and as a result it destroyed many lives'.[33] They continue:

> [n]o small part of the strategic license that enabled South Africa's minority government to destabilise the region in the 1970s and 1980s was the result of generation upon generation of South Africa's white youth learning – being taught – to look upon their neighbours as inferior and manipulated by external powers hostile to South Africa.[34]

As was illustrated in Chapter 5, the final dismantling of apartheid will also depend on education reform and the engendering of a new sense of dignity amongst many South Africans. The personal will help to secure the political. James Hamill, has looked at South Africa and Southern Africa in the transition from a state governed by realist principles to a situation of complex interdependence.[35] He argues that in the light of new dialogues of persuasion, and the recognition of the importance of economic development to peace and stability, the African National Congress (ANC) can be said to have used an holistic rather than a realist approach to security.[36] Hamill believes the focus should now be on economic development. The 'New' South Africa has no reason to invent itself as a stranded Western bastion to justify internal security. In the light of racism being dismantled and an internal defense force no longer prepared for civil war, the regional and international dynamics have

---

[31]   *Ibid.*

[32]   Elaine Tyler May, *Homeward Bound: American Families in the Cold War Era* (New York: Basic Books, 1988).

[33]   Ken Booth and Peter Vale, 'Critical Security Studies and Regional Insecurity: The Case of Southern Africa', in Williams and Krause, *op. cit.*, p. 330.

[34]   *Ibid.*, p. 331.

[35]   James Hamill, 'From Realism to Complex interdependence? South Africa, Southern Africa and the question of security', *International Relations*, Vol. XIV, No. 3, 1998.

[36]   *Ibid.*, p. 2.

thus changed. Economic development is now seen by many as the key to controlling poverty and unrest, and this will depend on navigating new understandings of societal stability rather than military security. Security is best understood as bestowed on and experienced by a whole community, and this includes children. This economic development will surely have to take into account the previously unrecognized presence of children.

The small world of everyday women and children was thus a vital part of the realization of apartheid and will continue to be the most crucial base from which to engender a sense of security. As Booth states 'the plain truth is that without the emancipation of women across Southern Africa there will not be regional security'.[37] Security begins at home. Men however are constituent within women's security interests, and vice versa. Women, if conceptualized as a special interest category, do not disturb the frameworks of power that subjugate them. The same can be said of children. 'The focus on women as a category keeps them segregated from "normal" International Relations conduct.'[38] Or as Booth puts it: '[t]o talk about security without thinking about gender is simply to account for the surface reflections without examining what is happening deep down below the surface'.[39]

Critical theorists in the third debate have similar priorities and goals as feminism but do not engage further with the subject of woman, either her specific insecurity or the gendering of traditional security concepts.[40] Andrew Linklater recognizes that theory plays a role in justifying, legitimizing and enabling forms of truth and forms of power. Theory in his eyes should recognize a project and if possible make this an emancipatory project.[41] As Christine Sylvester observes: 'We learn that supports and challenges to war – a core concern in International Relations – can be framed in gender terms' and that 'International Relations learns from everyday feminist theorizing how the conduct of international politics has depended on men's control of women, on gender mechanisms of power, and women as unheralded resources for men and their institutions.'[42]

Critical security studies can potentially expose and critique how the political and apolitical, the secured and the securing are constructed. Barry Buzan's People States and Fear,[43] for example is concerned with individual security and social threats, though his concept of security does not problematize the state.[44] Critical

---

[37]   Booth and Vale, *op. cit.*, p. 344.

[38]   Lara Stancich, 'Discovering Elephants and a Feminist Theory of International Relations', *Global Society* Vol. 12, No. 1, 1998, p. 132.

[39]   Ken Booth, 'Security and Self: Reflections of a Fallen Realist', in Williams and Krause, *op. cit.*, p. 101.

[40]   Christine Sylvester, *Feminist Theory and International Relations in a Postmodern Era* (Cambridge: Cambridge University Press, 1994), pp. 210–11.

[41]   Marysia Zalewski, 1996, *op. cit.*, p. 345.

[42]   Sylvester, in Smith, Booth and Zalewski (eds), *op. cit.*, pp. 266 and 267.

[43]   Barry Buzan, *People States and Fear*, 2nd edition (Hemel Hempstead: Harvester Wheatsheaf, 1991), p. 37.

[44]   Ed Cairns, *Children and Political Violence* (London: Blackwell, 1996), pp. 2–3.

Security Studies offers a way of seeing insecurity for families and children and by extension the community and state, as manifested within state practices traditionally thought of as contributing to their security.[45] Weak and damaged bodies, the disabled and the elderly all occupy apparently 'marginal' political spaces but with major implications. The impact of war on civilian mental health and mental health is vastly under researched compared to military mental health, despite civilians making up to 80 per cent of targets in war.[46] Psychiatry and psychology in particular have failed to address questions, or develop age based responses which are now crucial for the recovery of children. Children's resilience, and potential for resilience in all situations, with life long implications, is, like the Cinderella sister that is peace studies, also undervalued.

A more critical approach to security studies does focus on 'the powerless' for whom established world order is itself a source of insecurity, and recognizes that their insecurity contributes to world order.[47] Critical Security Studies promotes an emphasis on the individual, and the individual's condition as an indicator of security. A post-positivist feminist lens on the state, can reveal the structural violence of gender (and class) hierarchy, women's systematic insecurity as an internal and external dimension of state system.[48] Feminism can show how political power rests on and contains domestic and invisible power, in effect it masks and is parasitic on the most potent power at work.[49]

The children's world is largely that of the domestic sphere, traditionally separated from the international, the national interest and the 'political' proper. As a politicized group however children are posited in a feminine and domestic space naturally connected with women, the family and the home. Charlotte Hooper explains gender is not a variable one can add because 'gender constructions are relationally defined'.[50] As with critical and postmodern techniques, it is a matter of exposing and reidentifying what is already present. An analysis of gender at work requires an ontological and epistemological reconceptualization of what is already there.[51]

Less secure states or individuals may be constructed in political discourse as feminine and or infantile. As was illustrated in Chapter 1, the South/Third World, and its colonized populations have often been infantilized, either in racial caricature or in policies which render them naive and vulnerable and in need of patrimonial – Western – assistance. In aid programs and structural reforms, the Western model of

[45] Ken Booth, 'Security in Anarchy: Utopian Realism in Theory and Practice', *International Affairs*, Vol. 63, No. 3, 1991, p. 534.

[46] Cairns, *op. cit.*, p. 2.

[47] Richard Wyn Jones, 'Message in a Bottle? Theory and Praxis in Critical Security Studies', *Contemporary Security Policy*, Vol. 16, 1995, pp. 299–319.

[48] V. Spike Peterson, 'Security and Sovereign states', in V. Spike Peterson (ed.), *Gendered States: Feminist (Re) Visions of International Relations Theory* (Boulder: Lynne Rienner, 1992), p. 32.

[49] Marysia Zalewski (1996), *op. cit.*, p. 347.

[50] Hooper, *op. cit.*, p. 3.

[51] *Ibid.*, p. 1.

childhood, is the yardstick against which progress is measured, further contributing to the incommensurability of a universal human rights discourse, and condemnation of a Southern society held responsible for its 'out of place' children. In our simplistic way, we are motivated by 'disaster pornography' of these children[52] rescuing temporarily their innocence, asserting our political competence and equating 'development' with children's rights and children's development.[53]

Hooper writes of how International Relations has to reconsider its own responsibility in the fostering and 'shaping, defining and legitimating of such masculinity or masculinities' implicit in its own analysis' and suggests a move towards 'the (international) politics of identity construction'.[54] Such a move might be primarily concerned with deconstructing a core agenda in International Relations to reveal the ontological, methodological and epistemological limitations of mainstream approaches where research is limited to the 'public' if not the international levels of analysis. A sophisticated view of the construction of gender identity is that it is a multidimensional process, dependent neither solely on embodiment, institutional practices, or discourse/symbolism, but rather produced through the negotiation of all three.[55] Although the cases clearly show the state's reliance on the small world materially and theoretically, International Relations Theory does not yet sufficiently engage with this interdependence between the private and political spheres. A brief tour of the contending approaches in International Relations which aim to explore new referents and spaces, will illustrate the propensity of theories to construct and contain concepts of the political and the child. This snapshot of IR theory is post-Cold War and pre-9/11. It is also importantly pre-child.

As shown in Chapter Two, children's contribution to the global economy is vast, though there are few studies of how they are integral to it. If the International Political Economy 'denotes an area of investigation, a particular range of questions, and a series of assumptions about the nature of the international "system" and how we understand this system', it would be fair to assume that child laborers could be included in analysis.[56] That they clearly are not, may be seen as a consequence of the limited objectives in present theorizing of the international economy as a whole. Craig Murphy and Roger Tooze suggest that:

> in a fairly straightforward way, the construction of the universe of IPE reflects the policy concerns of the government of the United States throughout the era of US global supremacy and, especially, contemporary concerns about various challenges to that supremacy.[57]

---

[52]   On this theme see Erica Burman, 'Local, global or globalised? Child development and international child rights legislation', *Childhood*, Vol. 3, 1996, pp. 45–66.

[53]   Norman Lewis, 'The New Age of Interventionism: The Globalisation of American Liberal Discourse', 1996, British International Studies Association, unpublished paper.

[54]   Hooper, *op. cit.*, p. 4.

[55]   *Ibid.*, p. 6.

[56]   Craig Murphy and Roger Tooze, 'Introduction', in Craig N. Murphy and Roger Tooze, *The New International Political Economy* (Boulder: Lynne Rienner, 1991), p. 1.

[57]   *Ibid.*, p. 24.

They continue '[t]he principal issue so privileged in orthodox IPE is trade ... . That is international economy is the principal structure, and the international economy is trade between and among national economies'.[58] Trade of children's bodies is not included. The pluralist and liberal approaches to understanding the international economy thus far offer no explanation of children's roles in the International Political Economy. It was initiated as late as 1995 in the work of George Kent.[59] He argued that they are hidden there, just as they are hidden within national economies. Statistical information does not document the value of children's work because they are underage or unpaid, female, illegally employed or classed as informal laborers.

Identities, gendered and infantilized, are also constructed within the practices and structures of the economy. Indonesian factory workers are predominantly young and female and believe themselves to be subservient 'daughters' of the factory and 'daughters' of the state.[60] It is this patriarchal power relationship which legitimizes their slavery. They further limit their agency if they are disobedient or question their appalling working conditions. Stephen Roscow writes that '[s]ince women have rarely been regarded as participants within states, the recognition that women play significant and distinctive roles in global politics most easily dispenses with the traditional vocabulary and preoccupations of foundationalist themes in international political economy'.[61] But as Marianne Marchand writes, from the perspective of the developing world, this realization is late and only 'from the margins of feminist theory and the periphery of the global political economy'.[62] The recognition of 'women' in the economy is presumed to include children, though in many texts this may be unspecified, contributing both to children's invisibility, impotence and unwittingly rendering them as feminine, by conflating them with women. George Sorenson, in a paper titled 'Development through the eyes of the Child', also notes that in a key text on development, children are vaguely considered in chapters on population and education.[63] In such texts population policy, education and health practices are rarely recognized as vehicles of nationalization or militarization and are seemingly passed on or relegated to development studies rather than linked to broader issues of political stability and military security.

The specific placing of children into sub-sections of International Relations or World Politics is interesting for two reasons. It indicates where children are thought to have most relevance, and secondly, any inclusion of children, even in an 'associated' field contributes to a sense that they are recognized and they are not being ignored. Neither assumption may be justly made. As psychologist Erica Burman has shown,

---

[58]   *Ibid.*, p. 25.

[59]   George Kent, *Children in the International Political Economy* (Basingstoke: Macmillan Press, 1995).

[60]   Cynthia Enloe, University of Bristol, Feminism Symposium, 18 October 1997.

[61]   Roscow, *op. cit.*, p. 12.

[62]   Marianne H. Marchand, 'Latin American Voices of Resistance: Women's Movements and Development Debate', in Roscow, *op. cit.*, p. 56.

[63]   George Sorensen, 'Development through the eyes of a child', Development Research Series Working Papers, No. 19 (Denmark: Aalborg University, 1986) pp. 1–2.

the publicizing of child victims acts as a signal of concern and accommodation of a subject area, and is almost a substitute for further analysis or even action – too close to home. The iconography of victim children is but a superficial acknowledgement of their presence and underplays their potential political role. As contended throughout the volume the containment of the 'political' also keeps us from recognizing children as constructed political bodies.

New developments in International Relations do however aim to address the broadening out of the concept of the 'political' in that it can be seen as self reflective and aware of its own 'social construction'. This prominent new perspective is gaining ground as it finds interests and identities of states to be highly malleable and a product of specific historical processes and the impact of ideas. Two manifestations of this, evident in post-Cold War theorizing are the specifying of culture and identity in discourses of International Relations, particularly within new ethical or normative approaches. This new approach which claims to be concentrating on dominant factors constructing political identity might therefore offer an interpretation of children's political construction.

In a prominent text which attempted to significantly open out International Relations, 'The Return of Culture and Identity in International Relations', is heralded by Yosef Lapid and Friedrich Kratochwil in the opening line '[c]ulture's ship has finally come in, and the time is ripe for an inventory of its cargo'.[64] The title of the book merits the question of whose culture has returned. Culture has been present all of the time, in particular the culture of dominant International Relations Theory/theorists. Do we not in the West have a culture, or is it only to be found 'out there'? Culture and identity, of someone and somewhere are already present in any International Relations theory. To claim to be opening out 'the political' – by now stocking 'the cultural' – is claimed with all the subtlety of a market trader. Rather than attention going to what is missed out within theories – for example referents such as children, a new phenomenon seemingly from 'out there' is identified, celebrated and added. Culture and identity sound like the opium of the theorists, the feel good factor for theories, directly 'imported' from hot sunny places where 'ethnic', 'cultural' people live and keep dying, 'differently'.

The book is part of the project of social constructivism, though the referents and priorities remain distinctly realist and pluralist, and in their particular recognition of 'culture', the meaning of the word is seemingly lost. Certain identities and cultures such as British or American have been privileged throughout the writings of International Relations theory which has not been culturally sterile. The project of constructivism has been defined by Alex Wendt as the following:

---

[64] Yosef Lapid, 'Culture's Ship: Returns and Departures in International Relations Theory', in Yosef Lapid and Friedrich Kratochwil (eds), *The Return of Culture and Identity in International Relations* (London: Lynne Rienner, 1996), p. 3.

[F]irst states are the principal units of analysis for international political theory; second, the key structures in the international system are inter-subjective rather than material; and third, state identities and interests are an important part of these social structures, rather than given exogeneously to the system by human nature or domestic politics.[65]

Western, masculine, realist, military, senses of identity and culture have prevented theorizing about other culture's values and also prevented theorizing about children. Alex Wendt embraces culture by claiming to take a more sociological rather than economic approach. However, states are still the principal actors in the system he describes and identity is created by structures in the state system. In this theory there is still no room for children. The new phrase in this theory is 'culturally structured', but the political cultures of which children remain an unobserved part are not referred to. Given this definition of the new wave of constructivism, theories will continue to be contained.

Throughout his analysis Wendt does not include any further examples of the manifestations of culture though he later argues that 'a cultural understanding of international society means bringing ethical considerations back into the picture'.[66] Just because past theory does not use explicit ethical terms, does not mean that it has been non-ethical. Theorists have chosen what they want to explain, be it states, structure, bipolarity or nuclear deterrence. This selection of what to address and study is an ethical standpoint. The writings of International Relations are riddled with ethics. Ethical considerations might be better explained as previously conservative rather than non-existent. In Man the State and War, Kenneth Waltz concludes that '[a] foreign policy based on the image of International relations is neither moral nor immoral, but embodies merely a reasoned response to the world about us'.[67] The claim to theorize without ethical values is a highly positivistic notion. Such theorists have failed to realize that their theories are in fact infused with values and ethics. Their own interests and priorities live on within the theories. Academics in International Relations have recently argued that they have a duty to contribute to the strengthening of civil society.[68] But to achieve this they argue for a divergence of policy from theorizing, giving the latter 'practitioners' more room to expand their ideas, lengthen their journeys and presumably find new concerns, unforced by the direction of policy.

The next section of the chapter will demonstrate that theory and practice cannot be divorced in this way and are inextricably linked. It is the perception of theories of the political seemingly being divorced from political practices that also fosters the greater illusion of there being political and non-political spheres. This perception

---

[65]   Tim Dunne, *Inventing International Society, A History of the English School* (London: Macmillan, 1998), p. 36.

[66]   Naeem Ayatullah and David L. Blaney, 'Knowing Encounters: Beyond Parochialism in International Relations', in Lapid and Kratochwil, *op. cit.*, p. 82.

[67]   Kenneth Waltz, *Man, the State and War* (Columbia University Press, 2001), p. 238.

[68]   William Wallace, 'Truth and Power, Monks and Technocrats: Theory and Practice in International Relations', *Review of International Studies*, No. 22, July 1996, p. 309.

informs, reinforces and constructs identities and values about the political and the child, and underplays the connections made between their 'worlds'. Many practices involving children are constructed around a perceived separation of the children's world and the political world. The separation of the two constructs allows for their politicization, yet significantly underplays that politicization. The next section will further investigate the interdependence of the political world and the child's world, and how it is manifested.

Interdependence: The Child's World and The Political World

Security policy is a key way in which states control and fix their sense of identity. Societies create the threat 'other' against which the self is contrasted and similarly the state needs threats, a degree of insecurity in order that it generates security.[69] Similarly it can be seen that the 'self' is also given a stereotyped image, often a more aesthetic and childlike image than that of the 'other' or the threat. The image of the child has been instrumental in pleas to the national conscience, symbolic of life and society under threat. During the Cold War, nuclear war propaganda used by the United States and the Soviet Union featured sinister representations of Armegedon counterpoised with the blonde, beautiful child.[70] Similarly in 'mainstream International Relations we learn about a world of oppositions: us/them, west/east, soldiers/mothers, inside/outside: a world in which opposites are reified'.[71] In being presented with these oppositions, separateness and implied hierarchies we are also less able to imagine the interconnectedness and interdependency of these apparent oppositions. The Nazis in particular sustained the illusion of a non-political or private realm by drawing attention to the child's sphere as if it was separate and of high importance in itself, a subtle move away from recognizing reliance on the sphere.

By championing the mother's role the Nazis recognized that the private could be of political and international significance. This was easily achieved because of the previous presentation of the child's race, development and health being intrinsically linked with the state's future. As with other cases the domestic sphere was activated though at no point was its appropriation and damage seen by the state as also contributing to societal insecurity. The private sphere remained constructed as private, though in practice it was almost surgically removed. The separation of children from the political and the special attention given to them, can be seen to be parallel with the separation of the private from the political/public in International

---

[69]   See for example recent work by David Campbell, 'Political Prosaics, Transversal Politics and the Anarchical World', in M. Shapiro and H. Alker (eds), *Challenging Boundaries: Global Flows, Territorial Identities* (New York, Columbia University Press, 1995), pp. 24–45.

[70]   Sharon Stephens, 'Nationalism, Nuclear Policy, and Children in Cold War America', *Childhood: A Global Journal of Child Research*, Vol. 4, No. 1, 1997, pp. 103–23.

[71]   Marysia Zalewski, 'The Women "Women" Question in International Relations', *Millennium, Journal of International Studies*, Vol. 23, No. 2, 1994, p. 416–17.

Relations, and the special attention given to children in other subject areas. To find children as political bodies occupying both spaces simultaneously, and to find conflict prepared for and sustained in the home and civilian sphere in all the case studies, thus destabilizes core assumptions to be found in much contemporary International Relations and calls into question this relegation of the smaller world to outside political analysis. The political sphere is shown to be intimately connected to and dependent on the domestic sphere primarily though not singularly through the use of children.

Conflict, periods of military intensification, secession or disintegration, give rise to intensified practices of nationalization and militarization. The case studies show that practices of nationalization and militarization which involve appropriation of the child and familial sphere are often in place and active prior to the actual outbreak of conflict. The incorporation of children and the family into militarized practices, and the logical corollary of this, the targeting of the (enemy) civilian sphere dispels the myth that children are simply the protected or only victims. Children and their guardians are a form of security in themselves (whether alive or dead) and are clearly treated as such. Terrorism, civil war and total war, are dependent to varying degrees on the manipulation of children, and share similar rationales. Battles which use children's bodies and minds as effective weapons have so far taken place without being recorded in the pages of security textbooks and have remained outside the knowledge of those who accept the typically presented parameters and ontology of security. Women and children are still fought for as if they are 'safely inside' and away from the politics that will be acted out for them. To notice anything different would be to shatter this illusion. It is not that children are not thought about at all, it is that they are represented in such a way as to also serve political purposes. Our sympathy with them may conflate with feelings of militarized protection, or our attention on them may in Robert J. Lifton's words create a 'domesticisation of the unthinkable'.[72]

Lifton uses the term 'dissociated language' to describe how constructs of children function within language and are deliberately employed to counteract genocidal imagery. For example, nuclear weapons are described in terms of little boys and babies, explosions are likened to births, and nuclear capability associated with creative capacity, despite its destructive potential.[73] This is perhaps a classic example of the construct of the child to create 'dissociation' at the highest level of strategic or nuclear culture.

The case study of the child as a political body in Nazi Germany is also an account of constructed and converging subjects and referents of security practice. As one might expect of a totalitarian regime, almost every conceivable means of creating

---

[72]   Robert J. Lifton, cited in JoAnne Brown, ' "*A* Is for Atom, *B* Is for Bomb": Civil Defense in American Public Education, 1948–1963', *Journal of American History,* Vol. 75, No. 1, 1988, p. 84.

[73]   Robert Jay Lifton and Eric Markusen, *The Genocidal Mentality: Nazi Holocaust and Nuclear Threat* (London: Macmillan, 1990), pp. 214–15.

civil obedience and loyalty was put into practice. The political overhauling of every child's and family's everyday experience created absorbing compliance from anxious parents and a civil emotional distraction from more barbaric activities. The child's world was managed to an unprecedented degree, destroying a clear distinction between the personal and the political. Children were given political functions yet retained a non political identity.

The birth rate was a basic gauge of state strength and families and young children were recognized as raw material of defense. Scientific debate and the theories of eugenics, merged with security discourse and were simplified into public advice. Political motives or realist insecurities were to an extent concealed in the moral glare of child care policies and the simplicity of the appeal. From 1914, analogies were made of the state as a biological entity, subject to attack from outside, particularly if it fostered weak children inside. This articulation of the threat as beginning at home as well as close to home, allowed for greater infiltration and management of the personal sphere in the national interest. The child, and the child within women, embodied the future security of the state. Hitler made great play of the fact that he depended on the functioning of the domestic sphere to achieve his aims. However the mother's responsibility was matched by an equal measure of impotence. The laws on motherhood and the intense regulation of the domestic sphere became a scrutinized means and barometer of social cohesion, itself the basic component of a totalitarian project. Political socialization was disseminated through mothers and children. In the case of Nazi Germany, motherhood and the child were of political and patriarchal interest to the Nazi regime.

In Mozambique, the family was also an important military resource and target. Its destruction was often strategically managed in order that family unity was destroyed rather than all members killed. Through separation from their children, mothers were prevented from providing emotional support or skills and resources essential to everyday survival and family stability. In addition the separation brought with it social isolation and a lack of respectability. A particular practice of the military was to target the child so as to reach the parents, knowing that without their children they would no longer have a will to fight. In addition children were used to commit atrocities against their own families ensuring that they would not be able to return to their extended communities. The totality of these experiences was to create a denationalization of the state through the destruction of the family and manipulation of the child. Militarization of Mozambican children relied on the idea that they were far more malleable than adult soldiers, and both their use and their activities would destroy the family based fabric of Mozambican society. In Mozambique, children's presence outside of the family, and their engagement in warfare was invoked by Renamo as an indicator of societal instability. In turn the use of children can be shown to have been a cause of further instability within Mozambique. As in Nazi Germany and Northern Ireland child soldiers were described as if men, though the implications of their participation as 'children' were central reasons behind their forced involvement. In less written about practices in warfare, there may be little effort made by soldiers to conceal the use of the child.

In the Serbian occupied territories of Bosnia Hercegovina and Croatia, it is argued that the manhood of a soldier and the nationality of a country are simultaneously claimed through the rape of women and their impregnation. Serbian soldiers have talked of their desire to 'plant territory'[74] with new children, though in practice this description barely masks acts of barbarity, which have taken place involving all women, fertile or not. In Croatia, a legislative program to repopulate the nation has been attempted: the Croatian Movement for Demographic Renewal.[75] Non-mothers are referred to as 'non-women'; forced impregnation of women has been recorded and the legal directives on mothering increased. Women's identity is thus framed only in relation to their (future) children. The state is in essence personified or essentialised as the new-born child and the mother is conquered and appropriated as if national territory.[76] The identification of the Nazi mother as a soldier of race and an embodiment of national health was also central to Nazi perceptions of racial and military security.

The processes of nationalization explored in all the case studies show how women can reproduce nations, biologically, culturally and symbolically.[77] Women as mothers serve a political role as containers of the future nation or state. Nira Yuval-Davis argues that there are many ways in which this is manifested throughout political history: in the maintaining and enlarging of the national ideological and ethnic collective seen as vital for the national interest; in the reduction of the number of children as a means of preventing future national disaster; and when the 'quality of the national stock' is improved by encouraging those who are 'suitable' to have more and the others less.[78] In addition nationalist ideologies mobilize men to fight for the sake of 'women and children'. Each of these ways shows the strategic value of managed motherhood and cannot be analyzed without an understanding of the power of gender in discourse.[79]

At particular points in history, motherhood has been overtly drawn attention to as a site of nationalization. In Australia white women have been encouraged to produce more children and Aboriginal women discouraged.[80] Yuval-Davis has shown similar issues in the programs of both Israeli and Palestinian nationalists. The discourse of motherhood in Afrikaner nationalism and the African National Congress over

---

[74]   Roy Gutman, *A Witness to Genocide* (Shaftesbury, Dorset: Element, 1993), p. 76.

[75]   Jill Benderly, 'Rape Feminism, and Nationalism in the War in Yugoslav Successor States', in Lois West (ed.), *Feminist Nationalism* (London: Routledge, 1997), p. 65.

[76]   For a discussion of women as territory and women's bodies in boundary wars see Jan Jindy Pettman, *Worlding Women* (London: Routledge, 1996), pp .76 and 59–63.

[77]   Nira Yuval-Davis, *Gender and Nation* (London: Sage, 1997), pp. 2 and 22.

[78]   Nira Yuval-Davis and Floya Anthias, *Women-Nation-State* (London: Macmillan, 1989), p. 7.

[79]   Yuval-Davis, *op. cit.*, p. 195.

[80]   Jan Jindy Pettman, *Living in the Margins: Racism, Sexism and Feminism in Australia* (London: Allen and Unwin, 1992), p. 36.

the course of the twentieth century has also been instrumentalized in security practices.[81]

In Northern Ireland the civilian sphere and private sphere are the battleground of 'the troubles'. Nationalization is sedimented through the family and militarization made an extracurricular activity for children. The sectarian divided institutions give 'everyday' activities a political overtone. Terrorism and street fighting, violence or the threat of violence against the civilian population makes each individual a potential perpetrator or victim, leading Fraser to argue that children and parents are the combatants and there are no civilians in Ulster.[82] The roles are necessarily collapsed by the nature of the warfare. Terrorists aim at those with wives and children, the 'soft targets', and also use allegedly unpolitical bodies as a means of disguise, softening their intentions with innocent bodies. Because the familial sphere is under threat, and women and children perceived as soft targets, the perception of perpetrators in the conflict has remained gendered.[83] Naturally 'unpolitical' qualities assigned to women and children, has also enabled their use as paramilitary actors, above suspicion and below questioning. The smaller world, the unpolitical or softer world can thus be further appropriated as a resource for military and nationalist practices. Interestingly the killing of children is generally avoided in order to counter allegations of barbarity.[84]

Whilst within Northern Irish society 'politics' may not be spoken about in the home, it is lived in the home and the street. Terrorism uses small cells of individuals, often contained within the family, united against a common enemy: the 'other'. It has been understood that some children channeled their aggression into street fighting, riots and terrorist assistance, sharing a cause with their parents against mirror enemies and creating greater stability within family units. The conflict aptly illustrates the impossibility of separating a civilian from a military sphere, or finding a non-politicized child. Political socialization of children is unavoidable in the home or familial sphere. A dominant perception in Northern Irish society on both sides of the community is that the woman's contribution to the cause, and her primary role in society is to have children; a task which also serves to hinder her critical reflection of the situation. Similarly, Palestinian women's family responsibilities, and caretaking of children are allowed to become extremely woman-dependent activities, for the purpose of distracting, deterring and disassociating women from the other sites of political activities. Day-care centers for example are disallowed by

---

[81]   Deborah Gaitskell and Elaine Unterhalter, 'Mothers of the Nation: A Comparative Analysis of Nation, Race and Motherhood in Afrikaner Nationalism and the ANC', in Nira Yuval-Davis and Floya Anthias, *op. cit.*, pp. 61–3.

[82]   Morris Fraser, *op. cit.*, p. 8.

[83]   Begona Aretzaga, *Shattering Silence: Women, Nationalism and Political Subjectivity in Northern Ireland* (Princeton: Princeton University Press, 1997), p. 38.

[84]   Allen Feldman, *Formations of Violence: The Narrative of the Body and Political Terror in Northern Ireland* (Chicago: University of Chicago Press, 1991), p. 74.

the Israeli government. Children are seen and used as natural shackles on women in the community.[85]

In Mozambique, a developing country where the social memory was largely that of unsuccessful colonization and conflict, education was the only means of community identity and progress available. Children's education could determine their future potential. Renamo thus made the eradication of education facilities a military objective. They did not use education for renationalization, since they were a group committed to destruction rather than political socialization. In Northern Ireland by contrast the segregated school can be shown to politicize children's bodies by its very presence. The separation of children's learning in Northern Ireland substantially contributes to their perception of the 'other' as not part of their everyday present and therefore not part of their future. Postmodern and critical theorists have drawn attention to the ways that written history, of which school education may be considered a crucial conduit, is always partly an appropriation of the past for the purpose of the present. In Northern Ireland the most potent history is that which is also imagined and not committed to paper, the one that is acted out and reinvented through each generation. Memory and myth are also historical realities; the lies we tell ourselves are also truths, for we act upon them and are acted upon by them. History and myth were the cornerstone of the Afrikaner school socialization. The notion that the powerless have no history – a clear example of the big world creating itself using the little world – was pursued in Nazi Germany. Intellect was actively discouraged, text books destroyed and history 'rewritten'. The Nazi curriculum enabled the mass incubation of an invented past – that which served Nazi interests. Stories had a cartoon quality with good and bad characters, a focus on soldiers and fighting, glorious carnage and sacrifice. German success was a constant theme, or else successful battles in history. Coupled with the theme of spilt blood on the battlefield were racial theories of nationality and blood lineage.

As Marina Warner notes, 'folk tales powerfully shape national memory; their poetic versions intersect with history, and in the contemporary embattled quest for indigenous identity, under-estimating their sway over values and attitudes can be as dangerous as ignoring changing historical realities'.[86] In the former Yugoslavia, different factions have used oral folklore to raise heroes from the past into the present As Warner writes: 'There is nothing in the least childlike about fairy tales ... their task is to teach where boundaries lie.'[87] Stories told to children and stories they tell themselves easily lend themselves to political casting. In the playgrounds of Britain during 1992, school children pestered teachers to tell them that 'sadman insane' a demonized figure, would not reach them.[88] Nazis used folktales to substantiate racial fears of the other. Aryan fantasies employed an 'ancient enduring color code which

[85]   Enloe, *op. cit.*, p. 58.

[86]   Marina Warner, *From the Beast to the Blonde* (London: Chatto and Windus, 1994), p. 410.

[87]   Warner, *op. cit.*, p.xvi.

[88]   Jenny Murray, Radio 4, *Women's Hour*, 5 June 1998.

cast gods as golden boys and girls and outsiders as swarthy'. Blonde or golden color – which is typically bestowed on propagandized images of children, has a symbolic function. 'It was the imaginary opposite of "foul" it connoted all that was pure, good, clean.'[89]

In Northern Irish culture and historical recollection the myth has remained as powerful and educative tool as the history book. History is these children's shorthand for politics[90] and has emotional and theatrical overtones which help children to grasp and re-enact political grievances as if they were of today, thus making them of today. Simplified and cartoon-like management and presentation of the past and its divisiveness is rarely critiqued in formal literature though terrorists have cited their experience at school as having directed or prompted their future actions. Catholic schoolchildren in particular have politicized their play. The military figure could be easily imitated in street games of the children's own making and boys proved themselves by getting as close as possible to the real action and later by performing real terrorist roles.[91] In addition school children can use peer pressure or bully others into joining political associations and gangs. For children in such closely contained political quarters difference is easily spotted and difficult to conceal. The pseudo-military effects of the parade for adults are real military preparation for school children and give a certain legitimacy and adult quality to a typically childish experience.[92]

As with the game of 'cowboys and indians', boys learn that fighting the other and exploring and conquering as opposed to being explored is also available after they leave childhood. One of the 'naturalized' links between men and international relations, which has been forged through children is the association between adventure and masculinity also shown in the militarization of children's sport and leisure throughout the areas of the case studies.[93] Some children's more evident and prominent qualities such as a desire for adventure and excitement, high energy levels and interest in play and sport, were harnessed for military aims and also given a military significance. The ideal Aryan child was similar to the ideal Aryan soldier and an embodiment of the Aryan national body, the *volk*. To be fit and skilled militarily was more useful still. So children's sense of being childish was also manifested in citizenship. Fascism could be fun for children and adults. The Nazis applied the principle that political learning was a phenomenon of the mind and the body. Before they had much interest or understanding of politics, they were being conditioned to think of themselves as naturally bodies of the state, and their activities became part of the broader project of militarization. An increase in sports activity made

---

[89]   Warner, *op. cit.*, p. 364.

[90]   Aretzaga, *op. cit.*, p. 224.

[91]   Fraser, *op. cit.*, p. 148.

[92]   Neil Jarman, *Material Conflict: Parades and Visual Displays in Northern Ireland* (Oxford: Bergman, 1997).

[93]   See for example Helen Kanitkar, ' "Real True Boys" Moulding the Cadets of Imperialism', in Andrea Cornwall and Nancy Lindisfarne, *Dislocating Masculinity, Comparative Ethnographies* (London: Routledge, 1994), pp. 184–96.

playgrounds additional places of racial segregation, particularly for the disabled, thus firmly compounding the political hierarchy of healthy over damaged bodies. The aestheticization of violent death, and the construction of war as a fantasy was also allowed to flourish in youth groups. James Mangan writes that sport and play were one of the most informal and least explained transmitters of social and racial values throughout the time of the British Empire. Aspirations to the excellence of sport began at an early age and were equated with excellence of race, and had the additional benefit of improving the fitness of the nation.[94] The epitome of boy child qualities being required in the political world is demonstrated in the literature on India, and how its English administrators were trained. Sport (cricket) rather than political understanding was promoted amongst the Victorian middle classes and India was represented to them as an infantilized nation requiring an unintellectual administration. In their future role in India they were thus expected to carry on playing, at politics. It has been note of such men that:

> [i]n a very real sense the Victorian male was puer aeternus, the boy who never grew up. It was not just the all male society in which he functioned, it was also his preferred activities (hunting, empire building, exploring, warring) ... a striking feature of late Victorian culture was that its emotional focus was on boys.[95]

There are many examples of the political world also pertaining to and appropriating childlike qualities, and arguably some of these are stereotyped as boyish. Men it seems can be boys and boys men in many examples of political behavior. As was shown in Chapter One, the parameters and opportunities of boyhood are drawn much wider than for girls. This suggests that the contained child, in the sense of being in opposition to, protected by and not containing the political, is also likely to be imbued with feminine qualities. The next section brings attention on the theoretical construction of the child, in practices of nationalization and militarization, a child who is more likely to be presented as if infantile and also female and thus is described as embodying 'infant power'.

Infant Power

Put simply infant power describes practices motivated by children, with reference to children, or deploying infantilization of other constructs particularly in a military context. The construct of the child is typically a transhistorical, transcultural or essential infant. Infant power is a further example of the use of a private construction from the private sphere, often brought in and seemingly elevated to the political

---

[94]   See J.A. Mangan, *The Cultural Bond: Sport, Empire and Society* (London: Macmillan, 1992).

[95]   James A. Mangan and S. Walvin (eds), *Manliness and Morality: Middle Class Masculinity in Britain and America 1800–1940* (Manchester: Manchester University Press. 1987), p. 106.

sphere, though only in distinct and hierarchical relationship to the political and protectors.

This section looks at the ways in which the presence of the child is brought into play, and argues that children/infants are deeply embedded in security rationale. According to Anne Tickner: 'It is a world inhabited by diplomats, soldiers and international civil servants most of whom are men'.[96] A closer look however illustrates the deliberate positioning of the child close to political men.

Male politicians regularly kiss babies in public during their campaigns. In Bosnia, Ratko Mladic's troops handed out chocolates to Moslem children and patted their heads for the benefit of television, whilst removing and killing their fathers.[97] Politicians under threat commit family hug scenes for the camera men as a way of showing that they are still wanted, hanging on, secure in at least one sense. In numerous peace process discussions in Northern Ireland, tired ministers emerged and stated that they were doing this for the sake of the children, if no one else. In these scenes children become the visual equivalent of 'last words' in each case. Reference to children is used to indicate a sincerity of purpose that defies immediate rebuke. Similarly in a cine film discussion between Stalin and Lenin, it was the child on Stalin's knee that symbolized and answered the rhetorical question: 'why we are doing this?' One particular photograph of Stalin embracing a young girl was widely reproduced by Soviet propaganda agencies at the height of the purges, although the girl's father was later shot and her mother cast into the Gulag.[98] Flagging politicians commonly fall back on children for emotive moral mileage. Likewise terrorists in Northern Ireland have demonstrated their seriousness or need for media attention with child murders. Male birth imagery punctuated the language of the world's most deadly defense projects.[99] The practices of nationalization and militarization are often centered by the constructed infant.

So, where are these children, and the power invested in them in writings in International Relations? One of the most famous textbooks on security, the legacy of which has been its attention in International Relations up until the present day is Man, the State and War, by Kenneth Waltz. Waltz aimed to fully explain the international system with reference to three planes of analysis.[100] He contended that 'the most important cause of political arrangements and acts are found at the first level of political analysis in the nature and behavior of man'.[101] Man is Waltz's first image (person led) causal factor, and it is interesting that he does also speak of children many times, for example citing President Dwight Eisenhower who suggested that 'if the mothers in every land could teach their children to understand the homes

---

[96]   J. Anne Tickner, *op. cit.*

[97]   Jon Swain, 'Bosnia endures more atrocities', *Sunday Times*, 23 July 1995, pp. 1 and 13.

[98]   Norman Davies, *Europe: A History* (London: Pimlico, 1997), p. 1211.

[99]   Carol Cohn, 'Sex and Death in the Rational World of Defence Intellectuals', *Signs*, Vol. 12, 1987, pp. 687–718.

[100]   Waltz, *op. cit.*, p. 2.

[101]   *Ibid.*, p. 42.

and hopes of children in every other land – in America, in Europe, in the Near East, in Asia – the cause of peace in the world would indeed be nobly served'.[102] The civil defense programs, citizenship education and Cold War propaganda that Waltz himself was probably subject to is not mentioned.[103]

Waltz adds to this theme of political socialization by suggesting that '[i]f we could give Soviet children the kind of education the behavioral scientists might prescribe, then we might entertain some hope for a change in the Soviet government, say, twenty years from now'.[104] That children's education can create a more peaceful citizenship, makes sense to the author and this is evident by the brevity of the explanation. Waltz then refers to a psychologist, Gordon Allport and his suggestion of 'arranging the entrances to the General Assembly of the United Nations, the Security Council and UNESCO so that the delegates will have to pass through the playground of a nursery school on their way to their meetings'.[105] No more is said on this suggestion and this itself is interesting. Waltz assumes that the reader will have an understanding of how the construction of the peaceful child is an antidote to war. Presumably these children would be very different from the trigger-happy video game players that President Reagan addressed as the fighter pilots of the future. Thirty-five years later the same sentiments were expressed in the leader page of The Guardian: 'There should be a picture of a broken, mine damaged child on every defense Ministers desk'.[106] Waltz refers to this form of infant power as idealistic, peace-orientated and thus insignificant. He does not recognize this construction to be already central to his conceptualization of security. Such imagery and language relies on the assumption that we naturally nurture children – and leads us further away from questioning their involvement in the nurturing of war.

The separation of children from war is in part sustained by the association of the mother figure with the nation. Both are to be protected.[107] The nation is often personified as female and in turn the protector is male. Militarism and women are thus frequently separated. In Elshtain's well-known formulation, women are beautiful souls,[108] romanticizing the notion of war. Manhood and nationhood are asserted as the same; protecting the female nation is protecting the masculine self. Feminists play a key role in observing this gendered practice since they observe how women and children may be infantilized and feminized together. The argument that men take life while women give it remains a cornerstone of constructed gender differences and an idea central to warfare and the notion of women as non-combatants. The

---

[102]   On Eisenhower's address to the National Council of Catholic Women in 1954, cited in Waltz, *op. cit.*, p. 9.

[103]   JoAnne Brown, *op. cit.*

[104]   Waltz, *op. cit.*, p. 56.

[105]   *Ibid.*, p. 46.

[106]   Leader comment, 'The Forgotten Casualities of War', *The Guardian*, 12 December 1995, p. 14.

[107]   On the Theme of Nationalism and Sexuality, see *Feminist Review* Spring 1998, West, *op. cit.* and Yuval Davies, *op. cit.*

[108]   Jean Bethke Elshtain, *Women and War* (New York: Basic Books, 1987).

common view is that the 'manly urge is to serve their country and "protect" their female kin, with the one implying the other'.[109] The extension of this is that military service should act as a rite of passage for boys, where they are no longer protected but protecting. Weakened or damaged men – disabled ex-service men who cannot provide or protect – can become become marginalized and feminized in consequence. They can no longer protect and they have failed to protect themselves.[110] Similarly those who do not aspire to a military or masculine image are demasculinized, feminized or rendered childlike.[111]

During the Cold War a vigorous loyalty/security program sought to define dissenting Americans as 'pinko-liberal'.[112] In Nazi Germany the homosexual concentration camp members were given pink triangles to wear and in the first edition of Baden Powell's scouting manual for boys it is written: 'Every boy ought to learn how to shoot and obey orders, else he is no more good when war breaks out than an old woman'.[113] Baden Powell could not have said old man, since the military is full of them, neither could he have said young boy. He could have said girl. Infantilism is thus a carefully managed political tool, either justifying security practices and bestowed on the protected, or marking out those who cannot contribute to security and denigrating them.

Weakness, innocence and non-militarization are thought of as non-political qualities. Subjects who embody these are positioned diametrically from (thus framing) that which defines itself as political and protecting. Children are intimately associated with the domestic sphere and women, and are thought of as politically and often militarily weak. As the epitome of the weak civilian, they can be woven into powerful rationales for security behavior. It is also evident that non-political and sometimes specifically non-threatening (in a military sense) status is given by recourse to feminine or infantile qualities. This is a move which serves to further rationalize assumptions about the oppositional qualities of the political world, in short placing it a comfortable distance away from infantilized/ incomplete/feminine bodies, and the family or domestic context.

More recently, Kinsella in her work on the 'civilian', and Carpenter on 'vulnerable persons' have drawn attention to discursive practices which privileges some categories (of 'innocent') or persons over others.[114] All these social categories

---

[109]   J. Ann Tickner, in Lapid and Kratochwil, *op. cit.*, pp. 147–62.

[110]   Joanna Bourke, *Dismembering the Male, op. cit.*, p. 15.

[111]   Bourke, *op. cit.*, p. 21, see also David Campbell, *Writing Security: United States Foreign Policy and the Politics of Identity* (Manchester: Manchester University Press, 1992) p. 166.

[112]   *Ibid.*

[113]   John M. Mackenzie, 'The Imperial Pioneer and Hunter and the British Masculine Stereotype in Late Victorian and Edwardian Times', in J.A. Mangan and James Walvin (eds), *op. cit.*, p. 176.

[114]   See Kinsella, H., 'Securing the Civilian: Sex and Gender in the Laws of War', in M. Barnett and R. Duvall (eds), *Power and Global Governance* (Cambridge University Press, 2005) and Carpenter, C., '"Women, Children and Other Vulnerable Groups": Gender,

of 'other' civilians or other 'victims' are also worthy of opening and exploding. Who are 'the elderly' so frequently invoked in lists of the vulnerable? What do we mean by age? Are men and women afforded the same vulnerable or aged qualities? The majority of active men in politics and military echelons are elderly. Indeed disability is often anchored to, or drowned by constructs of vitality, ability and youth. In addition, 'different cultures' have different values of age and life spans, parenting and grand parenting, leadership and justice, and statesmen to name but a few.[115]

State interest in the personal sphere may carry with it the image of recognition and assistance, a legitimization of the personal sphere not a political appropriation of it. The pre-established boundaries between the domestic and political spheres, and their implicit hierarchy, can mask a political invasion into the domestic world by rendering the rationale as protective, personifying it as patrimonial, particularly in conflict. The German state prior to and during the Nazi regime specifically referred to children as a group, as a mass of bodies who could strengthen state security. The Weimar Republic had placed the interests of the child on an equal footing with national security. By improving children's welfare and monitoring parents, the state had acted as an additional parent and guardian, a role was easily disseminated to the population as it carried a moral (philanthropic/unselfish) credibility. The state was patrimonial and protecting, and to question its motivations would be difficult. Such 'security' thinkers publicly declared that the health of Germany's (young) population determined the state's strength, thus appealing for the public to accept their duty to nurture children and thereby strengthening her position in the international system. Child care was part of the language of state care and there was a circularity of consequence. If parents neglected their children then the state would suffer, and ultimately the state would not be able to protect children. It was emotive and simple instruction; children were a complement to the images of security.

As state security and the killing of children intensified, the presence of the mother was deliberately employed to mitigate the contradiction of the state as guardian destroying that which it also drew attention to as needing protection. By placing the child in an apparently caring sphere, for example in a maternity home, the state killed by proxy; mothers 'allowed' this to happen and medical science was seemingly unable to prevent their deaths. Outright killing of children may have been difficult for the Nazi conscience. Children's non-combatant status and weakness drew attention to the German soldier's role as protector of the vulnerable and civilian sphere, and consequently their difficulty in killing them led to the use of less direct killing through gas chambers in 1942. When women and children were killed throughout the camps they were collectively referred to as 'men, women and children'. The illusion of men's corpses also being present was a legitimizing device; 'easing' the isolation of women and children's deaths and making it less questionable. One of the greatest propaganda stories of recent times– manufactured by the American PR

Strategic Frames and the Protection of Civilians as a Transnational Issue', *International Studies Quarterly* (2005) 49, 295–334.

[115]   Helen Brocklehurst (*Children and War: An Unfinished Story,* forthcoming).

firm 'Hill and Knowlton' and paid for by the Kuwaiti Royal family – told of Kuwaiti babies forcibly removed from their incubators by Iraqi soldiers. The story succeeded in generating enormous Western support for military intervention.[116]

Hitler titled himself as father to thousands, and perhaps benefited personally from this invented role. Intense politicization of the family sphere and the guardianship assumed by the Nazi state may have acted as a smokescreen to barbarity. Rudolph Hoess amongst others remained convinced that his protection of his own family ameliorated his actions and rendered him normal.[117] There is no need to pursue a definition of normal here, what is interesting is how caring for a family distanced his mind/conscience from acts of barbarity against other families. The Weimar Republic and Nazi regime used childcare policies and practices as a pacifier of the people. The level of regulations in the child's interest provided a distraction for parents, as did the clear roles of men and women as protectors and nurturers. The reification of motherhood can be seen as the other side of a state dominated by patriarchal values or as Gisela Bock argues, a cult of fatherhood and masculinity.[118] The promotion of motherhood disguised an agenda of the fatherland. Motherhood was heavily propagandized as a natural and instinctive role, thus contradicting the rigorous training imposed on women. The amount of effort involved in constructing this child fantasy world can be seen as directly proportional to its fallacy, in other words mothers and motherhood were feared to work against the state. Tim Mason argues 'the nightmare Nazi world was parasitic on its ideological antithesis, the minute community of adults and children'.[119]

The Afrikaner mother was conceived by the state as a central figure in the socialization of the children into the volk. The home front in particular was seen as an area of social strength and also an area of additional if not already crucial military preparation and mobilization. The ideology of the *volks moer*, the silent soldier at home supplemented the rationale for the real soldiers. Militarization created a culture of masculinity and to this end the family was sanctified as a distinct sphere of peace and love in a culture of apartheid and violence. As in Nazi Germany women and children – the normal innocent sphere to be protected – were appealed to in later testimonies of violent action by Afrikaners. Yet as J. Ann Tickner notes that 'when we think about the definition of a patriot we generally think of a man, often a soldier who defends his homeland, most especially his women and children, from dangerous outsiders'.[120] Children and their perceived vulnerability are visibly

---

[116] Joel Bleifus, 'Happy Face Politics', *New Internationalist*, Issue 314, July 1999, http://oneworld.org/ni/issue314/happyface.

[117] Joachim C. Fest, *The Faces of the Third Reich*, translated from the German by Michael Bullock (London: Weidenfeld and Nicolson, 1970), p. 276.

[118] Gisela Bock, 'Antinatalism, Maternity and Paternity in Nationalist Socialist Racism', in Crew, David F. (ed.), *Nazism and German Society, 1933–1945* (London: Routledge, 1992), p. 129.

[119] Tim Mason, 'Women in Germany, 1925–1940: Family, Welfare and Work: Part II', *History Workshop* (1976), p. 24.

[120] Tickner, *op. cit.*, p. 3.

invoked by representatives of the state as reason to fight. This myth is sustained by the defense community and to an extent the language and codes of International Relations.

Mothers and their children can be designated as non political yet also made agents of the state through their bodies. The corollary is that they are not suspected of being politically motivated themselves. This is an 'I cannot see you so you cannot see me' situation. The assumption that women are also naturally unpolitical means that women are able to act politically, not necessarily on behalf of their children, but under the guise of their children. In Brazil, for example, women have chosen to take up practical political involvement in social movements, using to their advantage, the system that denigrates women and children. By inventing their own terminology on their own terms, they define themselves as a feminine movement, doing what they can do only as women, and in contrast to 'typical male activities in the public sphere'.[121] In Latin America and in South Asia, women have defined themselves as apolitical so as to avoid confrontation with politics and men. Their aims are political in that they wish to 'participate in the feminist movement and improve the living conditions for the whole family'.[122] The ingrained belief that women are indifferent to politics and that their concerns are apolitical[123] has allowed them to concretize their objectives undisturbed particularly under the unusual label of feminine. Similarly, Chilean mothers quietly demilitarize young people by discouraging imitation of practices of the Pinochet regime in their children's play.[124]

The *Madres de Plaza de Mayo*, are a protest movement of Argentinean mothers and grandmothers empowered through solidarity and anger over the fate of their missing grown-up children – sons and daughters who had taken a stand against injustice. One mother explained '[w]e began to realise that politics meant more than just the political parties. When we began to understand our children's real histories, their concern for social change, we began to make the same demands.'[125] The loss of their children powered their political objections and their relationship with their children was stronger than their relationship with the state. It is perhaps for this reason that states invent a patrimonial relationship with citizens. Gender-based subservience is a powerful tool of allegiance. Young, female Indonesian factory workers believe themselves to be subservient daughters of the factory as well as

---

[121] Hensman, in Afshar, *op. cit.*, p. 52.

[122] Stephen J. Roscow, Naeem Inayatullah and Mark Rupert (eds), *The Global Economy of Political Space* (Boulder: Lynne Rienner, 1994), p. 137.

[123] Rohini Hensman, 'The Role of Women in the Resistance of Political Authoritarianism in Latin America and South Asia', in Haleh Afshar (ed), *Women and Politics in the Third World* (London: Routledge, 1996), p. 52.

[124] Cynthia Enloe, *The Morning After: Sexual Politics at the End of the Cold War* (London: University of California Press, 1993), p. 100.

[125] Hensman, *op. cit.*, p. 3.

daughters of the state.[126] As Cynthia Enloe has argued, 'daughter', 'mother' and 'wife' are ideas on which the international political system today depends.[127]

Resistance to authoritarian regimes, as typified by women's movements like the *Madres de Plaza de Mayo* is 'rooted not in any notion of the rights of women but on the contrary, in a passionate love for their children'.[128] In 1990 the mothers and grandmothers took the seemingly small step of campaigning with photos of any of the children, not just their own.[129] The mothers' protection of their children extends beyond the imposed boundary of state authoritarianism, and towards other children. Robin Hensman believes that in countries of poverty, children are seen in a different way by their mothers. Their mothers associated them with the will to survive and the bond is one which transcends the hardship involved and is a source of inspiration.[130] Feminists and indeed critics of the military drew attention to the direct opposition between war-making and the care-giving of children.[131] Children can generate peaceful or non-militaristic tendencies – and a commitment not to neglect, in contrast to 'the willingness to burn, bury, cut, blow apart and starve bodies' that is essential to militarist enterprises.[132] The traditional cry 'womenandchildren' is graphic and shorthand for recognition of non-combatants, suggesting by default victims, casualties, refugees, and displaced, and the weak and feminine, the non-participants and therefore non political. During the Gulf War 'womenandchildren' rolled easily off network tongues.[133] Enloe points out that the running together of these two words by broadcasters and writers to mean victimhood renders both as child-like.[134] During the Vietnam war American troops were kicked into action by descriptions of their enemy as just a bunch of 'women and children'. The metaphor of 'women and children' implied easy targets, their military opposites, and later American troops were inspired and 'inflected by a desire to rescue and bolster American manhood after its humiliation at the hands of the Vietcong'.[135] The Irish Republican Brotherhood was formed after taunts of military ineffectiveness and

---

[126] Cynthia Enloe, Symposium, 'Inter-personal/Inter-national', University of Bristol, 18 October 1997.

[127] Cynthia Enloe, *Bananas, Beaches and Bases* (London: Pandora Press, 1989), p. 140.

[128] Hensman, *op. cit.*, p. 65.

[129] Jo Fisher, *Out of the Shadows: Women, Resistance and Politics in South America* (London: Latin American Bureau, 1993), p. 136.

[130] Hensman, *op. cit.*, p. 65.

[131] Sara Ruddick, 'Notes toward a Feminist Peace Politics' and 'Wars Wimps and Women: Talking Gender and thinking War', in Miriam Cooke and Angela Woolacott (eds), *Gendering War Talk* (Chichester: Princeton University Press, 1993), p. 120.

[132] Sara Ruddick, in Cooke and Woollacott, *op. cit.*, p. 120.

[133] Cynthia Enloe, *The Morning After: Sexual Politics at the End of the Cold War* (London: University of California Press, 1993), p. 166.

[134] *Ibid.*

[135] Marysia Zalewski and Cynthia Enloe, 'Questions about Identity in International Relations' in Smith and Booth (eds), *op. cit.*, pp. 10–11.

femininity; these became caricatures of the Irish.[136] In South Africa, Afrikaner white youth were militarized in the school and in youth movements, against the threat of otherwise becoming 'mommy's little boys', whilst girls were encouraged to become 'mommys'.[137] In Northern Ireland suffering and martyrdom have been internalized into male and female roles through religion and researchers question if the highly militarized and violent society may also reflect the breakdown of the traditional male role as a consequence of poverty and humiliation bestowed on sectors of the community throughout history.

Conclusion

In the American 'Cold War Consensus' of the 1950s and early 1960s the nuclear threat was personified as an iconographic image of vulnerable Western childhood. Sharon Stephens explains that:

> [c]hildren were widely depicted in the Cold War era as innocent beings at the heart of the contained domestic world, as objects of strictly gender-divided parental care and protection, and as the vulnerable core of American society, whose protection from foreign enemies required the construction of a vast and powerful nuclear defense system ... dominant Cold War images of abstract, generic children (invariably presented as white and middle class) [were counterposed with] the actual children most vulnerable to risks associated with nuclear weapons production and testing, and with government-sponsored radiation experiments. In various ways, these were all seen as 'deviant' children, whose lives could legitimately be put at risk in the interests of safeguarding 'normal' children at the heart of Cold War visions of American society.[138]

This example typifies how the construct of the political can be bolstered by the implication of its philanthropic objectives in the interests of the child – an example of infant power at work. The child performs additional 'political' activities, and yet children remain depoliticized and the underplaying of their political power actually contributes to their own insecurity. The power of the infant and the interdependence of the everyday child's world and the political world are not accounted for in traditional International Relations which also re-contributes to the containment of political and security practices.

The image of the victim child – the universal emblem of humanity – facilitates the perception that politics only impacts on children. Pictures of starving children dominated the film footage of the Ethiopian famine in 1985. When Russian troops invaded Chechnya in 1995, pictures of blood-smeared Chechen children were on

---

[136] David Fitzpatrick, *The Two Irelands* (Oxford: Oxford University Press, 1988).

[137] Jacklyn Cock, *Women and War in South Africa* (London: Gollancz, 1979), pp. 70–71.

[138] Sharon Stephens, 'Nationalism, Nuclear Policy and Children in Cold War America', *Childhood: A Global Journal of Child Research,* Vol. 4, No. 1, 1997, pp. 103–23.

the front pages of many British newspapers.[139] Similarly, British reporters of the Rwandan massacres have used the case studies of children to portray the crisis in graphical clarity.[140] Disaster imagery such as this invites motivation by pity, and superficial restorative measures, which do not account for deeper structural causes of inequality or instability, or children's political roles.[141] In South Africa, it has been argued that the culture of militarism, authoritarianism and apartheid has created adult children; it has removed the self identification and collective identification (other than race) necessary for people to survive and protect 'the self'.[142] South African leaders have been seen as fathers and the population as children and ever disappointed followers. Are we today any different?

Where children have been spoken of in their roles in conflict it is as political individuals, not as a collective group, or indeed as a politicized body.[143] In political violence however 'individualism and collectivism are not mutually exclusive', just as victims may also be perpetrators and adult and child identities may be embodied simultaneously.[144] Children's political roles tend to be thought of as a departure from or an extension to their everyday lives. Children are not recognized as politicized, nationalized and militarized bodies, and belonging to a political body. Thus to draw attention to or attempt to eradicate practices of their 'politicization' is unlikely to help children since their lives and experiences will largely remain unchanged. Children cannot be made more secure for example without first exposing the concepts and theories which presently construct children and politics, and which contribute to their insecurity. The reflections of Connolly, whose research is on sectarianism, also bear this out:

> Rather than being given the opportunity to raise and discuss what concerns them, the research has tended simply to probe the children about very specific issues that concern the researchers. Ultimately, this has led to a situation where researchers have used adult ways of thinking and making sense of the conflict to test children's attitudes and levels of awareness. The problem is that the conflict and social divisions associated with it may well exert a significant influence on children's lives but they could quite possibly think about and make sense of this in different ways to adults ... The danger exists, therefore, that because of this tendency to overlook the voices of the children themselves then we may

---

[139]   Andrew Higgins, 'Yeltsin takes over Army', *The Independent*, 12 January 1995, p. 1.

[140]   See for example Jenny Matthews, 'A Holocaust we Chose not to See', *The Observer*, 2 April 1995, p. 14 and Lindsey Hilsum, 'Rwanda's Time of Rape Returns to Haunt Thousands', *The Observer*, 26 February 1995, p. 17.

[141]   David Buckingham, *Moving Images: Understanding Children's Emotional Responses to Television* (Manchester: Manchester University Press, 1996), p. 184.

[142]   Leonard Bloom, *Identity and Ethnic Relations in Africa* (Aldershot: Ashgate, 1998) p. 122.

[143]   Ed Cairns, *Children and Political Violence* (London: Blackwell, 1996).

[144]   *Ibid.*

be underestimating the extent to which the conflict impacts upon their lives, especially for younger children.[145]

This last chapter has sought so far to illustrate how children are conceptually and theoretically contained within the discipline of International Relations and a starting point for a richer discipline is to expose them as such. Concepts and theories construct children as political bodies, and enable their nationalization and militarization whilst underplaying that politicization. What are the implications of this for our understanding of children as political bodies, conflict and ultimately ourselves?

---

145 Paul Connolly and Julie Healy (2004) *Children and the Conflict in Northern Ireland: The Experiences and Perspectives of 3–11 Year Olds.* (Belfast: Office of the First Minister and Deputy First Minister).

Conclusion

Politics and children

The volume has demonstrated practices which construct children as politicized bodies and explored concepts and theories which underplay that politicization. The first two chapters explored the construct of the child and revealed them to be socially and politically contested. Parameters and qualities of childhood were shown to vary with the priorities of society and providers of security. Conceptions of children, namely as diametrically opposed to adults, and as embodiments of weakness and innocence also serve to limit recognition of their acts as 'political'. Chapter 2 illustrated their material and theoretical presence in world politics and political constructions manifested in their roles. In particular children are invoked and involved in theories and practices of state building and state destruction. Asking the question 'where are the children?' found them to be central to practices of militarization and nationalization across the world and throughout history, though they are not recognized as such in literature about conflict; a core area of International Relations. Case studies then sought to provide substantial evidence of children's presence as political bodies in cases of conflict. Chapters 3, Four and Five together illustrated the central claim of the volume – that children and their everyday lives are politicized.

Chapter 3 made a detailed case of children's politicization in Nazi Germany. The link between children and state security, prior to and throughout the Nazi regime, was traced throughout the literature. Children were shown to be foundational to theories of nationalization, and subjected to intense political socialization and militarization. In addition they were used as an emotional sphere against which to normalize and legitimize violence. Chapter 4 moved on to illustrate similar perceptions, constructs and theories of the child as a political body employed in a very different society facing conflict.

In Chapter 4, children in Northern Ireland were shown to have participated in nationalist and military strategies both knowingly and unwittingly. Like Nazi totalitarianism, Northern Irish terrorism was seen to depend on the acquisition of the civilian sphere and use of 'soft tactics' – including the use of children's bodies, and the hearts and minds of their protectors. Terrorism depends on the constructed sphere of 'soft targets' such as children as a means of gaining publicity, generating fear in the community and by extension involving and inciting the protectors of dependants. Children in Northern Ireland are engendered with a political presence through their political socialization in communities, education and leisure activities which are particularly subject to sectarian socialization and military appropriation. Their identification as 'non-political' bodies, however, also allows them to perform additional political and military roles. The case illustrates that the everyday life of children and their families in Northern Ireland, sustains 'the troubles', and blurs the boundary between political and non-political spheres and activities.

Chapter 5 consolidated the evidence in the previous two cases. Its comparative analysis of Mozambican, African and Afrikaner children revealed their presence in practices of nationalization and militarization within the school and family. African and Afrikaner children were subject to politicized education and were militarily mobilized. Afrikaner nationalism was shown to have traditionally centered itself on the construct of the heroic and ideal mother. The central claim of the volume was also demonstrated in Mozambique, through Frelimo and Renamo's clear identification of the child and mother as the fulcrum of societal, and hence state stability.

In all cases children were shown to be subject to parallel practices of nationalization and militarization taking place in the social institutions of the family, school, leisure and youth movements. Children as political bodies, then, have a diverse material presence and a multiplicity of roles and functions in the everyday activities of the domestic/private sphere, and are interdependent with the international system. The detailed comparative analysis of children in Nazi Germany, Northern Ireland, South Africa and Mozambique showed the interconnectedness of the political and private spheres, in contradiction to the supposed containment of the political and the containment of the child which was demonstrated earlier. In showing that children's bodies have a political function and that children are a political 'body' or group, the volume brings into question how and why their politicization is played down, particularly in traditional International Relations literature.

The final chapter moves to examine the three themes of containment, interdependence and infant power, which run through the analysis, and shed light on how the child is politicized, but also rendered as unpolitical. These themes are interdependent though they have been clearly separated for the point of further analysis. The first theme, that of the 'containment' of concepts of the child and the political, was initially exposed in the study of constructs of the child and their various roles in global politics. It is shown that the two spheres are represented as mutually exclusive. The alleged separation of the child and the political, through their conceptual containment, enables the child to then be specifically brought in to the political, for example at times of national interest. The child's world is already interdependent with the political world, as the cases have shown. However, specific invocation of the child downplays the everyday conceptions and practices in which the child is constituted as a political body.

The construct and role of the child within an emotive raison d'être of security practices, is an example of infant power and interdependence specific to the construct of the child, and is common to the case studies. The use of children in security practices is shown to be further legitimized by the deliberate portrayal of them as under threat and in need of protection, even if this 'protection' also places them at risk. The essentialized, innocent, weak or victim child, found in nationalization discourse and security justifications is not, however, the same child who is encouraged to play war games – real or imaginary. Thus children's constructions are manipulated to political advantage. Adults too, have a multiplicity of roles and constructs in society, but unlike children, most of them are not also bestowed with an unpolitical identity which increases their potential for political instrumentalization, particularly in conflict.

The final chapter addressed how the dissociating of children from the political sphere allows for their greater instrumentality. The separation of the political and the child's world is shown to be founded on gendered perceptions about protection, nation-hood and power. That is, ways in which feminine and masculine spheres are constructed – the former classically rendered as being 'protected' through political means. These ideas are central to how the child is separated and then put to political use. The child is often conceptualized as a non-political extension of the non-political mother. Political practices can be justified by invoking the dual construct of the child and the mother–nation to be protected by the male adult and male/military power. Ideas from the third debate in International Relations make sense of the relationship between conceptions of the political and political practices. The power of the infant and the use of the everyday child's world for political purposes are as yet not accounted for in traditional or contemporary International Relations and this may also be seen as a factor which contributes to the containment of the political and the child.

Kids R' Us?

The volume shows that children's everyday activities can be politicized and harnessed to assist nationalization and militarization. Schools are sites of politicization. Nationalization is channeled through the familial sphere. Children may be militarized through social institutions and their aptitudes and interests harnessed for military ends. The evidence clearly shows that including children in our analysis can broaden and enrich our understanding of conflict. Not least, it exposes that children contribute to concepts and practices of security and insecurity. Exposing practices of child politicization, nationalization and militarization, may itself indicate how a state is securing itself and the degree of insecurity it is experiencing. The forced migration and renationalization of children by the Nazis, and by the British during the Empire, for example were aptly illustrative of perceived security needs. The intensity of political socialization that children are subject to, whether explicit or hidden, may suggest a state's sense of alienation or xenophobia, as in Cold War America and Afrikaner South Africa. It is also evident that many of the practices of politicization that children are subject to, are in place in peace-time and were intensified in conflict rather than invented out of necessity.

Thus, a significant theoretical point that the volume makes is to question the separation of the international, the political and the personal; the separation between conflict and peace-time, between adults and children, and between theory and practice. This is not to argue that these distinctions should or can be removed, but to show that parameters and barriers like these have served to contain concepts and theories of the political. This has ultimately contained our understanding of the child as a political body and the practices of which they are part, particularly conflict. A key theme that the volume exposes is infant power. Many more subjects than children have been politically denigrated, or rendered insecure by being constructed as 'child-like' and/or feminine; a phenomena which feminist approaches have thus far been more willing to expose than has critical security analysis. Gendered concepts are evident throughout the volume, exposing infantilization and infant power as political power, revealing the fluidity of personal and political spheres and disrupting dichotomies of state/public and home/ family/private which are thought of as autonomous in traditional academic International Relations.

The evidence in each case study reveals the fundamental importance of children's roles in conflict and challenges International Relations' comfortable and discernible distance from such material – a position which is perhaps reflective of the state or agenda of the discipline. In this way, the volume illustrates how when we learn about children, we learn about ourselves and to what effect we categorize and naturalize and neutralize ourselves and the 'other' and in effect patrol these boundaries in theory and in practice. International Relations' relationship with children is thus tense rather than healthy – strained by the energy taken up by non-recognition and misappropriation. As the volume shows, political children are already in International Relations, but unacknowledged within the structures of power it both describes and inhabits.

Children are already present in our conceptions of adults, in how we think about politics and how we think we can create security. Thus to not think about children, and where they are in International Relations is to not be thinking hard enough. International Relations is the sum of its practitioners and interpreters. Concepts and practices are a human creation and as such can be changed. Although we often do not want to believe that we are responsible for something problematic, the belated recognizing of children as political bodies, and the recognizing of how they disturb ways of thinking about the political, may help towards a better understanding of conflict and International Relations.

This book is but one beginning. The three themes pursued throughout the volume would suggest that there are many more trails to follow, before *Man the State and War* can be rewritten with an understanding of concepts, cases and theories of children as political bodies.

Bibliography

Andersson, Hillary (1992), *Mozambique: A War Against the People* (London: Macmillan).

Archard, David (2004), *Children, Rights and Childhood*, 2nd edition (London: Routledge).

Aretxaga, Begona (1993), 'Striking with Hunger: Cultural Meanings of Political Violence in Northern Ireland', in Kay B. Warren (ed.), *The Violence Within: Cultural and Political Opposition in Divided Nations* (Boulder: Westview Press).

Aretxaga, Begona (1997), *Shattering Silence: Women Nationalism and Political Subjectivity in Northern Ireland* (Princeton: Princeton University Press).

Aries, Philip (1973), *Centuries of Childhood* (Harmondsworth: Penguin).

Ayatullah, Naeem and David L. Blaney (1996), 'Knowing Encounters: Beyond Parochialism in International Relations', in Lapid and Kratochwil (eds).

Balakrishnan, Radhika (1994), 'The Wider Context of Sex Selection and the Politics of Abortion in India', in Gita Sen and Rachel C. Snow (eds), *Power and Decision: The Social Control of Reproduction* (Boston: Harvard School of Health).

Balch, Jeff, Phyllis Johnson and Richard Morgan (1995), 'Apartheid and Destabilisation in Southern Africa: The Legacy for Children and the Challenges Ahead', in *Transcending the Legacy: Children in the New Southern Africa* (AEI/SARDC/UNICEF: Amsterdam, Harare, Nairobi).

Ball, Stephen (1983) 'Imperialism, Social Control and the Colonial Curriculum in Africa', *Journal of Curriculum Studies,* No. 25, pp. 237–63.

Banfield, Jesse and Nevine Mabro (1997), 'Children in Statistics', *Index on Censorship*, 2.

Barry, Kathleen (1996), 'Pornography and the Global Sexual Exploitation of Women', in Diane Bell and Renate Klein (eds).

Barton, Keith C., and McCully, Alan W. (2005), 'History Education and National Identity in Northern Ireland', *International Journal of Historical Learning, Teaching and Research*, Vol. 5, No. 1.

Belfrage, Sally (1998), *The Crack, a Belfast Year* (London: Grafton).

Bell, Diane and Renate Klein (1996) (eds), *Radically Speaking: Feminism Reclaimed* (London: Zed Books).

Bellamy, Carol (1999), *The State of the World's Children 1996* (Oxford and New York: Oxford University Press).

Benderly, Jill 'Rape Feminism, and Nationalism in the War in Yugoslav Successor States', in Lois West (ed.), *Feminist Nationalism* (London: Routledge, 1997), p. 65.

Bessel, Richard (1995), 'The front generation and the politics of Weimar Germany', in Roseman (ed.).

Bloom, Leonard (1998), *Identity and Ethnic Relations in Africa* (Aldershot: Ashgate).

Bock, Gisela (1994), 'Antinatalism, maternity and paternity in National Socialist racism', in Crew, David F. (ed.).

Booth, Ken (1991), 'Security in Anarchy: Utopian Realism in Theory and Practice', *International Affairs*, Vol. 63, No. 3.

Booth, Ken (1995), 'Dare not to Know: International Relations Theory versus the Future', in Ken Booth and Steve Smith (eds), *International Relations Theory Today* (Oxford: Polity Press).

Booth, Ken, (1997), 'Security and Self: Reflections of a Fallen Realist', in Williams and Krause (eds).

Booth, Ken and Peter Vale (1997), 'Critical Security Studies and Regional Insecurity: The Case of Southern Africa', in Williams and Krause (eds).

Bowyer Bell, John (1997), *IRA Tactics and Targets* (Poolbeg Press, 1997).

Boyden, Jo (1990), 'Childhood and the Policy Makers: A Comparative Perspective on the Globalisation of Childhood', in Alison James and Alan Prout (eds), *Constructing and Reconstructing Childhood* (London: Falmer Press).

Boyden, Jo (2003), 'The Moral Development of Child Soldiers: What do Adults have to Fear?', *Peace and Conflict: Journal of Peace Psychology*, Vol. 9, No. 4, 343–62.

Boyden, Jo and Deborah Levison (2000), 'Children as Economic and Social Actors in the Development Process', Working Paper 1, Stockholm: Expert Group on Development Issues.

Brink, Elsabe (1990), 'Man-made Women: Gender, Class and the Ideology of the *Volksmoeder*', C. Walker (ed.), *Women and Resistance in Southern Africa to 1945* (London: James Currey).

Brocklehurst, Helen (2005), 'Just war? Just children?' in Mark Evans (ed.), *Just War Theory Reconsidered* (Edinburgh University Press).

Brocklehurst, Helen, *Children and War* (forthcoming).

Bronfenbrenner, Urie (1971), *Two Worlds of Childhood – USA and USSR* (London: George Allen and Unwin).

Brown, JoAnne (1988), '*A* is for Atom, *B* is for Bomb: Civil Defense in American Public Education, 1948–1963', *The Journal of American History*, Vol. 75, No. 1.

Brown, Margot and Ian Davies (1998), 'The Holocaust and Education for Citizenship: The Teaching of History, Religion and History in England', *Education Review*, Vol. 50, No. 1.

Bryan, Dominic and Neil Jarman (1997), 'Parading Tradition, Protesting Triumphalism: Utilising Anthropology in Public Policy', in Donnan Hastings and Graham McFarlane (eds), *Social Anthropology and Public Policy in Northern Ireland* (Aldershot, Hants: Avebury).

Buckingham, David (1996), *Moving Images: Understanding Children's Emotional Responses to Television* (Manchester: Manchester University Press).

Bunting, Brian (1964), *The Rise of the South African Reich* (Harmondsworth: Penguin).

Burleigh, M. and W. Wipperman (1991), *The Racial State: Germany 1933–1945* (Cambridge: Cambridge University Press).

Burman, Erica (1994), 'Innocents abroad: Projecting Western Fantasies of Childhood onto the Iconography of Emergencies', in *Disasters: Journal of Disaster Studies and Management*, Vol. 18, No. 3, pp. 238–53.

Burman, Erica (1996), 'Local, global or globalised? Child development and international child rights legislation', *Childhood*, Vol. 3, pp. 45–66.

Burman, Erica (1996), 'Constructing and Deconstructing Childhood: Images of Children and Charity Appeals', in J. Haworth (ed.), *Psychological Research: Innovative Methods and Strategies* (London: Routledge).

Burtonwood, Neil (1996), 'Culture, Identity and the Curriculum', *Education Review*, Vol. 48, No. 3.

Bush, Kenneth D. and Diana Salterelli (2000), Two Faces of Education in Ethnic Conflict (United Nations Children's Fund, Innocenti Research Centre, Italy).

Butalia, Urvashi (1997), 'So many Shivas', in *Index on Censorship*, 2.

Buzan, Barry (1991), *People States and Fear*, 2nd edition (Hemel Hempstead: Harvester Wheatsheaf).

Cairns, Ed (1987), *Caught in Crossfire: Children and the Northern Ireland Conflict* (Belfast: Appletree Press).

Cairns, Ed and Tara Cairns (1995), 'Children and Conflict: a Psychological Perspective', in Dunn (ed.), *Facets of the Conflict in Northern Ireland* (Houndmills: Macmillan Press).

Cairns, Ed, (1996), *Children and Political Violence* (London: Blackwell).

Caldicott, Helen (1984), *Missile Envy: The Arms Race and Nuclear War* (New York: Bantam).

Campbell, David (1992), *Writing Security: United States Foreign Policy and the Politics of Identity* (Manchester: Manchester University Press).

Campbell, David (1995), 'Political Prosaics, Transversal Politics and the Anarchical World', in Michael Shapiro and Hayward Alker (eds), *Challenging Boundaries: Global Flows, Territorial Identities* (New York: Columbia University Press).

Carlton-Ford, Steve, Anne Hamill and Paula Houston (2000), 'War and Children's Mortality', *Childhood*, Vol. 7, No. 4, pp. 401–19.

Carpenter, Charli, R. (2005), '"Women, Children and Other Vulnerable Groups": Gender, Strategic Frames and the Protection of Civilians as a Transnational Issue', *International Studies Quarterly*, 49, pp. 295–334.

Carrington, Bruce, and Geoffrey Short (1998), 'Reconstructing Multiracial Education: A Response to Mike Cole', *Cambridge Journal of Education*, Vol. 28, No. 2.

Carrington, Bruce and Geoffrey Short (1997), 'Holocaust Education Anti-racism and Citizenship', *Educational Review*, Vol. 49, No. 3.

Caul, Leslie (1993), *Schools Under Scrutiny: The Case of Northern Ireland* (London: Macmillan).

Childers, Thomas and Jane Caplan (1993), 'Introduction', in Thomas Childers and Jane Caplan (eds), *Re-evaluating the Third Reich* (London: Holmes and Meier).

Chisholm, Linda and Bruce Fuller (1996), 'Remember People's Education? Shifting

Alliances, Atate-building and South Africa's Narrowing Policy Agenda', *Journal of Education Policy*, Vol. 11, No. 6.

Clarke, Toby (1997), *Art and Propaganda in the Twentieth Century: The Political Image in the Age of Mass Culture* (London: Weidenfeld and Nicolson).

Clay, Catrine and Michael Leapman (1995), *Master Race: The Lebensborn Experiment in Nazi Germany* (BCA and Hodder and Stoughton).

Cock, Jacklyn (1992), *Women and War in South Africa* (London: Open Letters).

Cohn, Carol (1987), 'Sex and Death in the Rational World of Defence Intellectuals', *Signs*, Vol. 12, pp. 687–718.

Cohn, Carol (1993), 'War, Wimps and Women: Talking Gender and Thinking War', in M. Cooke and A. Woolacott, (eds), *Gendering War Talk* (Princeton: Princeton University Press).

Cole, Mike (1998), 'Re-establishing Multiracial Education; A Reply to Short and Carrington', *Cambridge Journal of Education*, Vol. 28, No. 3.

Comaccio, Cynthia R. (1992), 'The Infant Soldier: Early Child Welfare Efforts in Ontario', in Valerie Fildes, Lara Marks and Hilary Marland (eds), *Women and Children First: International and Infant Welfare 1870 –1945* (London: Routledge).

Conflict Archive on the Internet (CAIN), cain.ulst.ac.uk.

Connolly, Paul and Julie Healy (2004), *Children and the Conflict in Northern Ireland: The Experiences and Perspectives of 3–11 Year Olds* (Belfast: Office of the First Minister and Deputy First Minister).

Connolly, Paul (2003), 'The Development of Young Children's Ethnic Identities: Implications for Early Years Practices', in Carol Vincent (ed.), *Social Justice, Education and Identity* (London: Routledge).

Corsaro, William A. (1997), *The Sociology of Childhood* (Thousand Oaks, California: Pine Forge Press).

Coulby, David (1997), 'European Curricula, Xenophobia and Warfare', *Comparative Education*, Vol. 33, No. 1.

Crew, David F. (ed.) (1994), *Nazism and German Society* (London: Routledge).

Cunningham, William G. (1988), *Conflict Theory and Conflict in Northern Ireland*, M.Litt Thesis, University of Auckland, CAIN [website] http://cain.ulst.ac.uk/conflict/cunningham.html.

Cunningham, Hugh (1995) *Children and Childhood in Western Society Since 1500*, (London and New York: Longman).

Daly, Bridget and Jenny Vaughan (1988), *Children at War* (London: Macdonald).

Darby, John (1976), *Conflict in Northern Ireland: The Development of a Polarised Community* (Dublin: Gill and Macmillan).

Darby, John (1995), 'Conflict in Northern Ireland: A Background Essay', in Seamus Dunn (ed.), *Facets of the Conflict in Northern Ireland* (Houndmills: Macmillan Press).

Darby, John and Seamus Dunn (1987), 'Segregated Schools: The Research Evidence', in Osbourne R.D., Cormack, R.J., and Miller, R.L. (eds), *Education and Policy in Northern Ireland* (Belfast: Policy Research Institute).

Davies, Norman (1997), *Europe: A History* (London: Pimlico).

de Clerq, Francine (1997), 'Policy Intervention and Power Shifts: An Evaluation of South Africa's Education Restructuring Policies', *Journal of Education Policy*, Vol. 12, No. 3.

de Mause, Lloyd (1976), *The History of Childhood* (London: Souvenir).

de Paor, Liam (1970), *Divider Ulster* (Harmondsworth: Penguin).

Dean, Jacqueline and Robert Sieborger (1995), 'After Apartheid: The Outlook for History', *Teaching History*, No. 79, April, pp. 32–8.

Defence For Children International (1990), *The Convention on the Rights of the Child* (Geneva).

Devetak, Richard (1996), 'Postmodernism', in Scott Burchill and Andrew Linklater (eds), *Theories of International Relations* (London: St Martin's Press, 1996).

Dodge, Cole P., and Magne Raundalen (1991), *Reaching Children in War: Sudan, Uganda and Mozambique* (Bergen, Norway: Sigma Forlag).

Dowler, Lorainne (1998), 'And They Think I'm Just a Nice Old Lady : Women and War in Belfast, Northern Ireland', *Gender, Place and Culture*, Vol. 5, No. 2.

du Toct, Marijke (1992), '"Dangerous Motherhood": Maternity Care and the Gendered Construction of Afrikaner Identity, 1904–1939', in Valerie Fildes, Lara Marks and Hilary Marland (eds).

Dunae, Patrick, A. (2001), 'Gender, Generations and Social Class: the Fairbridge Society and British Child Migration to Canada, 1930–1960', in Jon Lawrence, Pat Starkey (eds), Child Welfare and Social Action in the Nineteenth and Twentieth Centuries: International Perspectives (Liverpool: Liverpool University Press).

Dunn, Seamus, John Darby and K. Mullan (1984), *Schools Together?* (Coleraine: Centre for the Study of Conflict).

Dunne, Tim (1998), *Inventing International Society, A History of the English School* (London: Macmillan).

Edgerton, Lynda (1986), 'Public Protest, Domestic Acquiescence: Women in Northern Ireland', in Rosemary Ridd and Helen Callaway (eds), *Caught Up In Conflict, Women's Responses to Political Strife* (Basingstoke: Macmillan).

Education for South Africa: The 1961 Education Panel First Report (Witwatersrand University Press: Johannesburg, 1963).

Eekelaar, John (1994), 'The Interests of the Child and the Child's Wishes: the Role of Dynamic Self-determinism', in Phillip Alston (ed.), *The Best Interest of the Child: Reconciling Culture and Human Rights* (Oxford: Clarendon Press, UNICEF).

Elshtain, Jean Bethke (1987), *Women and War* (New York: Basic Books).

Elshtain, Jean Bethke (1990), *Power Trips and Other Journeys: Essays in Feminism as Civic Discourse* (London: University of Wisconsin Press, 1990).

Elshtain, Jean Bethke (1992), 'Sovereignty, Identity, Sacrifice', in V. Spike Peterson (ed.), *Gendered States: Feminist (Re)Visions of International Relations Theory* (Boulder CO: Lynne Rienner).

Encyclopedia Britannica Micropedia (1989), Vol. 3, 15th edition.

Enloe, Cynthia (1989), *Bananas, Beaches and Bases* (London: Pandora Press).

Enloe, Cynthia (1993), *The Morning After: Sexual Politics at the End of the Cold War* (London: University of California Press).

Enloe, Cynthia (1996), 'Margins, Silences and Bottom Rungs: How to Overcome the Underestimation of Power in the Study of International Relations', in Smith, Booth and Zalewski (eds), *International Theory: Positivism and Beyond* (Cambridge: Cambridge University Press).

Esposito, John. L. (1982), *Women in Muslim Family Law* (New York: Syracuse University Press).

Farson, Richard (1974), *Birthrights* (London: Collier Macmillan).

Fataar, Aslam (1997), 'Access to Schooling in a Post Apartheid South Africa: Linking Concept to Context', *International Review of Education,* Vol. 43, No. 4.

Fay, Marie-Therese, Mike Morrissey and Marie Smyth (1999), *Northern Ireland's Troubles: The Human Costs* (London: Pluto Press).

Feldman, Allen (1991), *Formations of Violence: The Narrative of the Body and Political Terror in Northern Ireland* (Chicago: University of Chicago Press).

Fest, Joachim C. (1970), *The Faces of the Third Reich*, translated from the German by Michael Bullock (London: Weidenfeld and Nicolson, 1970).

Fields, Rona M. (1973), *A Society on the Run*: *A Psychology of Northern Ireland* (Harmondsworth: Penguin).

Fildes, Valerie, Lara Marks and Hilary Marland (1992) (eds), *Women and Children First: International and Infant Welfare 1870 –1945* (London: Routledge).

Fisher, Jo (1993), *Out of the Shadows: Women, Resistance and Politics in South America* (London: Latin American Bureau, 1993).

Fitzpatrick, David (1988), *The Two Irelands* (Oxford: Oxford University Press).

Fleming, John, 'Children in Bondage: Young Soldiers, Labourers, and Sex Workers', *Sunday Independent*, Johannesburg, 13 August 1995, reproduced in *World Press Review*, January 1996, p. 9.

Franca, Valerie and Joachim de Carvalno, 'Children in Bondage', from *Veja*, Sao Paulo, 30 August, reprinted in *World Press Review*, January 1996, Vol. 43, No. 1, pp. 10 and 11.

Frankel, Mark *et al.*, 'Boy Soldiers: Special Report', *Newsweek* , 7 August 1995, p. 15.

Frankel, P. (1984), *Pretorias Praetorians: Civil–Military Relations in South Africa* (Cambridge: Cambridge University Press).

Fraser, Lyndley, (1957) *Propaganda* (London: Open University Press).

Fraser, Morris (1973), *Children in Conflict* (Harmondsworth: Penguin)

Freeman, M. (1987), *The Atlas of Nazi Germany* (London: Croom Helm).

Friedlander, Henry (1995), *The Origins of Nazi Genocide, From Euthanasia to the Final Solution* (Chapel Hill and London: University of North Carolina Press).

Furley, Oliver (1995), 'Child soldiers in Africa', in Oliver Furley (ed.), *Conflict in Africa* (London: Tauris).

Furley, Oliver (1995), 'Introduction: Africa: The Habit of Conflict', in Oliver Furley (ed.), *Conflict in Africa* (London: Taurus).

Furley, Oliver (1995), *Child Soldiers and Youths in African Conflicts: International Reactions*, African Studies Centre, Occasional Papers Series, No. 1.

Gaitskell Deborah and Elaine Unterhalter (1989), 'Mothers of the Nation: A Comparative Analysis of Nation, Race and Motherhood in Afrikaner Nationalism and the ANC', in Nira Yuval-Davis and Floya Anthias (eds), *Woman–Nation–State* (London: Macmillan).

Gerwel, Jakes (1994), 'Education in South Africa: Means and Ends', in Jack E. Spence (ed.), *Change in South Africa* (London: RIIA:Pinter).

Goddard, Jim, Sally McNamee, Adrian James and Allison James (eds) (2005), *The Politics of Childhood: International Perspectives, Contemporary Developments* (Houndsmills, Basingstoke: Macmillan).

Goodwin-Gill, Guy and Ilene Cohn (1994), *Child Soldiers* (Oxford: Clarendon Press).

Goonesekere, Savitri (1994), 'The Best Interests of the Child: A South Asian Perspective', in Phillip Alston (ed.), *The Best Interest of the Child. Reconciling Culture and Human Rights* (Oxford: Clarendon Press, UNICEF).

Graham-Brown, Sarah (1991), 'Battling for Survival: War, Debt and Education in Mozambique Nicaragua and Sudan', in *Education in the Developing World: Conflict and Crisis* (London and New York: Longman).

Grant, James P. (1994), *The State of the World's Children 1994* (New York: Oxford University Press).

Green, Duncan (1998), *Hidden Lives: Voices of Children in Latin America and the Caribbean* (London: Cassell).

Grosman, Cecilia P. (1996), 'Argentina – Children's Rights in Family Relationships: The Gulf between Law and Social Reality', in Michael Freeman (ed.), *Children's Rights: A Comparative Perspective* (Dartmouth, Aldershot: University College London).

Grosvenor, Ian and Maria Green (1998), 'Making Subjects: History Writing, Education and Race Categories', *Paedegogica Historica,* Vol. 33, No. 3.

Grunberger, Richard (1974), A *Social History of the Third Reich* (Harmondsworth: Penguin).

Grundy, Kenneth W. (1996), *The Militarisation of South African Politics* (Oxford: Oxford University Press).

Gutman, Roy (1993), *A Witness to Genocide* (Shaftesbury, Dorset: Element).

Guyver, Robert (1997), 'National Curriculum History: Key Concepts and Controversy', *Teaching History,* No. 88.

Hamill, James (1998), 'From Realism to Complex Interdependence? South Africa, Southern Africa and the Question of Security', *International Relations*, Vol. XIV, No. 3.

Hamilton, Carolyn (1995), 'Children in Armed Conflict – New Moves for an Old Problem', *The Journal of Child Law*, Vol. 7, No. 1.

Hanlon, Joseph (1984), 'From Marx to the mixed economy', *South*, December, p. 25.

Harris, Jennifer (1998), 'How Ireland's Women won the War for Peace', *Women's Journal*, August.

Harvey, Elizabeth (1993), *Youth and the Welfare State in Weimar Germany* (Oxford: Clarendon Press).

Harvey, Rachel (2003), Children and Armed Conflict: A Guide to International and Humanitarian Human Rights Law (Essex University and the International Bureau of Children's Rights: The Children and Armed Conflict Unit).

Hederman, Mark Patrick (1982), 'Paolo Freire's Pedagogy of the Oppressed', in *The Crane Bag: Latin American Issue*, Vol. 6, No. 2.

Hendrick, Harry (1994), *Child Welfare in England, 1872–1989* (London: Routledge).

Hensman, Rohini (1996), 'The Role of Women in the Resistance of Political Authoritarianism in Latin America and South Asia', in Haleh Afshar (ed.), *Women and Politics in the Third World* (London: Routledge).

Hewitt, James (1986), *Flashpoints in the Irish Question* (Wayland: East Sussex).

Higonnet, Anne (1998) *Pictures of Innocence: The History and Crisis of Ideal Childhood* (London: Thames and Hudson).

Hitler, Adolf, *Mein Kampf,* with an introduction by D.C. Watt, translated by Ralph Manheim (London: Hutchinson, 1969).

Hoffman, Mark (1987), 'Critical Theory and the International Politics Debate', *Millennium: Journal of International Studies*, Vol. 16, No. 2, pp. 231–49.

Høiskar, Alstri Halsan (2001), 'Underage and Under Fire: An Enquiry into the Use of Child Soldiers 1994–1998', *Childhood*, Vol. 8, No. 3.

Holland, Patricia (1992), *What is a Child? Popular Images of Childhood* (London: Virago Press).

Holland, Patricia (2004), *Picturing Childhood: The Myth of the Child in Popular Imagery* (London: I B Tauris).

Hooper, Charlotte, 'Masculinities, International Relations and the Gender variable: A Cost-Benefit Analysis for Sympathetic Gender Sceptics', Department of Politics, University of Bristol, July 1997, unpublished paper.

Horrell, Muriel (1968), *Bantu Education to 1968* (Johannesburg: South African Institute of Race Relations).

Housden, Martyn (1997), *Resistance and Conformity in the Third Reich* (London: Routledge).

Human Rights Watch Africa (1995), *Children of Sudan: Slaves, Street Children and Child Soldiers* (USA: Human Rights Watch Africa).

Human Rights Watch Africa (1995), *Easy Prey: Child Soldiers in Liberia* (New York).

Human Security Report 2005 Canada.

IDAF (1988), 'Apartheid's Violence Against Children', Fact paper on South Africa, No. 15, p. 7.

IDAF (1989), *Subverting Apartheid: Education, Information and Culture under Emergency Rule* (London: IDAF Publications).

Irwin, Colin (1997), 'Social Conflict and the Failure of Education Policies in Two Deeply Divided Societies: Northern Ireland and Israel', in Donnan Hastings and Graham McFarlane (eds), *Social Anthropology and Public Policy in Northern Ireland* (Aldershot, Hants: Avebury).

James, Alison and Alan Prout (eds) (1990) , *Constructing and Reconstructing Childhood: Contemporary Issues in the Sociological Study of Childhood* (London: Falmer Press).

Jarman, Neil (1997), *Material Conflict: Parades and Visual displays in Northern Ireland* (Oxford: Bergman).

Johnson, S. (ed.) (1992), *South Africa: No Turning Back* (London: Macmillan).

Johnston, Anton (1990), 'The Mozambican State and Education', in Martin Carnoy and Joel Sarnoff (eds), *Education and Social Transition in the Third World* (Princeton, New Jersey: Princeton University Press).

Jowett, Garth S. and Victoria O'Donnell (1957), *Propaganda and Persuasion* (London: Sage, 1992).

Kallaway, Peter (1995), 'History Education in a Democratic South Africa', *Teaching History*, No. 78, January.

Kanitkar, Helen, '"Real true boys": Moulding the cadets of Imperialism', in Andrea Cornwall and Nancy Lindisfarne (eds) (1994), *Dislocating Masculinity, Comparative Ethnographies* (London: Routledge).

Kennedy, Liam (2001), *They Shoot Children Don't They? An Analysis of the Age and Gender of Victims of Paramilitary 'Punishments' in Northern Ireland*, Report prepared for the Northern Ireland Committee against terror and the Northern Ireland Affairs Committee of the House of Commons, CAIN [website] http://cain.ulst.ac.uk/issues/violence/docs/kennedy01a.htm.

Kent, George (1995), *Children in the International Political Economy* (London/New York: Macmillan/St. Martin's, 1995).

Kershaw, Ian (1998), *Hitler, 1889–1936: Hubris* (London: Allen Lane).

King, Edmund (1979), 'Afrikaner Education', *International Review of Education*, Vol. 25.

Kinsella, Helen (2005), 'Securing the Civilian: Sex and Gender in the Laws of War', in M. Barnett and R. Duvall (eds), *Power and Global Governance* (Cambridge: Cambridge University Press).

Knight, Derrick (1988), *Mozambique: Caught in the Trap* (Christian Aid).

Konner, Melvin (1991), *Childhood* (Boston: Little Brown and Company).

Koonz, Claudia (1987), *Mothers in the Fatherland: Women, the Family and Nazi Politics* (London: Methuen).

Koonz, Claudia (1993), 'Eugenics, Gender and Ethics in Nazi Germany: The Debate about Involuntary Sterilization', in Childers and Caplan (eds), *Re-evaluating the Third Reich* (New York: Holmes and Meier, 1993).

Kotze, Hennie (1995), 'South Africa's youth in transition', in Ursula J.Van Beek (ed.), *South Africa and Poland in Transition: A Comparative Perspective* (Pretoria: Human Sciences Research Council).

Laffan, Michael (1999), *The Resurrection of Ireland: The Sinn Fein Party, 1916–1923* (Cambridge University Press).

Lapid, Yosef (1996), 'Culture's Ship: Returns and Departures in International Relations Theory' in Yosef Lapid and Friedrich Kratochwil (eds), *The Return of Culture and Identity in International Relations* (London: Lynne Rienner).

Lapid, Yosef and Friedrich Kratochwil (eds) (1996), *The Return of Culture and Identity in International Relations* (London: Lynne Rienner), pp. 3–20.

Laurence, John (1979), *Race Propaganda and South Africa* (London: Victor Gollancz).

Lewis, Norman (1996), 'The New Age of Interventionism: The Globalisation of American Liberal Discourse', British International Studies Association, unpublished paper.

Lifton, Robert Jay and Eric Markusen (1990), *The Genocidal Mentality: Nazi Holocaust and Nuclear Threat* (London: Macmillan), pp. 214–15.

Mackenzie, John M. (1987), 'The Imperial Pioneer and Hunter and the British Masculine Stereotype in Late Victorian and Edwardian Times', in J.A. Mangan and James Walvin (eds), *Manliness and Morality: Middle Class Masculinity in Britain and America 1800–1940* (Manchester: Manchester University Press).

Magee, J. (1970), 'The Teaching of Irish History in Irish Schools', *The Northern Teacher*, Vol. 10, No. 1.

Mangan, J.A. (1992), *The Cultural Bond: Sport, Empire and Society* (London: Macmillan).

Mangan, J.A. (1993), 'Images for confident control', in J.A. Mangan (ed.), *The Imperial Curriculum: Racial Images and Education in the British Colonial Experience* (London: Routledge).

Mangan, J.A. and S. Walvin (eds) (1987), *Manliness and Morality: Middle Class Masculinity in Britain and America 1800–1940* (Manchester: Manchester University Press).

Manicom, Linzi (1992), 'Rethinking State and Gender in South African History', *Journal of African History*, Vol. 33, No. 3, pp. 441–65.

Marchand, Marianne H., (1994), 'Latin American Voices of Resistance: Women's Movements and Development Debate', in Roscow, *et al.*, (eds).

Marks, Monique (2001), *Young Warriors: Youth Politics, Identity and Violence in South Africa* (Johannesburg: Witswatersrand University Press).

Marks, Shula and Stanley Tripido (1987), 'The Politics of Race Class and Nationalism', in Shula Marks and Stanley Trapido (eds), *The Politics of Race, Class and Nationalism in Twentieth Century South Africa* (Harlow: Longman).

Mason, Tim (1976), 'Women in Germany, 1925–1940: Family, Welfare and Work: Part I', *History Workshop Journal*.

Mason, Tim (1976), 'Women in Germany, 1925–1940: Family, Welfare and Work: Part II', *History Workshop Journal*.

Matsushima, Yukiko (1996), 'Controversies and Dilemmas: Japan Confronts the Convention', in Michael Freeman (ed.), *Children's Rights: A Comparative Perspective* (Dartmouth, Aldershot: University College London).

McLoughlin, Eithne (1992), 'Women and the Family in Northern Ireland: A Review', *Women's Studies International Forum*, Vol. 1, No. 4.

Miles R.C. Hewstone and Rupert J. Brown, (1986) 'Contact is not Enough: An Intergroup Perspective on the Contact Hypothesis', in Miles R.C. Hewstone and Rupert J. Brown (eds.), *Contact and Conflict in Intergroup Encounters* (Oxford: Blackwell).

Moeller, Susan D. (2002), 'The Media's Use of Children in the Telling of International News', *Press/Politics*, Vol. 7, No. 1, pp. 36–56.

Moorhead, Caroline (1997), 'All the world's children', in *Index on Censorship*, 2.

Morgan, Valerie and Grace Fraser (1995), 'Women and the Northern Ireland Conflict: Experiences and Responses', in Dunn, Seamus (ed.), *Facets of the Conflict in Northern Ireland* (Houndmills: Macmillan Press).

Muianga, Lucienga (1995), 'Rehabilitation and Empowerment of the Victims of War and Violence in Southern Africa' in *Transcending the Legacy: Children in the New Southern Africa* (AEI/SARDC/UNICEF: Amsterdam, Harare, Nairobi).

Murphy, Craig and Roger Tooze (1991), 'Introduction', in Craig N. Murphy and Roger Tooze (eds), *The New International Political Economy* (Boulder: Lynne Rienner).

Murray, Dominic (1983), 'Rituals and Symbols as Contributors to the Culture of Northern Ireland Primary Schools', *Irish Educational Studies*, Vol. 3, No. 2.

Murray, Dominic (1985), 'Identity: A Covert Pedagogy in Northern Irish Schools', *Irish Educational Studies*, Vol. 5, No. 2.

Murray, Dominic (1993), *The Chance of a Lifetime: An Evaluation of Project Children* (Centre for the Study of Conflict: University of Ulster).

Nenadic, Natalie (1996), 'Femicide: A Framework for Understanding Genocide', Diane Bell and Renate Kline, *Radically Speaking: Feminism Reclaimed* (London: Zed Books).

Newsweek, 19 April 1971, p. 22.

Noakes, John and G. Pridham (eds) (1984), *Nazism: 1919–1945,* Vol. 2., *State, Economy and Society 1933–1939* (Exeter: University of Exeter).

Nordstrom, Carolyn (1999), 'Visible Wars and Invisible Girls, Shadow Industries and the Politic of Not-Knowing', *International Feminist Journal of Politics*, Vol. 1, No. 1.

Nossent, Natasja (1996), 'When the Division of Child Labour in Gendered, but Civil Society's Approach to this Phenomenon is Not', unpublished paper (University of Amsterdam).

O' Neill, Sean (1991), *Northern Ireland* (East Sussex: Wayland).

Ottunu, O. (1999), 'Protection of Children Affected by Armed Conflict: Note by the Secretary General', United Nations General Assembly', 1 October, 99-28333.

Otunnu, O. (2000), 'The Impact of Armed Conflict on Children: Filling Knowledge Gaps, Draft Research Agenda.' [website]: http://www.mofa.go.jp/policy/human/ child/survey/annex2.html.

Peterson, V. Spike (1992), 'Security and Sovereign States' in V. Spike Peterson (ed.), *Gendered States: Feminist (Re)Visions of International Relations Theory* (Boulder: Lynne Rienner).

Peterson, V. Spike (1992), *Gendered States: Feminist (Re)Visions of International Relations Theory* (Boulder: Lynne Rienner).

Pettman, Jan Jindy (1996), *Worlding Women* (London: Routledge).

Pettman, Jan Jindy (1992), *Living in the Margins: Racism, Sexism and Feminism in Australia* (London: Allen and Unwin).

Peukert, Detlev (1991), *The Weimar Republic: The Crisis of Classical Modernity* (London: Allen Lane).

Pine, Lisa (1997), 'Nazism in the Classroom', *History Today*, April, pp. 22–7.

Pine, Lisa (2003), 'Creating Conformity: The Training of Girls in the *Bund Deutscher Mädel*', *European History Quarterly*, Vol. 33, No. 3, pp. 367–85.

Plowright, John (1991), 'Teaching the holocaust: A Response to the Report of a Survey in the UK', *Teaching History*, No. 45.

Pollock, Linda (1983), *Forgotten Children: Parent–Child Relations from 1500–1900* (Cambridge: Cambridge University Press).

Proctor, Robert N. (1998), *Racial Hygiene: Medicine Under the Nazis* (Cambridge, Mass: Harvard University Press).

Pupavac, Vanessa (1997), 'The Deviant South: The Globalisation of Childhood and the Creation of a New Moral Order', paper presented to British International Studies Association.

Quine, Maria Sophia (1996), *Population Politics in Twentieth Century Europe* (London: Routledge).

Reese, Dagmar (1995), 'The BDM Generation: A Female Generation in Transition from Dictatorship to Democracy', in Mark Roseman (ed.), *Generations in Conflict: Youth Revolt and Generation Formation in Germany 1770–1968* (Cambridge: Cambridge University Press).

Reulecke, Jurgen (1995), 'The Battle for the Young: Mobilising Young People in Wilhelmine Germany', in Mark Roseman (ed.).

Review Committee on Curriculum 2005 (2000), South African Curriculum for the Twenty First Century: Report of the Review Committee on Curriculum 2005, Presented to the Minister of Education, Professor Kader Asmal, Pretoria, 31 May 2000.

Riley, Denise (1983), *War in the Nursery: Theories of the Child and Mother* (London: Virago).

Roscow, Stephen J., Naeem Inayatullah and Mark Rupert (eds) (1994), *The Global Economy of Political Space* (Boulder: Lynne Rienner).

Roseman, Mark (ed) (1995), *Generations in conflit: Youth revolt and generation formation in Germany 1770–1968* (Cambridge: Cambridge University Press).

Rowland, Robyn and Renate Klein (1996), 'Radical Feminism: History, Politics, Action', in Diane Bell and Renate Kline (eds), *Radically Speaking: Feminism Reclaimed* (London: Zed Books).

Ruddick, Sara (1990), Maternal Thinking: Towards a Politics of Peace (Boston, Mass: Beacon Press).

Rwezaura, B. (1994), 'The Concept of the Child's Best Interests in the Changing Context of Sub-Saharan Africa', in Philip Alston (ed.), *The Best Interest of the Child. Reconciling Culture and Human Rights* (Oxford: Clarendon Press, UNICEF).

Sales, Rosemary (1997), *Women Divided, Gender, Religion and Politics in Northern Ireland* (London: Routledge).

Sandstrom, C.I. (1968), *The Psychology of Childhood and Adolescence* (Great Britain: Pelican Books).

Sawyer, Roger (1993), *We Are But Women: Women in Ireland's History* (London: Routledge).

Seamus, Dunn (1986), 'The Role of Education in the Northern Ireland Conflict', *Oxford Review of Education*, Vol. 12, No. 3, pp. 234–6.

Searle, Chris (1977), 'Classrooms of Freewill', *New Internationalist*, August, p. 9.

Seatlholo, Khotsio (1980), 'Black Schools in Uproar' *South*, December, p. 18.

Shakry, Omnia (1998), 'Schooled Mothers and Structured Play: Child Rearing in Turn-of-the-Century Egypt', in Lila Abu-Lughod (ed.), *Remaking Women. Feminism and Modernity in the Middle East* (Princeton University Press).

Sherington, G. (2003), ' "Suffer Little Children": Between Child Migration as a Study of Journeyings between Centre and Periphery', *History of Education*, Vol. 32, No. 5, pp. 461–76.

Siegfried, Klaus-Jorg (1996), 'Racial Discrimination at Work: Forced Labour in the Volkswagen Factory', in Michael Burleigh (ed.), *Confronting the Nazi Past: New Debates on Modern German History* (New York: St. Martin's Press).

Simao, Pinda (1995), 'Education in Angola in the Post-Apartheid Era: Overcoming Physical and Spiritual Destruction', in *Transcending the Legacy: Children in the New Southern Africa* (AEI/SARDC/UNICEF: Amsterdam, Harare, Nairobi).

Singer, P.W. (2005), 'Western Militaries Confront Child Soldiers Threat', Jane's Intelligence, *Review*, Vol. 17, No. 11.

Singer, P.W. (2005), Children at War (Pantheon).

Singer, Peter W. 'Caution: Children at War', Parameters, Winter 2001–02, pp. 40–56, at http://carlisle-www.army.mil/usawc/Parameters/01winter/singer.htm accessed (20/10/04).

Sisson, Elaine (2004), *Pearse's Patriots: St Enda's and the Cult of Boyhood* (Cork University Press).

Smith, Steve (1995), 'The Self-Images of a Discipline: A Genealogy of International Relations', in Ken Booth and Steve Smith (eds), *International Relations Theory Today* (Cambridge: Polity Press).

Smyth, Marie (1998), *Half the Battle: Understanding the Impact of the Troubles on Children and Young People* (INCORE, University of Ulster: Derry Londonderry).

Sorensen, George (1986), 'Development Through the Eyes of a Child', Development Research Series Working Papers, No.19 (Denmark: Aalborg University).

Stachura, Peter D. (1975), *Nazi Youth in the Weimar Republic* (Oxford: Clio Books).

Stancich, Lara (1998), 'Discovering Elephants and a Feminist Theory of International Relations', *Global Society*, Vol. 12, No.1.

Stephens, Sharon (1997), 'Nationalism, Nuclear Policy and Children in Cold War America, *Childhood: A Global Journal of Child Research*, Vol. 4, No. 1, pp. 103–23.

Stephens, Sharon (1995) *Children and the Politics of Culture* (Princeton: Princeton University Press).

Stephenson, Jill (1996), 'Women, Motherhood and the Family in the Third Reich', in Michael Burleigh (ed.) *Confronting the Nazi Past: New Debates on Modern German History* (London: Collin & Brown).

Stephenson, Jill (1996), 'Women, Motherhood and the Family in the Third Reich', in Michael Burleigh (ed.), *Confronting the Nazi Past: New Debates on Modern German History* (London: Collin & Brown).

Stewart, A.T.Q. (1977), *The Narrow Ground: Aspects of Ulster* (London: Faber and Faber).

Stone, Lawrence (1977), *The Family, Sex and Marriage in England 1500–1800* (New York: Harper and Row).

Stone, Norman (1997), 'The New Age of Interventionism: the Globalisation of American Liberal Discourse', paper presented to the British International Studies Association.

Sylvester, Christine (1994), *Feminist Theory and International Relations in a Postmodern Era* (Cambridge: Cambridge University Press).

Sylvester, Christine (1996), 'The Contributions of Feminist Theory to International Relations', in Smith, Booth and Zalewski (eds), *International Theory: Positivism and Beyond* (Cambridge: Cambridge University Press).

Tajfel, H. (1981), *Human Groups and Social Categories* (Cambridge: Cambridge University Press).

Teitelbaumn, Michael S. and Jay M. Winter (1985), *The Fear of Population Decline* (Orlando: Academic Press).

Thomas, John W. and Merilee S. Grindle (1994), 'Political Leadership and Policy Characteristics in Population Policy Reform', in Jason L. Finkle and C. Alison McIntosh (eds), *The New Politics of Population: Conflict and Consensus in Family Planning* (New York: Oxford University Press).

Thompson, Leonard and Andrew Prior (1982), *South African Politics* (London: Yale University Press).

Tickner, J. Anne (1992), *Gender in International Relations: Feminist Perspectives on Achieving Global Security* (New York: Columbia University Press).

Trew, Karen (1989), 'Evaluating the Impact of Contact Schemes for Catholic and Protestant Children', in Harbison, J.I. (ed.), *Growing Up in Northern Ireland* (Belfast: Stranmillis College).

Tyler May, Elaine (1988), *Homeward Bound: American Families in the Cold War Era* (New York: Basic Books).

Urban, Mark (1992), *Big Boys' Rules, the SAS and the Secret Struggle Against the IRA* (London: Faber and Faber).

Van Beuren, Geraldine (1995), *The International Law on the Rights of the Child* (Netherlands: Martinus Nijhoff).

Van Bueren, G. (1998), 'Opening Pandora's Box' in G. Van Bueren (ed.), *Childhood Abused: Protecting Children Against Torture, Cruel, Inhuman and Degrading Treatment and Punishment* (Dartmouth: Ashgate).

Vines, Alex (1991), *Renamo: Terrorism in Mozambique* (London: James Currey).

Vittachi, Anuradha (1989), *Stolen Childhood: In search of the Rights of the Child* (Cambridge: Polity Press).

Vittachi, Tarzie (1989), *Making Reality of Children's Rights* (Stockholm: Radda Barnen).

von Saldern, A. (1994), 'Victims or Perpetrators? Controversies about the Role of Women in the Nazi State', in Crew, David F. (ed.) *Nazism and German Society* (London: Routledge).

Walker, Cherryl (1990), 'Building a nation from words: Afrikaans Language Literature and Ethnic Identity, 1902–1924', in C. Walker (ed.), *Women and Resistance in Southern Africa to 1945* (London: James Currey).

Walker, R.B.J. (1990), *Inside Outside: International Relations as Political Theory* (Cambridge: Cambridge University Press).

Wallace, William (1996), 'Truth and Power, Monks and Technocrats: Theory and Practice in International Relations', *Review of International Studies*, No. 22.

Warner, Marina (1994), *From the Beast to the Blonde* (London: Chatto and Windus).

Watson, Alison M.S. (2004), 'Seen But Not Heard: The Role of the Child in International Political Economy', *New Political Economy*, Vol. 9, No. 1.

Wedekind, Volker, Cassius Libisi, Ken Harley and John Gultig (1996), 'Political Change, Social Integration and Curriculum: A South African Case Study', *Journal of Curriculum Studies*, Vol. 28, No. 4.

Weindling, Paul (1989), *Health, Race and German Politics between National Unification and Nazis, 1870-1945* (Cambridge: Cambridge University Press).

Welch, David (2004), 'Nazi Propaganda and the *Volksgemeinschaft*: Constructing a People's Community', *Journal of Contemporary History*', Vol. 39, No. 2. pp. 213–38.

Weldon, Gail (2005), 'Thinking Each Other's History: Can Facing the Past Contribute to Education for Human Rights and Democracy?', *International Journal of Historical Learning, Teaching and Research*, Vol. 5, No. 1.

Whyte, John (1990), *Interpreting Northern Ireland* (New York: Oxford University Press).

Williams, Michael C. and Keith Krause (eds), (1997) *Critical Security Studies: Concepts and Cases* (London: University College London).

Wilson, Gillian (1986), ' History – Ours or yours? Pt 1', *Teaching History*, No. 19.

Wolpe, Harold and Elaine Unterhalter (1991), 'Reproduction Reform and Transformation: Approaches to the Analysis of Education in South Africa', in Elaine Unterhalter *et al.*, (eds), *Apartheid Education and Popular Struggles* (London: Research on Education in South Africa).

Woodhead, Martin, Paul Light and Ronnie Carr (1991), *Open University: Child Development in a Social Context. Vol. 3, Growing up in a Changing Society* (London: Routledge).

Worden, Nigel (1995), *The Making of Modern South Africa: Conquest, Segregation and Apartheid* (Oxford: Blackwell).

Wyn Jones, Richard (1995), 'Message in a Bottle? Theory and Praxis in Critical Security Studies', *Contemporary Security Policy*, Vol. 16, pp. 299–319.

Wyn Jones, Richard (1996), 'Travel without Maps: Thinking about Security after the Cold War', in Richard Wyn Jones and M. Jane Davis (eds), *Security after the Cold War* (Brookfield, VT: Edward Elgar).

Wyness, M., Harrison, L, Buchanan, I (2004), 'Childhood, Politics and Ambiguity: Towards an Agenda for Children's Political Inclusion', *Sociology*, Vol. 38, No. 1.

Yuval-Davis, Nira (1997), *Gender and Nation* (London: Sage).

Yuval-Davis, Nira and Floya Anthias (1989), *Women–Nation–State* (London: Macmillan).

Zalewski, Marysia (1994), 'The Women "Women" Question in International Relations', *Millennium, Journal of International Studies,* Vol. 23, No. 2, pp. 416–17.

Zalewski, Marysia (1995), 'Well What is the Feminist Perspective on Bosnia?', *International Affairs* Vol. 71, No. 2, pp. 339–56.

Zalewski, Marysia (1996), 'All these Theories Yet the Bodies Keep Piling Up', in Smith S. Booth K., and Zalewski M. (eds), *International Theory: Positivism and Beyond* (Cambridge: Cambridge University Press).

Zalewski, Marysia, and Cynthia Enloe (1995), 'Questions about Identity in International Relations', in Ken Booth and Steve Smith (eds), *International Relations Theory Today* (Oxford: Polity Press).

Index

1857174364
11/06/01
£11.99
SM00007446
STMARSO-93A
HHV 6E
(Kin)
Ref.

Health Care UK
Spring 2001

The King's Fund review of health policy